READING, WRITING, AND RITUALIZING

RITUAL IN FICTIVE, LITURGICAL, AND PUBLIC PLACES

RONALD L. GRIMES

The Pastoral Press
Washington, DC

Cover background pattern was designed by a group of public school teachers during a workshop on rites of passage sponsored by the Minnesota Humanities Commission and led by the author.

Back cover photo by Susan Shantz.

ISBN: 1-56929-007-5

The Pastoral Press
225 Sheridan Street, N.W.
Washington, D.C. 20011
(202) 723-1254

The Pastoral Press is the publications division of the National Association of Pastoral Musicians, a membership organization of musicians and clergy devoted to fostering the art of musical liturgy.

Printed in the United States of America

Contents

Preface

I AM GRATEFUL TO PASTORAL PRESS, PARTICULARLY ITS PRESI-
dent, Virgil Funk, for hearing in words that I have spoken and
pieces that I have written something akin to a musical sensibility and aspiration. That the National Association of Pastoral
Musicians should offer to publish the uncollected essays of a
musically illiterate, not very churchly scholar of ritual is delightful in its irony, since I only aspire to musicality. Unable
either to carry a tune or play an instrument, I nevertheless repeatedly find myself in the company of musicians, conversing
with them as if we spoke a common language. They range
from the African American drummer who beats out the
rhythms in my female-led African dance class to Christian musicians who accompany classical Roman, male-dominated liturgies on European-crafted, antique organs.

Sometimes I joke, "If I knew how to make music, I would
give up scholarship." But I don't, so the bridge between musicality and me is necessarily built of words—more specifically,
scholarly words about ritual actions. The distance is so great
that it generates considerable torque on the words I employ.
At worst it twists them into academic obscurity. At best it teases them in the direction of poetic prose. Reading and writing
about ritual on the edge of poetry, I come as close to music as I
will ever get.

Even though I may be more poet than musician, I am still no poet. I am scholar, with a scholar's drive to explain, convince, schematize, and make clear. However much I imagine myself as moving ritual aspirants beyond words with the magic and unspeakable power of flute or drum, I will have to appear on judgment day (if such there is) even more bereft than the Little Drummer Boy. I will have only prose to present as a gift.

These essays, then, are no symphony, metaphoric or otherwise. Occasionally, they approach making a "joyful noise" (as the Psalms enjoin). But more often the tones are too various and the voices too dissonant to be worthy of musical metaphor. I have made no attempt to homogenize the voices or delete the refrains. The popular pieces remain popular; the academic pieces remain academic.

Since these chapters are collected and written in retrospect, one has to be careful in attributing either too much or too little coherence to them. They all concern ritual and in this sense share a common, deliberate leitmotif. But I would be attributing too much coherence if I claimed that they were all fragments of an internally consistent theory of ritual that lurks in some Platonic fashion behind or below them. However, I would be attributing too little coherence if I ignored the repetitiveness with which certain notions and images recur in my own writing. Collecting these essays, public lectures, and unpublished writings, I have more than once been surprised to discover that I have already said something that I supposed I had only recently imagined. The imagination (or at least, my imagination) is remarkably curvaceous. It returns more often than I like to territory already traversed. So, like any other reader, I have had both to invent and to discover the links among these chapters and the various voices that permeate them.

The three sections differ according to audience as well as assumed social space. Section one assumes a mixed audience of ritual scholars, liturgists, and liturgical theologians (or, liturgiologists). The locus of debate is the space between what are too conveniently called "church" and "world." Section two addresses curators, shop owners, artists, tourists, and other sorts of pilgrim-observers, and the implied meeting place is the museum, studio, gallery, or tourist site. The last section addresses literary critics, authors, and characters. The space in which such conversation happens is imaginative or virtual, the "heterocosmic" space of fiction.

The first section plays two ritual modes off one another. Ritualizing, the deliberate attempt to cultivate rites, is made both partner and worthy opponent of liturgy, the most established and most obviously religious form of ritual. The examples of ritualizing are typically North American and contemporary, because this is the area of my own research. The examples of liturgy are typically Roman Catholic, because Roman Catholics have most often invited me into their conversations, seminars, and symposia.

Whereas section one concentrates on two ritual modes, section three collects essays on ritual components, specifically ritual objects, ritual places, and ritual actions. This section concerns the concrete stuff of ritual, those dimensions of it that can be photographed, owned, bought, mapped, made, or traversed.

The final section may surprise readers of *Beginnings in Ritual Studies* or *Ritual Criticism*, two previously published collections. These chapters have nothing to do with fieldwork, an emphasis that strongly marks the other two books. Instead, they are on texts, specifically works of fiction or autobiographies. The sort of ritual that is their subject matter is fictive. Fictive ritual is different from what I usually call "ritualizing," though the two notions are obviously related: both are emergent or nascent forms. Whereas ritualizing is the act of deliberately constructing and self-consciously enacting ritual processes, fictive ritual is imagined but not performed (or, if it is performed, the medium is the written page not the human body in motion).

What do the fictive, liturgical, and public have to do with one another? Especially the notion of fictive ritual will seem far-fetched to some. Fictional space is on the other side of the mirror, beyond what we comfortably define as everyday reality. But then so is liturgical space; we step aside from the quotidian in order to enter it. Public space, we fancy, is another matter. We like to imagine it as the space where all meet, regardless of "race, color, or creed." But some public spaces, such as museums, are quite a distance beyond the surface of the mirror that separates the real from either the fictive or the transcendent. Enter a gallery full of exotic masks imported from Africa, or stroll among sacred objects stolen and bought cheaply from tribes closer to home. Then, public spaces, will seem more fictive than fiction, more liturgical than liturgy.

Part I

Emergent Ritual
and
Liturgical Authority

Part I

Emergent Ritual and Liturgical Authority

INTRODUCTION

THE THREE CHAPTERS IN PART ONE ARE ABOUT RITUAL PRACTICE, ritual norms, and ritual criticism. The first one is addressed primarily to theorists. The remaining two arise out of conversations with doers of ritual rather than those who want to theorize about it. My aim in them is not to describe but to implicate practice. This is a goal that some ritologists eschew, leaving such tasks to liturgical theologians or drama critics, but a growing minority of social scientists are refusing the safety and purity supposedly provided them by the brackets of objectivity. Those who think of themselves as doing what is sometimes called "critical ethnography"[1] or engaging in "praxis-oriented" anthropology, consider research itself a politically, if not ontologically, laden activity and thus argue that scholars should assume responsibility for the values advocated by, and social consequences of, their scholarship.

In "Reinventing Ritual," the first chapter, I propose an alternative understanding of ritual that takes issue with some of the commonly held assumptions about its nature and thereby lays the groundwork for some the critiques that follow. Specifically, I question whether rites are necessarily collective, pre-critical, or meaningful. Definitions and theories of ritual often assume that they are. In the process of articulating a view of ritual that allows for its individual, critical, and "meaningless" variants, I hope to comprehend embodiment, tradition, and memory as a foundations for a theory of ritual.

"Emerging Ritual" was a topic on which I was asked to speak by the North American Academy of Liturgy. Members of the Academy were interested in "emergent ritual's" promise and threat to established liturgy. I approached this topic on the basis of research at the Ritual Studies Lab and summarized a few of its key principles in order to invite comparisons with liturgical principles. Thus chapter two, originally a plenary address, retains its oral style. In addition, it is followed by two brief sections that attempt to capture some of the process in which the address was embedded. My presentation was followed by small-group discussions based on questions requested by Academy organizers and formulated by me. Both my questions and some of those posed by participants follow the body of the address.

"Liturgical Supinity, Liturgical Erectitude" was originally a lecture presented at a conference on liturgical authority at the University of Notre Dame. It is the most polemical and playful piece in part one, concerned as it is with the politics and power plays of liturgical practice and theory. Though feminist concerns have often lay behind what I write, this was the first occasion on which I made them so overt.

1

Reinventing Ritual[2]

NORTH AMERICA IS PRESENTLY RIFE WITH INVENTED RITES, SOME of which one might want to regard as good examples of ritual creativity and some of which one might want to castigate as evidence of widespread cultural neurosis. There is a growing popular literature on these rites, and, implicitly, it calls into question some key scholarly assumptions about ritual. Virginia Hine refers to the phenomenon as "self-generated" ritual and "self-created" ceremony.[3] I use the term "ritualizing" to denote emergent or newly constructed ritual.[4] Ritualizing is the activity of incubating ritual; it the act of constructing ritual either self-consciously and deliberately or incrementally and editorially, as it were. The gerund form ("ritualizing") is a reminder that I am highlighting the processual phase in the life history of a rite. Whatever one calls it, there are many manifestations of it. For example, feminist accounts of self-consciously constructed ritual are multiplying rapidly.[5] Though much feminist ritual draws on traditional resources, much of it is the result of spontaneous improvisation and imaginative effort. There is a smaller but growing body of psychological literature on the development of ritual for purposes of family therapy and intergenerational transition-making.[6] Proponents work with families to construct rites that reveal, diagnose, or heal dysfunctional aspects of a family system. Another body of literature is ethnographic, and it includes numerous works that

5

depict ritual in the context of colonialism and other culture-contact situations.[7] This kind of ritual arises as critical and creative response to radically altered social configurations. Ritual emerging under the pressures of intercultural conflict is necessarily self-conscious, because ritual construction often occurs within a few years, in a single lifetime rather than across generations or aeons. The ethnographic literature on ritual creativity also includes works by anthropologists themselves who imaginatively reconstruct and re-enact rites they have studied in the field.[8]

With almost no exceptions scholarly theories of ritual do not take into account this emergent ritualizing. We scholars do not like to think of our theories and definitions as reflections of popular culture. And if we are convinced of the efficacy of ideas, we may even want to believe that our definitions and theories transcend all forms of culture, popular as well as elite. Theories are not supposed to reflect culture, rather they are supposed to account for, or lay the grounds for evaluating, it.

But theories and definitions change, usually in patterns consonant with changed cultural practices. One particularly striking contemporary example is the theory and definition of ritual. Since the mid-1960s the understanding of ritual (which includes not only its definition and theory but its image and sense) has been undergoing a dramatic shift. One way to account for the shift is to treat it as a consequence of Victor Turner's theories, particularly his widely known and appropriated notions: liminality, communitas, ritual process, and social drama. Before Turner ritual was static, structural, conservative. After Turner it is imagined as flowing, processual, subversive. In effect he reinvented ritual.

There is considerable truth in this account, which attributes changed sensibility to changed theory, but the account is half-truth. The other half of the truth is that Turner's theorizing was itself goaded by much that we associate with the popular culture of late 1960s: experimental theater, popular psychology, feminism, hippies, festivals, travel, pilgrimages, entertainment, counterculture politics. The reinvention of ritual was already taking place in the culture and era in which Turner wrote.

Whether shifts in theory lead or follow cultural changes is a chicken-egg problem I have no desire to solve, but I do think it important to examine conceptions of ritual that have not caught up with the popular phenomena they should account for. Even Victor Turner's formal definition of ritual lagged behind his sense and theory of it.[9] If he had adhered to his own definition, he would never noticed most of what he argued was distinctive about ritual.

Despite Turner's effect on the North American sense of ritual, it is still rather typical of scholarly theories and definitions to maintain that ritual is collective rather than individual and traditional rather than invented. This view is held not just as true but as true by definition: an action will not be recognized as ritualistic unless it meets these two criteria, collectivity and traditionality. There are two corollaries. One is that ritual consciousness is pre-critical. A second is that ritual is meaningful and that meaning consists of the words or ideas to which ritual acts refer.

The view of ritual as traditional (rather than invented), collective (rather than individual), pre-critical (rather than self-conscious and reflective), and meaningful (that is, referential), is so widespread and unquestioned as to make it virtually sacrosanct, hence the necessity of critique. No single theorist espouses all these criteria in a definition of ritual, but its several features are widely stated or implied.

Is Ritual Necessarily Traditional?

The rhetoric of ritualists (people who engage in ritual practices) has several strategies for denying the inventability of ritual. One, for example, is to claim, "It has always been done this way" or "Our grandparents did it this way" or simply "It is traditional." In effect this kind of statement is used to deflect explanation of ritual. It is a quasi-explanation that makes ritual a kind of, or consequence of, tradition.

Another strategy, which raises the ante considerably, is to claim for a rite the status of a sacrament instituted by some divine figure, often in the beginning or in the time before this time. This is the more radical form of denying the inventability of ritual. Both strategies put ritual considerably beyond the range of mere human creativity and thus beyond the reach of criticism.

The rhetoric of ritologists (people who study ritual) has parallels to that of the practitioners. For some ritual and tradition are virtual synonyms, or if not that, then partners for life: ritual is the enactment of tradition, or, put more synchronically, the enactment of convention or custom. For instance, Stanley Tambiah defines ritual as

> a culturally constructed system of symbolic communication. It is constituted of patterned and ordered sequences of words and acts, often expressed in multiple media, whose content and arrangement are characterized in varying degree by formality (conventionality), stereotypy (rigidity), condensation (fusion), and redundancy (repetition).[10]

Although Tambiah does not use the word "tradition," he implies it in several terms: "culturally constructed," "formality," "conventionality," and perhaps even "stereotypy." Often implicit in the assumption that ritual is traditional, customary, or conventional is the denial that it is creative (or, if this is too romantic a notion, then, invented).

I do not want to argue that ritual cannot be traditional, only that it is also invented and that it can be creative. Certainly, it may not *seem* that we who are not shamans or liturgists invent ritual, any more than it *seems* that we nonpoets invent language. It *seems* that we merely inherit and use both languages and rites. It may even seem this way to shamans and liturgists. But this seeming givenness is an illusion. Like the illusion that believes a clock's hands do not move, this illusion arises from too short a view of the process. A longer view would reveal a process beneath an apparently timeless, motionless structure.

Just as language is always being invented in the process of using it, so ritual is always in the process of being created as ritualists enact it. However typical it may be to deny the inventability of ritual, there is good reason for contesting the denial. One reason is that the history of any rite known to us always reveals it as changing, and these changes are typically congruent with others, which suggests that ritual is a fully historical, fully cultural process. As soon as one admits that ritual is fully historical and cultural, the door is open to admitting that it is constructed and on occasion, constructive. A major problem is that we have very few long-range historical accounts of rites, which gives the illusion of stasis and thus eternality.[11]

However much one might be justified in debating whether the self-generated rites reported in feminist, psychological, and ethnographic literature are authentic, good, or successful, there is less room for debate about whether they are ritual. We must be wary of allowing descriptive definitions to function normatively. To say that an invented rite is ineffective is one thing; to say that it is not ritual at all is another.

In most cultures ritualizing is socially anomalous. It happens in the margins, on the thresholds; so it is stigmatized by liturgical classicists and eulogized by ritual romantics. In either case it makes havoc of theories and definitions of ritual if we have built into them the notions of tradition, repetition, and collective participation.

If we admit the possibility that ritual can be invented, then ritualizing requires a revised understanding of tradition if we are to retain it as a feature of ritual. Tradition must be understood not merely as cultural inertia but as a mode of active construction. The work that has most thoroughly examined the relation between tradition and ritual invention is the collection of essays, *The Invention of Tradition*. In it Eric Hobsbawm says, "Inventing traditions . . . is essentially a process of formalization and ritualization characterized by reference to the past, if only by imposing repetition."[12] For Hobsbawm invented tradition is any set of practices governed overtly or covertly by a set of rules and worked out symbolically or ritually in order to inculcate values and behavior by establishing continuity with the past.[13]

Hobsbawm's understanding of both ritual and tradition is conditioned by the kinds of ritual he and his associates choose as examples. All the instances are of civil or royal ceremony. Hobsbawm and company study the invention of Bastille Day in 1880, ceremonies of the Daughters of the American Revolution, May Day, the Olympic Games, royal weddings,[14] and other devices of decadent colonialism and emergent nationalism.

Hobsbawm distinguishes tradition from custom. Custom is loosely held and comparatively flexible.[15] Tradition, on the other hand, is rule-bound; it has the aura of invariance; it boasts "the sanction of perpetuity."[16] Custom is, for example, what British judges *do*. What judges do is not invariant (a society is lucky if it is even consistent). However, says Hobsbawm, what judges *wear* (wigs and robes) is invariant; this is tradition. In Hobsbawm's model ritual serves tradition rather than custom.

There are two problems with Hobsbawm's view of tradition. One is that he denies its flexible, adaptive aspects. The other is that he regards the invention of tradition only as a symptom or as an ideology-perpetuating tool of political establishments and revolutions.[17] There is little doubt that the mass-produced, state-sponsored traditions that he examines cover up the traces of their own inventedness, but there is doubt whether this is the only form that the invention of tradition can take. Furthermore, Hobsbawm seems to imply that invented rites are effective only if ritualists are self-deceived: traditions publicly known to have been invented are not effective. "Where the old ways are alive," he says, "traditions need to be neither revived nor invented."[18] In his view invented tradition is not so much creative as manipulative. Or if it is creative, it is so within very narrow limits. Traditions, like tastes and fashions, he suggests, can only be created after they have been discovered in popular culture. Unfortunately, Hobsbawm and associates say little about either the limits or dynamics of ritual creativity. If they were to do so, they would, I presume, have to deal with ritual "custom;" it is the stuff that is flexible and therefore alive.

Is Ritual Necessarily Collective?

Much contemporary ritualizing is focused on the body and articulated using the rhetoric of the self. This focus and rhetoric give emergent ritual a distinctively individualistic ethos that sets it in opposition to the standard scholarly view of ritual as a group-oriented phenomenon that is essentially collective and necessarily social.

Often ritualizing individuals claim to tap the depths of the unconscious, and then they pit the results against the breadth of conventional social wisdom as represented in collective rites. One tactic of ritualized individualism is to mythologize the practices in Jungian, Eliadean, or, more recently, Turnerian terms. Accordingly, the zones of ritual creativity are named "the collective unconscious," "the mythic center," or "liminality." Deep, centered, or liminal ritualizing functions as an alternative to both the merely conventional and the traditional, and it allows individuals outside the confines of institutions or sometimes even groups to engage in ritual practice. Scholarship itself is appropriated and used mythically against scholars who would use it critically against emergent ritual.

There is a sizeable literature on individualism and self-culture, the most penetrating example of which is *Habits of the Heart* by Robert Bellah and his associates.[19] Virtually all of this literature is prescriptive and critical, and virtually none of it considers the ritual manifestations of individualism. Consequently, many students of ritual overlook or reject ritualizing on definitional grounds ("It is not really ritual") or moral and psychological grounds ("It is neurotic and narcissistic").

Theologically or anthropologically trained critics worry about the ethical and psychological liabilities of ritualizing, which they assume is narcissistic because it is said to serve that mythical entity, the self. But the self itself is a cultural construction, so one could just as easily argue that self-generated rites are a form of social expression. There is no such thing as an unsocialized individual, therefore no such thing as an asocial rite.

A major problem for theorists of ritual is how to conceive the relation between self and society. Too often individual and group are construed as mere static opposites when in reality they are dialectical pairs that presuppose and require one another. Theorists of ritual too often set ritual on the collective side of an individual/collective split, but we should reject the dualism this action presupposes, because taking seriously either term in the self/society pair always leads to the other term: bodies are encultured and cultures are embodied. For this reason it is necessary to reject much that is assumed about ritual and the individual, for example, that private ritual is inherently neurotic or that all ritual is by definition collective. It is *necessarily* collective only in the sense that anything human is: nothing escapes socialization. Societies have their most persistent root in the human body itself, and the body is always— no matter how closeted or private—socially inscribed.

Theories that deny the possibility of individual ritual are too undialectical in their conception of the relation between self and society. Even Roy Wagner, who has most adequately theorized the inventability of cultural forms, flounders on this score. He describes the self/society dynamic as cyclical—one would assume, dialectical.[20] However, he characterizes the cycle as moving sequentially from everyday consciousness to ritual consciousness, a movement, in his view, from differentiating to collectivizing. For Wagner the everyday is individualistic, while ritual is collectivistic. His understanding of ritual is still unable to embrace the possibility of individual ritualizing. In contemporary North American ritualizing we find the opposite of the movement he describes. Here ritual for many of the makers of new rites is an expression of their individualism, and the everyday is an expression of their collective existence. So deciding whether ritual is the tool of collectivizing or of individualizing is not a matter of theory or definition but a matter of observation of actual behavior. No theory or definition of ritual ought to preclude the possibility of individualistic ritualizing, since we know that hunting cultures, for example, emphasized ritual individualism.[21]

I am not offering an apologetic for private ritual, but I am criticizing theories that make ritual by definition a form of group behavior. I am the first to admit that what Jung called "self culture" is dangerous. The temptations to ego-inflation, intercultural imperialism, and self-deception are high, especially if a self introjects the notion that it is *the* source of ritual. Certainly, both the notion and the experience of the self need considerable refinement, or ritualizing can, in fact, feed neurosis, but this danger does not obviate the validity of individual ritual.

Are Ritualists Necessarily Pre-critical?

Assuming that ritualists—at least when they are engaged in the act of performing rites—exist in an unself-conscious, precritical state of mind is widespread. Jack Goody, for instance, defines ritual as "a category of standardized behavior (custom) in which the relationship between the means and the end is not intrinsic."[22] Defining ritual as outside of means/end logic implies that it is irrational and therefore incapable of grounding critique. For romantics this absence of means/end reasoning would be a virtue, but for Goody and others it is not. In such views ritualists are assumed to be in the body and therefore not in the mind. The new ritualizers as well as the old theorists of ritual sometimes lapse into this assumption that ritual is a way of embodiment, therefore a way of "getting out of the head." This way of speaking about the effect of ritual is probably a popularized version of the practice in Gestalt therapy that chides patients for speaking merely from their heads.

The implication that ritual is a pre-critical activity takes many forms. For instance, Hobsbawm's arguments that ritual functions like ideology in its tranquilizing of criticism implies this attitude. Roy Wagner and Paul Connerton hold a similar view. Wagner believes self-consciousness about the invention of culture has a shattering effect. He says,

> Of course, a realization of this fact by the symbolizer would be deadly to his [or her] intention: to see the whole field at once, in all its implications, is to suffer a "relativization" of intention, to become aware of how gratuitous a part it plays in the activation of symbols. Thus the most compelling necessity of action under these circumstances is a restriction of vision. . . .[23]

Applied to ritual, this view would suggest that recognition of the inventedness of ritual is too critical an activity for ritualists to engage in. Self-consciousness would amount to a kind of unmasking that undermines motivation.[24] Wagner implies that it is possible for him, the scholar, to see ritual's inventedness, but not for the dancers themselves to see it. When ritual is relativized by being conceptualized as *in*vention rather than *con*vention, says Wagner, the result appears "'forced,' 'commercialized,' 'too serious,' or sacrilegious.'"[25]

Wagner suggests that taking oneself too seriously as an inventor of culture produces not invented but counterfeit culture, with guilt as the primary motivation to action.[26] Self-invention—though perhaps a necessity in some cultural contexts—is a flirtation with neurosis, and, he says, those who aspire to professional ritual creativity can be virtually assured of neurosis. So, although Wagner does not say that ritualists cannot be self-conscious and critical, he clearly implies that the consequences of doing so would be destructive to ritual.

The belief that ritual is a pre-critical activity is often linked to the fact that ritual is embodied and to a view of the human body as a non-cognitive entity. The most astute theorist of the relations between memory, embodiment, and ritual is Paul Connerton. In *How Societies Remember* he tries to formulate a theory of memory that utilizes Hobsbawm's view of tradition-inventing and takes seriously both ritual and the body. At first, Connerton seems more promising than Hobsbawm. Part of his strategy is to distinguish "incorporating practices" from "inscribing practices."[27] Incorporating practices are performative—smiling and hand-shaking, for example. Inscribing practices are textual, for instance, depositing information in print, computers, tapes, files, and other sorts of knowledge traps.[28] For Connerton general bodily practices such as decorum and habit and specific commemorative practices, rites, for example, are instances of incorporating practices that enable societies to remember.

Connerton attacks the cognitive imperialism of linguistic models when used on bodily practices.[29] And in applying performance theory to ceremonies, he explicitly rejects symbolic or semantic interpretations of ritual.[30] In his view commemorative ceremonies are "acts of transfer" that depend on "habit-memory," as distinct from personal and cognitive memory.[31] Embodied memories are those that enable performers to reproduce a certain kind of performance. Like typing or riding a bicycle, performing rites depends on embodied knowledge, which is tacit and does not depend for its effectiveness on ritualists' ability to do an exegesis of it.

Although I accept Connerton's central claim that ritual embodiment is a primary means through which societies remember and thus create tradition, I reject his understanding of the body and of ritual. Rites do not "transfer" either memories or knowledge. Neither knowledge nor memory is a quantity deposited somewhere, for example, in texts or computers. The container/contained metaphor is contrary to his own theory of incorporating practices.[32] The theory requires a performative model in which rites improvise and thus reinvent. Unfortunately, Connerton lapses back into inscription language, the very model he criticizes. In his epistemology the body is a "sedimentation" of the past, and memory is the "transmission" of the past. For him performance is the way such transmission occurs. Unfortunately, he ignores the transformative activities of both body and memory.

The view of ritual that emerges from Connerton is much like Hobsbawm's, if not actually borrowed from Hobsbawm. Connerton says,

> Newly invented rites, spring up and are instantly formalized ... That is why invented rites, involving sets of recorded rules and procedures, as in modern coronation rites, are marked out by their inflexibility. By virtue of their procedural inflexibility they are held to represent, as nowhere else, the idea of the unchanging for a society of institutionalized innovation. Their intention is reassurance and their mood is nostalgic.[33]

The kinds of invented rites Connerton studies—coronations, for example—determine his conclusions. I would have no problem with his argument if he recognized that his is a view appropriate only to certain kinds of invented rites, in certain kinds of societies, during certain historical periods. But he ignores processes of tacit ritual revision and adaptation that mark some traditional societies, as well as the ad hoc (rather than rule-bound) ritual inventiveness in self-conscious subcultures in our own society. The problem his view presents for theorizing about ritual is that it assumes invented rites are necessarily specious. Unlike Connerton I do not know of any *un*invented traditions.

Connerton says,

> Both commemorative ceremonies and bodily practices contain a measure of insurance against the process of cumulative questioning entailed in all discursive practices. This is the source of their importance and persistence as mnemonic systems. Every group, then, will entrust to bodily automatisms the values and categories which they are most anxious to conserve. They will know how well the past can be kept in mind by a habitual memory sedimented in the body.[34]

This is an interesting idea—that groups hide important memories from the great search light of critical consciousness by stashing memories in the body. But it is one Connerton assumes, not one he demonstrates. For him the body is a kind of repository—a bank or library—that works on the basis of "automatisms" (a bank with an automated teller, one supposes).

Connerton does not look for evidence that the ritualizing body can be either cognitive or critical; he simply assumes cultures use bodies to house a collection of treasures thus protecting them from being raided by critical questions. He might, for instance, have considered Hopi women, who have a fall ceremony in which they mock the sacred winter ceremonies controlled by Hopi men. He might have considered Pueblo clowns who regularly perform their critiques in the midst of the most solemnly sacral rites.

One place to look for evidence that people perform their rites with some measure of critical awareness, not necessarily with self-deception, is in the rites themselves, rather than in what people say about those rites. Even though Connerton rightly recognizes the bodily foundation of social memory, his view of the body is that it is a habituated, mindless object; he implies that it is essentially passive and stupid. He fails to comprehend the creative, cognitive, critical functions of the ritualizing body.[35] The human body is not only object, but subject. It has its own way of questioning, arguing, asserting, thinking—its own form of wisdom. The body is cognitive, not stupid; and conversely, the mind is embodied.[36]

In my view ritualizing is not incompatible with criticism, nor a sense of mystery with iconoclasm, provided self-critical actions are embedded in rites themselves, and provided the timing of criticism is carefully chosen. Criticism itself can take the form of an action, a gesture. It need not take the form of an intellectual operation separate from ritual performance, an operation that forces it to stand apart as literary criticism sometimes does from literature or as religious criticism (that is, theology) sometimes does from liturgy. We are used to thinking of ritual and criticism, if not as opposites, then as an unhappily married pair. We worry that criticism may destroy mystery, or mystery befog criticism. But it is quite possible to develop forms of critique that do not depend on the ideology of objectivism with its penchant for distancing, or on dividing up social roles into critics, on the one hand, and ritualists, on the other.

In the Ritual Studies Lab, which I direct and where we experiment with ritual in a highly self-conscious environment, two sorts of criticism transpire: acted out critique and verbal, expository critique. Whatever we enact seriously we later invert and thus criticize. Whatever is revelatory is later fictive, and vice-versa. The effect is much like that of Hopi Kachina initiation: enchantment is held in constructive tension with disenchantment—an important skill in a society highly susceptible to romantic mystification, on the one hand, and cynical disenchantment, on the other. Much depends on the timing of criticism. If we separate the formal critique and analysis of an event from the experience of it by an hour or week, most participants eventually learn to hold two attitudes simultaneously: reverence and iconoclasm.

Cultural processes, including ritual, are human constructions, and awareness of this fact does not automatically imply the death of them. Religious studies and anthropology have tended to identify as religious those elements of culture that its participants are least able criticize. To some practitioners, as well as to some scholars, religious culture (ritual, for example) is a given—its sources out of reach and its authority beyond question. However, improvisation and revision are essential parts of many, if not most, ritual traditions, not just the ritual experiments and ad hoc rites I have mentioned. An adequate theory of ritual should take into account the revision, improvisation, and invention of cultural forms. All such processes imply that ritualists are not uncritical of what they perform.

Although we may think that self-consciousness in ritual performance and construction is something new, arriving in North America in the 1970s, reflexivity is not new nor confined to this continent. Reflexivity is to a culture what self-consciousness is to an individual. When a society enacts itself in ritual, it is able to see itself mirrored. Far from tranquilizing critique or immobilizing performance, such reflexivity, especially heightened in festive and initiatory rites, can serve as a strong motive for criticism and stimulus for enhanced performance.

Counterculture ritualizing, for instance, that of feminists, is sometimes torn between a sense of the importance of ritual and a self-consciousness about the contrivance of enactment. But it is not *necessarily* the case that either self-awareness or consciousness of invention means the death of ritual, any more than breaking symbols or demythologizing myths prevents their reappropriation in an attitude of second naivete. Sam Gill has illustrated how ritual disenchantment can, in fact, enhance ritual performance and tradition.[37]

Roy Wagner distinguishes between cultural change that only amounts to an alteration of imagery and change that alters the line between the given (what Wagner refers to as "innate") and the invented.[38] The latter is a fundamental shift of sensibility. Presently, we are, I believe, in the midst of such a fundamental change in our attitude toward ritual. Gestures once regarded as innate and scenarios once treated as sacrosanct are now understood as cultural constructions.[39] But I do not believe that the death of supposedly primordial actions or revealed rites spells the death of ritual practice any more than doubt necessarily destroys faith. Reflexivity, the awareness of performance by one who is performing, does not have to precipitate the demise of ritual; it can become part of the work of ritual. It may even be that ritual is a primary cultural means whereby participants learn to comprehend and criticize the constructedness of what are taken to be cultural facts.

The claim that people cannot live with ritual criticism or with the knowledge that rites are invented is exaggerated and not based on much field observation. Clerics, shamans, and scholars disenchant ritual all the time. Calling attention to the symbolic nature of the realities negotiated by ritual is one of the primary functions of ritual leaders. People's capacity to incorporate critical self-consciousness depends mostly on their having experienced rites that weave criticism, self-parody, and humor into the fabric of the ritual system itself.

One of the most powerful presentations of critical, self-conscious, but nevertheless effective, ritualizing is by Barbara Myerhoff in her ethnographic classic *Number Our Days*. Regarding a made-up rite for senior citizens, the Graduation-Siyum, she writes,

> All rituals are paradoxical and dangerous enterprises, the traditional and improvised, the sacred and secular. Paradoxical because rituals are conspicuously artificial and theatrical, yet designed to suggest the inevitability and absolute truth of their messages. Dangerous because, when we are not convinced by a

ritual we may become aware of ourselves as having made them up, thence on to the paralyzing realization that we have made up all our truths; [that] our ceremonies, our most precious conceptions and convictions—all are mere invention, not inevitable understandings about the world at all but the results of mortals' imaginings.[40]

Like Wagner, Myerhoff seems to imply that an awareness of invention and a recognition of the role of imagination, is devastating for ritualists, yet she documents ritual activities that illustrate the contrary. She herself participates in made-up rites, aware of their constructedness and taking them seriously at the same time.[41] The assumption by scholars that second naiveté is possible for themselves but not for ritualists is astonishingly ethnocentric. Second naiveté is as possible in performing ritual as it is in appropriating ancient myth, and it is as possible among ordinary participants as among scholarly participant-observers.

Is Ritual Necessarily Meaningful?

The phenomenon of ritualizing not only implies revisions of our understanding of tradition, collectivity, and critical self-consciousness but also of meaning. Conceptions of meaning are closely linked to symbol theory. Three widespread assumptions about ritual are (1) that its building blocks are symbols, (2) that symbols are the carriers of meaning, (3) that the meaning of a symbol is that to which it refers, and (4) that ritualists "believe in" these meanings.

If one asks ritualists what their rites and symbols mean, one quickly finds that there is little connection between how much people can articulate about a symbol's referents and how meaningful it is to them. The usual social scientific way of handling this conceptual dilemma is to resort to function. Thus, a ritual becomes meaningful by virtue of what it does socially, not just by virtue of what it refers to. Victor Turner, for example, makes "operational" (that is, functional) a category of meaning alongside "exegetical" (or referential) meaning.[42]

I do not deny that ritual symbols either refer or do, but the problem with both semantic and functional theories is that either they set us looking outside of ritual for the meaning of

ritual or they lead us to believe that meaning is a kind of referentiality.[43] One of the most insightful theorists for helping
articulate questions about conventional theories of ritual
meaning is Dan Sperber. In *Rethinking Symbolism* he suggests
that the search for symbolic meanings in ritual is fundamentally wrongheaded, because it makes us think ritual is a set
of coded messages.[44] But inevitably when we decode them,
they seem banal—counterfeit inventions, to use Wagner's
term. The expectation that rites have meaning in a semiotic,
or referential, sense is an expectation of *our* culture, says
Sperber.[45] Thus, it may be ethnocentric to try applying it
elsewhere.

He argues that what ritualists offer as interpretations of
symbols are usually as opaque as the symbols themselves, and
that they are not really interpretations at all but further acts of
symbolizing. Interpreting, or doing exegesis of, ritual symbols
amounts to the reinvention or recreation of them in another
form;[46] it is not an explanation of their meaning. In short,
meaning does not consist of "indigenous exegesis" (Victor
Turner's term) or what members of multinational Western religious traditions like to call "theology." It is not a matter of
explicating referents.

Sperber makes a provocative claim: that smells are symbols
par excellence.[47] Symbols work like smells, he suggests. They
evoke rather than refer. Olfaction is our least rationalized
sense; its way of meaning is tied more immediately to primary
bodily responses than those rooted in other senses. The smells
of freshly baked bread or of burning flesh reach the guts (that
is, the cerebral cortex) directly; they evoke, in the one case
hunger, in the other revulsion.

Sperber claims that, "when Westerners speak in a vague
way of meaning, they are really talking about evocation."[48]
Smells, he argues, are difficult to recall (we usually resort to
visual symbols instead), but they are extraordinarily powerful
in the area of recognition and evocation.[49] We can recognize a
smell arising from an old drawer even though we cannot recall where we originally encountered such a smell. Then, as if
by magic, here comes a whole set of memories from the distant past; we did not know we had them. Ritual symbols, understood according to this Sperberian, olfactory logic, focalize

attention and evoke memory; they do not leave us with religious ideas or political statements that constitute their meaning.

In Sperber's view evocation is the re-collecting of some initially unfulfilled condition, in other words, a defect, a break. Sperber thinks the defect is conceptual. And here I begin my departure from him. I think this is only one among several possibilities. His understanding is more exclusively cognitive than mine.

In any case, symbols in this view are part of a system of implicit knowledge, and ritual is an improvisation, reconstruction, or anticipation based on that knowledge.[50] It is not merely a repetition of it. Sperber says,

> The cyclical movement of cultural symbolism might seem absurd if it were not precisely for the constructive character of remembering. Indeed, it is not a question here of the endless quest for an impossible solution, but rather of a repeated work of re-organization of the encyclopedic memory. Each new evocation brings about a different reconstruction of old representations, weaves new links among them, integrates into the field of symbolism new information brought to it by daily life: the same rituals are enacted, but with new actors; the same myths are told, but in a changing universe, and to individuals whose social position, whose relationships with others, and whose experience have changed.[51]

Sperber's argument implies that ritual, by virtue of its olfactory-like symbolization, is not just occasionally creative, as in the case of experimental ritual, but regularly so. Ritualists do not merely discover the meaning of symbols but, by improvising with them ritually, invent "a relevance and a place in memory for them despite the failure in this respect of the conceptual categories of meaning."[52]

Like Sperber I believe that the most interesting cultural knowledge is tacit, which is to say, preconscious, implicit, and embodied. When knowledge becomes explicit, he says, it can be learned by rote, but when it is tacit, it cannot; it must be reconstructed, improvised, or reinvented in each new enactment.[53]

At first it may sound as if Sperber, like Wagner, Hobsbawm, and Connerton, is suggesting that ritual consciousness is uncritical because it is embodied and that the body is noncognitive. But he is not. Tacit knowledge is still knowledge.

The knowledge in a surgeon's or artist's hands is no less knowledge because it is embodied, and it is no less critical because its criticism takes the form of action rather than verbal articulation.

If ritual meaning is anything like what I have implied by appropriating some of Sperber's views of symbols, then belief is not quite the right word for what one does as a ritualist. Would we want to speak about believing a smell, as we might speak of believing a statement? Does the surgeon "believe in" her hands, or the artist, his? I think not. We must give up the linguistic analogies that have formed the basis for much theorizing about ritual. But then what? If ritual is not message or communication, we will have to become more articulate about it as play, performance, and practice. But that is another essay.

To conclude, I have argued that contemporary invented rites are precipitating a corresponding conceptual reinvention of ritual. Whereas previously we may have insisted that ritual is *necessarily* traditional, collective, precritical, and meaningful, we now have to say, "'Taint necessarily so." The result of sustained ritualizing and revised theory of ritual to account for it is likely to be the bleeding of genres—the fuzzing of boundary lines that separate ritual from art, theater, politics, and therapy—but this bleeding of boundaries may not be a loss. It may represent instead ritual's reconnection with some of its vital sources and tributaries.

2

Emerging Ritual[54]

YOU HAVE ASKED ME TO SPEAK ON THE TOPIC, "EMERGING RITU-al." Since this august body is reputed to be a bastion of liturgical classicism (with its penchant for ritual understatement, noble simplicity, and a wise and chastened sense of limits), I should be wary that you have handed me such a topic fraught with ritual romanticism (with its penchant for ritual hyperbole, meaning-laden complexity, and a tendency to soar on the wings of rebellious individualism and exotic syncretism).

Instead of resisting, I have decided to assume the role you have implicitly assigned me: that of ritual romantic in a den of liturgical classicists. Unlike Daniel I do not imagine my safety to lie in successfully shutting the lions' mouths but in tempting them to fill their mouths with more questions than they can chew.

What is "emerging ritual?" I should ask you. You assigned me the topic. Since you handed me neither definitions nor illustrations, I assumed I was free to make up my own. So let me begin by enumerating a few examples so the phrase seems less vague.

Emerging ritual is what transpires when an intertribal group of Native Canadians and Native Americans has to invent a rite to rebury ancestral bones repatriated from the 18,000 Native skeletons held by the Smithsonian institution.

Emerging ritual is what happens when anthropologist Vic-

23

tor Turner dies and has a funeral with two phases, one Catholic, the other Ndembu, or when he enacts an Ndembu rite in a workshop in New York City with a theater director.

Emerging ritual is what occurs when Jews join Christians or Lutherans join Orthodox in makeshift, one-time, inevitably awkward celebration or prayer.

Emerging ritual is what must happen to commemorate, grieve, and resist the anti-feminist murder of fourteen women in Quebec.

Emerging ritual is bound to happen when Buddhists, Cree, Christians, and "Others" beat the *dharma* drum, burn sweet grass, and chant lines from St. Francis in honor of the Dali Lama's reception of the Nobel Peace Prize.

It is also what happens when a wife invents a turning-forty party for her husband, a therapist puts a family to making and dancing masks of its members, or Rites of Passage, Inc., (of California, of course) takes teenagers on vision quests.

The list could go on. Some of the instances are inspiring; some embarrassing. The principles that inform them are not uniform. What all these have in common is that scholars ignore or look down on them, which is to say, they do not pay serious ethnographic or theoretical attention to them. They do not seem to be ritual in the fullest sense of the word; they are new, self-conscious, disestablished. Either they are small and therefore not important, or they are secondary because they are not enduring. My aim is to call attention to them and to persuade you that they merit theoretical and ethnographic attention.

What you have called "emerging ritual" I usually call "ritualizing." The gerund form is to call attention to the activity of deliberately cultivating rites. Ritualizing is not often socially supported. Rather it happens in the margins, on the thresholds; so it is alternatively stigmatized and eulogized.

In contrast, "rites" are the classical paradigms, the full-blown instances of ritual with claims to longevity or legitimacy. In this usage Jewish or Christian worship is a rite. Ritualizing, on the other hand, is "romantic," still "wet behind the ears"; it is the stuff born out of wedlock in a society in which the life-expectancy for newborn ritual is typically brief.

Some Principles of Ritualizing

Usually, I have spoken and written abut ritual as a theorist or field worker (my wife Susan calls me a "professional ignorant observer"). But I have decided for this occasion to take off my honorary anthropologist's hat and my ritual critic's hat and to put on my ritual plumber's hat. Rather than speaking generally about the social and political conditions of ritualizing, I will speak specifically as a maker of rites, a ritualizer, (if you will pardon the awful term) a role parallel (but certainly subordinate to) that of liturgist. Most of you do your ritual work in churches or synagogues. Most of mine is in either domestic or academic space. Since I have already described some of the activities of the Ritual Studies Lab in *Ritual Criticism*, I will not do so again here but will try to summarize some of the principles that have emerged from research there. Most of you are teachers of ritual. Either you are practicing liturgists or liturgiologists who teach in seminaries. Many of you play both roles. So I address you as one teacher of ritual to another, even though I am aware that the ways we frame and value ritual differ considerably, even radically. I will state the principles briefly, because my primary aim is not to lecture but to enter into conversation.

1. The principle of ritualized pedagogy: The form of ritual pedagogy more profoundly shapes the attitudes of students of ritual than the content of it does. Process is determinative. One may adequately teach students the data, history, and theory of ritual by reading and lecturing, but if one cares about formation—that is, with people's *sense* of ritual—the form is what shapes basic attitudes, which are always both bodily and spiritual. Teaching itself *is* ritualized whether or not we intend it. If you think it is not, you should read Peter McLaren's book, *Schooling as a Ritual Performance*. In the Lab our aim is to make this fact evident and then to change the values that are ritualized. Thus it is obvious that there is not only a purpose to what we do but a socially critical one.

One enduring characteristic of the Ritual Studies Lab that results from its pedagogical setting is experimentalism, its incessant trying, testing, criticizing, and reimagining. One danger in experimenting with ritual in a lab is that participants can begin to value experiment for its own sake. And the demand that ritual, like the market-at-large, provide something forever new and exciting could be destructive to ritual itself.

Another of the dominant formal characteristics of work in the Lab is our ritualizing of passage. Rites of passage depend on a great deal of mystification of authority. Even though this mystification is opened up periodically to question and to overt iconoclasm in the end, it can easily create a false picture. Designing, executing, and evaluating a rite is not nearly as exciting as being led through it. Students who take subsequent courses on the theory, field study, or construction of ritual sometimes find it hard to marshal the necessary energy and motivation for wading through the infinite list of details required to facilitate or study a rite. A rite of passage has a certain drama to it that is missing from more repetitive ritual forms such as worship and meditation.

2. The principle of embodied criticism: Ritualizing is not incompatible with criticism, nor a sense of mystery with iconoclasm, provided self-critical actions are embedded in ritual itself. Criticism itself can take the form of an action, a gesture. We are used to thinking of ritual and criticism, if not as opposites, then as an unhappily married pair. We worry that criticism may destroy mystery, or mystery befog criticism. But it is quite possible to develop forms of critique that do not depend on the ideology of objectivism with its insistence on sheer distance. Pueblo ritual clowns are a classic example.

In the Ritual Studies Lab whatever we enact seriously we later invert. Whatever seems revelatory is later seen as fictive, and vice-versa. The effect is much like that of Hopi Kachina initiation: enchantment is held in constructive tension with disenchantment—an important skill in a society highly susceptible to manipulation and exploitation by ritual means.

Much depends on the timing of criticism. If we separate the formal critique and analysis of an event from the experience of it by an hour or week, most participants eventually learn to hold two attitudes simultaneously: reverence and iconoclasm.

3. The principle of attunement: Ritualizing most effectively transpires on the basis of some form of meditative practice. I do not mean only traditional forms of it. Rather, I mean any way of cultivating an attitude of bodily responsiveness and attentiveness that minimizes one's sense of separation from the objects of contemplation and undermines sole dependence on symbolization and referentiality. Sometimes in the Lab we use a musical analogy and speak of it as "attunement." We also call it simply "following," after the analogy of following one's breath in Zen practice.

Celebrations and other ritual forms we utilize at the Lab are more likely to work well if they are constructed with a minimum of verbalization and a maximum of "following." The incubatory process of ritualizing requires a protected space between social institutions such as universities and churches. Such work as ours happens most effectively at the edge of paradigmatic rites such as official liturgies. Yet, despite all this mystical-sounding language, attunement can be taught, and its absence can be readily be detected by students who have absorbed this form of ritual knowing. Obviously, I consider ritual, not merely a form of expression but a legitimate, in fact, essential way of knowing. It has cognitive, not merely aesthetic, import.

The ethos and outcome of attuned interactions have no adequate name. They are experienced as off the map of usual categories: ritual, drama, game. One cue that we are on track in the Lab is when we have no name for what transpires. (However, the difficulty with a refusal to name as a strategy is that grocery stores have made "No Name" into a brand name.)

4. The principle of gestural ordinariness: The ground of ritualizing is "interaction ritual" (Erving Goffman's term), the stylized, repeated scenarios of everyday life. If attunement gives ritualizing its mysterious quality, the principle of bodily—gestural and postural—ordinariness gives it its basic grounding, its root. Appropriate sources of symbols for use in ritualizing are those elemental to ordinary life or those that come from the refuse of the culture.

Although we use in the Lab ritual motifs that remind some participants of those in specific religions, we never borrow directly, nor do we enact rites taken from another culture. We build on simple actions like walking, sitting, eating, and we use junk from dumps or unclassifiable keepsakes from the backs of people's drawers to make our "treasures" and "icons."

There are many ways to call attention to ritual ordinariness. One is to refer to ritualizing as "work." Another is to frame it as "play." But if these are only metaphors, that is, if there is no sustained exertion nor any pervasive frolicing and enjoyment, we have cut an essential lifeline for ritual.

5. The principle of body/culture dialectic: Body and culture, self and society, are not merely opposites; they are dialectical pairs. Taking seriously one term in each pair always leads to the other term. For this reason I reject much that is assumed about ritual and the individual, for example, that ritual is by definition collective. It is *necessarily* collective only in the sense that anything human is: nothing—not the body, not the self escapes culture. And culture has its most persistent root in the human body itself. If bodiliness is central to ritualizing, then ritual action is essentially gendered. Any and all bodily features—weight, health, size, skin color, hair texture—may exercise considerable force in one's ritual formation, with or without one's consent.

Theologically or anthropologically trained critics worry about the ethical and psychological liabilities of ritualizing that takes individual persons seriously. These critics assume such ritual is narcissistic. But psychologizing and excessive self-preoccupation can be reoriented by the use of specific techniques, so I argue that ritualizing is not *necessarily* self-focused. It has taken me years to learn how to do so, but there are many ways. One is to play off the materialistic preoccupation of our culture and substitute what D.W. Winnicott would call "transition objects" for the self: let this wooden egg, not your self, occupy your attention. Another way is to teach eye decorum. People lose interest in the state of their psyches if they cannot peer into one another's eyes hoping to see their own reflections. The same is true if they learn a rhetoric that displaces the agency of action from the self to the space, to an object, or to an action itself: "The blank scroll called for a signature in the bottom left corner; the rhythm of the drum wanted us to move counterclockwise," and so on. Animistic language facilitates transference onto things and places rather than onto a therapist. The dangers of projection are, of course, ever present.

6. The principle of momentary community: Community does not have to be enduring to be real. What Victor Turner called *communitas* is, in fact, temporary. And it always requires its opposite, social structure. But nothing requires that a ritual community also be the community of work and play, though most of us wish this were the case. We have yet to learn how to deal with ritual in a highly segmented, socially differentiated society like ours. So I am least sure about the implications of this principle except to reject the typical anthropological assumption that rites of passage, if not all ritual, is really at home in small-scale tribal cultures and cannot really thrive in societies such as ours.

The segregation of one's ritual community from one's community of work and one's neighborhood certainly has its dangers. The most persistent problem at the Lab is on this point. Students sometimes cling to it, hoping for more permanent community. I repeatedly ask myself whether such a course raises unfillable expectations and thereby plays into the decadence of the late twentieth-century, workshop-circuit spirituality. Students who take the course are sometimes tempted to try continuing the Lab experience nostalgically in other contexts. Much of what they learn is portable, but the experience of community, at least this specific community, is not.

By now you are probably asking, What are these students being initiated *into*? They are being initiated into the community and tradition of this class and thereby the study of ritual. Of course, the process is not the same as being initiated into a religion. The class has a limited lifespan and it offers no ongoing community. Part of the message of the course is that much human ritualizing is predicated on the fact that all things, including communities and courses, die.

7. The principle of performance-dependence: Ritualizing exists in the doing; like rites, plays, and games it is a species of action. Not being primarily dependent on either ritual texts or ritual traditions is simultaneously its strength and its liability. All ritual lives in the performance of it, but when a traditional rite ends, a participant is surrounded by a blanket of symbols, stories, icons, and other ritual fragments; texts and traditions reinforce the performance. But when ritualizing ends, there is a void. There are small traditions perhaps but not large enduring ones. As with all voids, we are tempted to fill them compulsively rather than dwell in their emptiness. For this reason we practice dwelling in emptiness in the Ritual Studies Lab. We practice waiting expectantly with out expecting anything in particular.

The performance ethic underlies advertising as surely as it does ritual, and there is a growing, sometimes disturbing, literature on the use of ritual in business and in family therapy. We must be vigilant that the current hunger for ritual, theories of ritual process, and experimentation with ritual do not make us even more susceptible to the consumer ethic or lead to cross-cultural religious imperialism. One has to ask whether ritualizing, particularly if it is experiential, performative, and experimental, is merely one more symptom of the shift from salvation to self-realization that occurred in North America between the 1880s and the present.

8. The principle of ritual inventability: People can be taught to incubate rites; traditions can be invented. As Roy Wagner has shown, there is little question that humans do, in fact, invent culture, which is simply tradition viewed synchronically. What varies is the degree of self-awareness with which people do so. Religious studies and anthropology have both tended to identify as religious those elements of culture that we are least able, or least likely, to regard as inventable. To some practitioners, religious culture seems given. However, improvisation is an essential part of many, if not most, ritual traditions. This does not mean new rites are created whole cloth but that the incubating of new rites utilizes a nest of old "parts" from dismembered older rites. Just as a literary work is written, not out of experience alone, but out of other works of literature, so we should recognize the ways that new rites emerge out of other rites.

In research at the Lab we have been able to construct activities in which the given and the made-up are not experienced as mutually exclusive. Consequently, participants are less torn between their study of ritual and their practice of it. After almost fifteen years the Lab itself is (or has) a miniature tradition of sorts. Participants leave ritual objects for the next year's class. Stories and lore accumulate. Some of it is passed from student to student; some, through the lab assistant and me, to the next "generation" of students.

There are other principles; I could go on. I could supplement the list of principles with stories, narrative accounts. But what would it all amount to? My experiments with ritual, though sustained for over fifteen years, have been small-scale. And fifteen years is a mere pittance in the face of traditions such as yours that extend for millennia and involve millions. So obviously, I am not holding up ritualizing in the Ritual Studies Lab as a model for either Christian or Jewish worship. I am claiming, however, that we may be witnessing the emergence new forms of ritual practice and consciousness that are consonant with life in a world that is increasingly pluralistic in its ritual practices. What we know about the histories of Jewish and Christian liturgy clearly illustrates that fundamental liturgical principles, not mere adiophora, have changed as ritual traditions have migrated across cultural boundaries and passed across eras. One of the forces with which those interested in the enculturation of liturgy must come to terms is the growing wave of ritual practice outside ecclesiastical space. Enculturation is not merely what happens when liturgies enter Third World countries, it is what ought to happen here. Here in North America, I think, one of the central issues is, or will soon be, learning how to engage in liturgy while remaining aware of its fictive, or, if you prefer, made up nature. One of the most convincing and moving presentations of emerging ritual is that of Barbara Myerhoff in her ethnographic classic *Number Our Days*. I conclude with her observation, which immediately follows an account of a made-up rite for senior citizens, the Graduation-Siyum:

> All rituals are paradoxical and dangerous enterprises, the traditional and improvised, the sacred and secular. Paradoxical because rituals are conspicuously artificial and theatrical, yet designed to suggest the inevitability and absolute truth of their messages. Dangerous because when we are not convinced by a ritual we may become aware of ourselves as having made them up, thence on to the paralyzing realization that we have made

up all our truths; our ceremonies, our most precious conceptions and convictions—all are mere invention, not inevitable understandings about the world at all but the results of mortals' imaginings.[55]

Some Discussion Questions
Based on the Principles of Ritualizing
and Considered by Academy Participants

Note: Where there are questions marked "a" or "b" the first calls for a more imaginative response; the second, for a more analytical response to the same topic.

1. The principle of ritualized pedagogy: The form of ritual pedagogy more profoundly shapes the attitudes of students of ritual than the content of it does.

a. Imagine the form of ritual pedagogy that most completely denies or undermines what you consider most important to say about liturgy.

b. Assume this principle may be as true of liturgies as it is of ritualizing, what kind of ritual sensibilities are inculcated by the ritual pedagogies of contemporary synagogues, churches, or classrooms?

2. The principle of embodied criticism: Ritualizing is not incompatible with criticism, nor a sense of mystery with iconoclasm, provided self-critical actions (e.g., ritual clowns in Pueblo rites) are embedded in ritual itself.

a. Identify some facet you are critical of in the liturgy you are most committed to. Now imagine doing what you are not likely to do, namely, acting out that critique in the middle of the rite itself.

b. In your own tradition, and outside formal theological contexts, what are the means for the criticism of ritual?

3. The principle of attunement: Ritualizing most effectively transpires on the basis of some form of meditative practice.

a. Suppose for a moment that the most apt image of attuned interaction is that of a flock of geese or a school of fish. Imagine away, item by item, anything in a liturgy that would obstruct such behavior.

b. In your own experience where do you come nearest this image of attunement or "following?" Where is such experience the least likely?

4. The principle of gestural ordinariness: The ground of ritualizing is ritualization, specifically the kind Erving Goffman calls "interaction ritual," the stylized, repeated scenarios of everyday life.

For the sake of the discussion assume a pair of polarities, at the one of which is the "grounded" rite rooted in elemental things of everyday life; at the other end is a "rarefied" rite elevated above them. What phases of the liturgy you know best cluster at which ends of the polarity?

5. The principle of the body/culture dialectic: Body and culture, self and society, are not merely opposites; they are dialectical pairs.

a. Imagine that your body is a repository, a container, and that cultural items are deposited in it. What cultural "things" (from out there) do you most readily imagine as residing in the container? Where, specifically, in your body are they?

b. Take a position pro or con regarding this principle and illustrate your answer, not with arguments, but with examples.

6. The principle of momentary community: Community does not have to be enduring to be real.

Tell about ritually significant examples of formative, but momentary, community that are outside the context of what you consider normative, religious community.

7. The principle of performance-dependence: Ritualizing exists in the doing; like rites, plays, and games it is a species of performance.

Choose a liturgy with which you are familiar. Imagine that you are a theater director and not bound by theological or congregation expectations. What part of the liturgy would you redesign and how would you do it?

8. The principle of ritual inventability: People can be taught to incubate rites; traditions can be invented.

Narrate and evaluate one instance in which you were involved in a made-up rite or in an activity that one might at least imagine as a rite.

Some Questions Asked of the Presenter
Publicly and Privately

Note: The following questions and answers are reconstructed from memory, condensed, anonymous, and rearranged.

Q: You ask us to imagine our bodies as containers. When women have been imagined as containers, the result has been destructive. We are not just receptacles of culture or men's bodies. We are producers of culture and givers of life. Wouldn't the metaphor of giving birth be less susceptible to violation?

A: In the Ritual Studies Lab I do a critique of the container metaphor, because, like you, I believe it is misleading and dangerous. But it is one of the most common metaphors. I hoped imagining it would lead to a critique of it.

As for birth, the metaphor recurs regularly at the Lab without my prompting. However, as a man, I am a bit shy about appropriating it, even though I venerate it.

Q: You are obviously in control of the Lab. And there seems to be a clear hierarchy between you and your female lab assistant. Have you thought about gender and power relations? And have you considered a more collaborative model?

A: Yes, to both questions. As long as I have to give grades, I have no choice but to work in a less than collaborative fashion. It is true that there is a lot of mystification of power in this course. In others I use more collaborative models.

As soon as some of the female assistants finish their Ph.D.s, they will no doubt look for male teaching assistants, and some aspects of the problem will then shift.

In Journey, which concludes one of the courses at the Lab, I play Old Man Death. As for the hierarchy between Old Man and Young Woman, who's at the top of the totem pole? For

Journey she is top dog, good guy, savior; the students bond with her and kill Death. (Of course, I have to admit that Death, like Milton's Satan, is more interesting than Life, like Milton's God). So the anthropologist in me would even sharpen your question: Does this inversion of hierarchy dissolve it or only reinforce it?

Q: I am not happy with your answer to your own question, What are these students being initiated into? Surely, it is inadequate to say that they are being initiated into the temporary community of the class.

A: Perhaps. But it's true. There is no more: student's are initiated into the course, nothing else.

Q: But doesn't that drive your students into the workshop circuit?

A: I don't think so. Students who are on the circuit before the course are on it after, and students in traditional churches or synagogues are in them afterward. What I notice is that both sorts of students become more critical of whatever sort of ritual they are involved in; a few also become more imaginative.

Q: What you're really saying is that this is a course that advocates ritual without theology or myth.

A: What I am really saying is that theology can work just as effectively when it has to be inferred from action as when it is explicit and precedes action. There is myth, or something like myth, in the course. I've just chosen not to talk about it here.

Q: Isn't your course really a Zen course?

A: My Zen master wouldn't think so. But perhaps it is. If so, it is also a Christian course, a Pueblo course, a Poor Theater course, and so on. I do not deny that my own Zen training shapes the course. How could it not? But there are many other influences as well. Isn't this also the case in any course that you might teach, say, on Lutheran liturgy? Surely, the fact that you are male, from the upper Midwest, and so on, would be evident in the way you teach such courses.

Q: Can you really have ritual without shared meaning?

A: There are shared meanings in the Lab; it is just that I don't determine all of them or impose them. They develop rapidly from shared experience. I suspect there is more shared meaning in the Lab than you'd guess and that the meanings of Roman Catholic liturgy are less shared than you'd guess. In any case, I distinguish meanings that arise from actions and meanings that are applied to or imposed on them.

Q: You've asked us to consider how applicable your ritualizing principles are to liturgy. What is your view of their applicability?

A: I don't know. Ritualizing is most effective at the edge of social institutions. In the center there is too much light. The intellectual, theological, and ecclesiastical-political spotlight is always on liturgies, especially in ritually "monocentric" traditions such as Catholicism and Lutheranism. In polycentric ritual traditions ritualizing can better survive. Ritually speaking, after Vatican II there was only ritual center, not much ritual circumference. The ritual circumference will have to be reinvented. For instance, there is a growing need for domestic ritual. I work better on this more local scale than on the scale of multi-national religious traditions, though doing so is more an expression of my limited abilities and temperament than any principle.

Q: Much of what you say is a critique of talk. And yet, what you have presented us is talk.

A: A meeting of the NAAL is a liturgizing of talk. The traditions represented here are traditions of the book and thus of talk. When in a liturgical situation, behave liturgically and with appropriate decorum. In other situations, Buddhist ones, for instance, I talk less.

Q: What's an example of "embodied criticism"?

A: The best one happened right in front of us when the entire Teaching Feminist Liturgy Group stood up during the question period and suddenly and visibly sent out two messengers like doves from the ark. Although the feminist delegates asked questions about containers, power, and gender relations, the ritual point was made before they ever said a word. Everyone recognized it. Otherwise, the audience would not have laughed when I yielded the platform and sat down in an audience member's seat.

3

Liturgical Supinity, Liturgical Erectitude: the Embodiment of Ritual Authority[56]

A CENTRAL THEME IN RITUAL STUDIES, AT LEAST AS PRACTICED IN the field of religious studies, is embodiment. When embodiment is given a position of theoretical primacy, posture and gesture emerge as crucial considerations in the interpretation of a rite. Posture and gesture, though micro-units in a ritual enactment or ritual tradition, assume considerable importance, because they encode both intended and unintended meanings—meanings "transmitted" as well as meanings "given off." We use the term "posture" in two ways. On the one hand, it refers to one's physical posture (as in, "That child has poor posture"). On the other, when we speak of "political posturing," the phrase refers to one's ideological commitments and ways of displaying them. A posture is not only one's manner of physical comportment (how one parks the body, so to speak) but also one's attitude—one's manner or style in the world. "Attitude" denotes the spiritual counterpart of posture, though even this term has both psychological and physiological connotations. We speak of "mental attitudes" but also of the attitude, or tilt, of a sailboat. A mental or spiritual attitude is indicated by our tilt or cant—that is, the way we sit, walk, or move. The terms "attitude" and "posture," then, refer to the same thing except that "attitude" emphasizes the psychological and spiritual dimensions, while "posture" connotes the physiological and ideological dimensions.

In liturgies participants assume postures that both reflect and cultivate attitudes. When deeply embodied, these attitudes become determinative metaphors that permeate the intellectual, social, and spiritual lives of those who practice them. Here, I want to consider two liturgical postures and their corresponding implications for our understanding of ritual authority, the topic of this symposium. I am being both playful and polemical when I dub them "erectitude" and "supinity."

Liturgical erectitude is a style typified by poise and verticality. When we embody it, we stand up straight; we process with a noble simplicity. We rise above our surroundings with a quiet and confident dignity—the fruit of age, tradition, and reflection.

Liturgical supinity, on the other hand, is characterized by its flexibility and its closeness to the ground. Supine, the spine hugs the earth. Supine, we are integrated with our surroundings. We are attuned to them, but our openness leaves us in danger of violation.

Described in this general and abstract manner neither posture is particular to a specific person, gender, or tradition. Buddhists may assume either or both attitudes. So may Jews or Christians, though a given tradition may cultivate one of the attitudes more deeply than the other. All of us can probably imagine persons who more obviously typify either erectitude or supinity, and we may suppose that one is more characteristic than the other of a specified gender, but in theory no person, gender, or tradition "owns" either posture.

However, my reflections on the two attitudes did not arise in the abstract, so, lest these characterizations seem disembodied in the very moment that I propose to discuss embodiment, I will situate them more concretely. Recently, two queries regarding ritual authority arrived at my desk. The first came in the proposal for this symposium, which bears the title, "Reclaiming Our Rites," and which originally bore the subtitle "Reasserting Ritual's Authority in a Pluralistic, Privatized Culture." This proposal embodies the posture that I am calling liturgical erectitude, so I will spend most of my energies considering it.

The proposal asks specific questions and assigns me the task of addressing them from the point of view of ritual studies. I was given the tentative title (and implicit question): "What 'ritualizing' can teach 'rites' and 'liturgies.'" My job description implicitly calls these terms into question by framing them with quotation marks, and yet it elevates "ritualizing" (which I suspect is associated with my own writing) to authoritative status by assuming that it has something to "teach" rites and liturgies (which, I assume, is associated largely with Christian, perhaps even Roman Catholic, liturgy).

The synopsis of the symposium contains these two paragraphs:

> The liturgy is no longer seen as an established pattern of invariable words, music and gestures, but as a freely improvised service that varies enormously from parish to parish—or from Mass to Mass within the same parish. While such innovation may showcase the skills of some parish members (e.g., the presiding priest, the musicians), it also risks subverting the larger community's participation in the ritual action. For a primary purpose of ritual is surely to enable to the participation of everyone by creating a pattern of familiar, repeated actions that can be "done by heart," without artifice of self-conscious display.

> This rather widespread disregard for the integrity and authority of ritual . . . is a principal reason why the Center for Pastoral Liturgy has chosen to host this symposium on the problem of ritual's declining authority in both church and society. It is not so much that our churches—or our cultures—lack rituals, but that these rituals lack authority. Unlike those of archaic peoples, our rituals (whether those of the rock concert, the football stadium, or the church) seem quite improvisatory and provisional. We often "make them up" at will, without invoking ancestral precedent or tradition, and we just as often discard them in favor of "new and improved rites."[57]

The second query, which I will use to illustrate the posture of liturgical supinity, arrived in the form of a phone call from a woman I had not met and whom I will call "Renata." She is, let us say, from Tucson. Renata wanted some advice about an initiation rite that she was constructing for half a dozen girls between the ages of twelve and fourteen. She had roughly the month of August during which to construct the rite, prepare the girls and their mothers, and perform the ceremony. She had been reading books on women and ritual having to do with menstruation, female body imagery, "croning," and other such matters of ceremonial importance to contemporary North American women, and she wanted my reactions to the scenario for the ceremony. Clearly an intelligent and articulate woman with considerable initiative, she had made phone calls to adults actively involved in creative forms of initiating adolescents into adulthood. Unfortunately, they were all men. Even though she knew many ritualizing women, she could find no groups of women who were designing rites for groups of girls.

In talking with me she was obviously not escaping her dilemma, so I put her in touch with the only local woman I knew who had any experience with initiating girls. For the duration of our first conversation I mostly asked questions, for example, What was the sequence of actions? Her plan, still in very provisional form, was to have several discussion meetings in town. After that she, the girls, and their mothers would go on a brief retreat to the mountains, where they would "die" by entering a darkened sweat lodge and then "rise" into womanhood by coming out into the light. This was to be the central ritual act. All the other gestures would be tributaries to this paradigmatic ritual act.

I asked more questions: What was her goal?

To initiate the girls into adulthood.

Who would effect this transition?

She would, assisted by the girls' mothers.

What had been the role of the mothers so far—were they actively involved in the planning?

No, not really.

Was she a mother of one of the girls?

No.

Was this initiation authorized by the church in which the discussions would occur?

No.

These two queries were the sources of the two polarized voices I heard as I began to reflect on the question of ritual authority. When I was feeling playful and a bit perverse, I sometimes reduced each inquiry to a single question. The question for this symposium became: How can a massive, centuries-old, multi-national religious institution maintain its ritual authority among highly pluralistic, materialistic, individualistic, mobile parishioners living in a racist, militaristic, deeply psychologized society? And I rendered Renata's inquiry this way: How can a young adult woman with few degrees, no children, no formal religious sanction, and no "grandmothers" successfully initiate half a dozen girls in the four weeks that compose the month of August?

Despite my hyperbolic reframing of the essential questions, I take both queries with equal seriousness. I probably do what the symposium organizers suspected I would do, since, in describing my task, they posed this question, "To what degree—and in what ways—does the field of ritual studies (with its habit of 'phenomenological levelling,' its penchant for taking the Tennessee snakehandler's ritual as seriously as the bishop's solemn ministrations) challenge the (Christian) liturgist's affection for norms, paradigms and 'privileged moments' of history?"

The question of religious authority is a classical Western one, and it has traditionally been framed in ways that are not only culture-specific but androcentric. I am not referring only to the obvious historic exclusion of women from positions of liturgical authority, but to the inscription of masculine postures and attitudes in liturgical practice and theology. For instance, I cannot imagine Renata's being the least interested in a liturgy whose symbols and gestures (as described by the symposium organizers) are "hearty" and "robust." Not only would she question whether the liturgy is, in fact, hearty and robust, she would probably hear in both adjectives an old-boys'-club rhetoric that fails to grasp the tenor of her aspirations. Heartiness and robustness are among the virtues of liturgical erectitude. In the current North American cultural situation, they are expressions of an androcentric liturgy. Even more directly to the point, I cannot imagine Renata's agreeing with the claim that when a "liturgical order" is enacted, those who engage in it indicate—to themselves and to others—that they *accept* whatever is encoded in the canons of the liturgy they are performing. In short, they acceded to the liturgical rite's *authority*, an authority that yet remains independent of those who participate in it.[58]

For what gives liturgical rites their authoritativeness is not, ultimately, the participants' approval or fidelity. What makes the liturgy *socially and morally binding* is not the participants' private, prayerful sentiments (however worthy these may be), but *the visible, explicit, public act of acceptance itself.*[59]

These two statements seem to me a fundamental premise and undergirding value of this conference. It is the tip of an iceberg, a flag signalling a view that is gaining momentum in the wake of post-Vatican II disenchantment and the waning authority of traditional Euroamerican masculinity. It is a very Catholic view (though, of course, there are other Catholic views), and it is set squarely against the individualistic "habits of the heart" (that Robert Bellah was probably invited to this conference to criticize). I am intrigued by the fact that the claim is buttressed not by arguments from scripture or Catholic theologians but by anthropological theory, especially that of Roy Rappaport. My objection is not to the use of anthropological theory as such but to the uncritical appropriation and reactionary use of it. Rappaport's work seems to me fundamentally descriptive and analytical in intent; whereas, this use of it is undeniably normative. The logic seems to be: "Ritual *is* like this, therefore liturgy *must be* like that." Rappaport says ritual insulates "public orders from private vagaries," thus, the proposal for this symposium concludes that the liturgy is inherently superior to personal prayer, popular devotions, and made-up rites.[60]

I am sympathetic with the insistence that Christian liturgy ought to assume a critical, prophetic posture toward middle-class American popular culture. Certain aspects of American culture certainly deserve sustained spiritual critique, and liturgical enactments have on historic occasion provided an effective platform from which to launch such an attack: "The Liturgy of the Christian assembly stubbornly resists the manipulations of both politics and civil religion."[61] No doubt, it sometimes does. However, no doubt, it sometimes does not. My claim that it sometimes does not is central to a deep disagreement with the aim of this symposium: "reclaiming our rites" understood as a reassertion of liturgical authority. Who are numbered among the "our?" Christians, clearly. Catholics, clearly. But how can women, who have been systematically denied liturgical authority, be counted among those privileged with inclusion in the first person plural? Women can hardly be imagined as wanting to *re*claim what they have not had. So I confess that, whatever the intentions of the title of this symposium, I cannot help hearing in such words a nostalgia for pre-Vatican II days when the liturgy was the liturgy and lay people knew their place. Neither can I help hearing it as a parallel to complaints by men that their authority in families and jobs has been eroded by women, particularly feminists. Perhaps it is the "re-" in "reclaiming" and "reassertion" that conjures such connotations. In any case, I first coined the term "liturgical erectitude" after I read the symposium proposal, because in the current cultural and ecclesiastical climate liturgical authority is largely and obviously masculine.

Many who assume the posture of liturgical erectitude are busy appropriating a host of allied theological and anthropological notions, for instance, tradition. Liturgical erectitude maintains a proper relation to tradition:

> Understood correctly, tradition is a word denoting those aspects of a group's social compact which have managed to survive the traumas of history *because they work in maintaining the social group as a whole*. It is by this compact that the group coheres and is thus able to survive. Because of this, the social compact—however it is stated or left unstated—is the result of the entire group and its deliberative processes. Responsibility lies with the group itself and cannot be appealed to anyone's private "revelation," nor ought it to be taken from the group and handed over to anyone less than the total body politic.

> Thus differing from mere custom and convention, tradition frees from the tyranny of the present: it also protects against aggression by the compulsively articulate, as well as against opportunism by unchecked authority.[62]

I hear such claims as aspirations rather than descriptions, so

I would have to shift into the subjunctive in order to affirm them: "Oh, *if* liturgical tradition were consistent in delivering us from the tyranny of the present! Oh, *if it were only true* that liturgical tradition represented the *total* body politic? *Don't we all wish* we could be sure that structures which have enabled us to survive would continue to do so!"

If we couple unquestioning trust of liturgical tradition with this symposium's statements about ritual authority, Renata's kind of ritualizing is reduced to caricature and made a symbol of the "tyranny of the present." As a middle-class woman she becomes an example of *embourgeoisement*.[63] She is taken to be an instance of "private ritual vagaries."[64] If one adds to this multi-layered critique a definition of ritual that takes it to be "the performance of more or less invariant sequences of formal acts and utterances not encoded by the performers," Renata's ritualizing is not only caricatured and devalued but defined out of existence, a situation all too familiar to women and one that I find both morally and theoretically intolerable.[65]

Though it may hope to claim anthropological support, a liturgical theology which holds that a rite's authority transcends its ambient culture and the social relationships on which it is based is not likely to receive much support from anthropologists themselves. Such a theology probably derives from buttressing theological images and ideas, such as that of a god who transcends the land. This god, of course, is metaphorically male. This "god of the gaps" (to appropriate Dietrich Bonhoeffer's well-worn term) will be increasingly relegated to the edges of the cosmos, not so much because he is male but because he is fundamentally removed and essentially unrelated. My prediction is that in North America a ritual authority that is not grounded in the social relationships on which it depends will suffer the same fate as the god of the gaps, and not at the hands of feminists alone. Renata, along with many other women and a growing number of men, would insist that the authority (if they would even use such a term) of ritual is *dependent* on—in fact, ought to grow organically out of—those who participate in it. This view is not without its difficulties, but it a cogent option.

Another feature of liturgical erectitude is what we might call "liturgiocentrism," by which I mean theological ideologies that treat "the" liturgy as both the single center of the ritual tradition in which it is embedded and as the norm for judging its ambient culture. Several assumptions and axioms are regularly associated with liturgiocentric theologies and obviously present in the proposal for this symposium: (1) that "public orders," such as the liturgy, are by their very nature superior to personal or private ones; (2) that Christian liturgy is somehow above its ambient culture (called in the proposal for this symposium, "the social contract"); (3) that Christian liturgy is "invariable";[66] (4) that ritual invariance (if there were such a thing) guarantees the authority of the liturgy.

The fact that Christian liturgy has a history at all means that it is variable, changing, fluid. Even if it is a stream that flows more slowly than all others, it nevertheless changes, and its changes are often consonant with other cultural and historical changes. Though a liturgy may criticize and judge social structures, it also reflects them. In short, the liturgy is a cultural process, itself in need of constant reformation and revision. The liturgy, like persons, can err. It can and does embody oppressive structures. If in aspiration it has overcome racism and nationalism, it has not in fact. And it has not overcome sexism even in aspiration, except on rare occasion. The liturgy is not, at least in moral terms, superior to some of the private, invented rites celebrated in homes, convents, forests, and urban work places. Some of these kinds of ritualizing judge the liturgy. Renata's attempt to initiate six girls into the mysteries of menstruation and womanhood, flawed though it may be, judges the baptismal rites of a church in which there are no huts, no nests to which women may have repose in order to bleed, write theology, weave, or draft resolutions. Nothing guarantees that "*Liturgy* is what underwrites [that is, is the standard for] the social contract."[67] Sometimes the social contract functions as a standard for evaluating liturgy. One ought only to decide which underwrites which after observing actual instances of liturgy/culture interaction. One ought not assume, for theological or other reasons, the priority of public liturgy since it has at times in its history proved itself culture- and gender-bound. It has proved itself faithless for the same reason that any rite does: because it does *not* transcend the people who engage in its performance.

If my language seems too strong and too theological, then let us at least admit that the process of ritual revision, in which many, if not all, religious groups engage, implies the necessity of ritual criticism and the possibility of ritual infelicity. And let us recognize that, even though liturgy sometimes earns the right to be the "model for" a culture, it is also a "model of"[68] culture, and thus it participates in the foibles, injustices, and contradictions of culture.

In 1990 Helen Ebaugh delivered a presidential address called, "The Revitalization Movement in the Catholic Church: The Institutional Dilemma of Power."[69] Her address is about the dilemma of hierarchical authority precipitated by Vatican II. Though the article says little about ritual, some of its conclusions are germane to our consideration of ritual authority. Ebaugh's argument is that personalized religious individualism was one of the *results* of Vatican II, this "revitalization movement."[70] Far from setting Catholic liturgy with its collective sensibility against or above American cultural individualism, she sees the church and its liturgy as one of the *sources* of that individualism. The relationship is not antithetical but circular; there is no pure or simple division between liturgy and culture, religion and society. In Ebaugh's view "selective Catholicism" (picking and choosing which aspects of Catholicism one will participate in) is another *result* of Vatican II. I mention Ebaugh's argument because we are so used to hearing accounts that blame these qualities on American culture rather than the church.[71] I do not intend simply to reverse the causal sequence by blaming the church rather than the culture but rather to argue against any dualistic understanding of liturgy and culture.

Vatican II left largely untouched the gender arrangements that underwrite Roman liturgy. Insofar as the church has begun to challenge such arrangements, it has, by and large, followed the lead of culturally informed critics. Joan Laird, for instance, has mounted a powerful critique of the gender arrangements presupposed by most traditional ritual systems, among which we must count Roman Catholic liturgy as well as much that remains of Protestant and Jewish liturgy. She argues that these arrangements "leave men free to design rituals of authority that define themselves as superior, as special, and as separate," and "because men can be separate, they can be 'sacred.'"[72] Thus, she concludes that, "since rites of passage are important facilitators in the definition of self in relation to society, there is clearly a need for women to reclaim, redesign, or create anew rituals that will facilitate life transitions and allow more meaningful and clear incorporation of both familial and public roles."[73]

I believe Laird's conclusion is essentially correct. I see no way to refute the core of feminist critique of ritual authority and no reason to obstruct women's attempt to claim (or reclaim, if they ever had control of) their rites. In fact, liturgy, liturgical theology, and ritual theory, ought to be put in the service of this critique rather than having to be the repeated objects of it. There is a tacit but fundamental conflict between the project to "reclaim our rites," the stated aim of this symposium, and the feminist attempt to reclaim ritual, so let us not pretend this is not a power struggle.

So far I have not engaged in critique of the assumptions about authority implicit in the ritualizing represented by Renata. If she were in attendance at this symposium, I would do so, but its presuppositions exclude her. If I were addressing, say, a New Age convention in Boulder, Colorado, at which she might be present, I would challenge at the least following problematic assumptions: (1) that personal insight and private passion, such as one finds in contemporary Anglo-American ritual groups, are by their very nature more authentic than public liturgical orders; (2) that women's concerns, merely because they are rooted in women's bodies, (or men's concerns merely because they are rooted in men's bodies) are universal and timeless—the same now as in ages past and in other cultures; and (3) that ritual creativity or authenticity displaces the need for ritual authority in the more public or conventional sense; (4) that all ancient or Native American symbols are available for mining by the White middle class for use in its ritualizing. I will not argue each of these points here. My aim is simply to illustrate that I am not uncritical of contemporary ritualizing and its assumptions about authority.

In Christian history the usual sources of authorization for anything, liturgy included, have been the Bible, tradition, and the hierarchy (pastoral as well as papal and gender-based ones

as well as ecclesiastical ones). But I have not yet tackled directly the evasive theoretical question: What is ritual authority?
There are multiple candidates for an answer to it. Ritual authority might be, for example, whatever

1. is endorsed (by the gods, elders, officiants, or other
   kinds of participants);

2. is traditional (usually done, done for generations);

3. is performed according to the rules (contained in sacred
   and/or liturgical texts);

4. functions (that is, fits the social context) or works (to
   achieve explicit goals);

5. is just (according to moral criteria).

Distinguishing kinds or levels of authority at least would
enable us to notice that the symposium organizers emphasize
#1 and #2 (what is endorsed and traditional), whereas Renata
is more interested in #4 (what functions or works), and feminist critiques of mainline liturgy often question its moral authority (#5). Such emphases are, of course, not mutually exclusive, so there is no *necessary or logical* conflict between the
three positions (that of established liturgiology, that of feminist liturgical theology, and that of private ritualizing outside
the ecclesiastical context). The very complexity of ritual precludes any simple answer to the question, What is ritual authority? But we will do much talking past each other if we do
not distinguish at least among these sorts of authority. Furthermore, there are different kinds of ritual, and these probably entail different sorts of ritual authority.

The notion of ritual authority conceals at least two, circular-
ly related questions. The first is this: What authorizes ritual?
by which is meant, Where does it come from, how does it
arise, who warrants it? The stated intention of this symposium
seems to emphasize this aspect of current liturgical difficulties
in North America. The organizers appear interested in fostering a liturgy that has public, not merely private, validity
and that arises out of time-tested, ecclesiastically grounded
tradition. The second question is this: What does ritual authorize? by which is meant, What does it do, achieve, or enable?

Renata is primarily interested in this question. She wants to construct a rite that will, in fact, enable girls to become women. A serious problem, as I see it, is the divorce between these questions that ought to be dialectically related. If we make the mistake of focusing entirely on the first one (what ritual authorizes), treating ritual solely as a pragmatic tool, we are tempted to ransack the world's ritual traditions for symbolic goods, much as we once plundered the globe for spices and gold. If we over-emphasize the second one (what authorizes ritual), treating liturgy solely as a paradigm or norm (with authority over participants and culture), we attribute to it a false, heteronomous transcendence removed from criticism but also from relevance and cultural roots. So in my view those who practice liturgical supinity (a posture emphasizing attunement to cultural currents and ecological realities) as a way of fostering ritual creativity need to attend to ritual traditions, especially their own. Those who defend liturgical erectitude (a posture emphasizing public accountability and traditional integrity) as a way of consolidating ritual authority need to attend to ritual generation, especially that of women and other groups marginalized by mainline liturgical activity.

I am calling, then, for a reframing of the question of ritual authority. Since the notion of authority is so contaminated with androcentrism, I prefer to change the terms of reference altogether. We might, for instance, speak of "felicitous" and "infelicitous" rather than authorized (or authoritative) and unauthorized (or "unauthoritative") ritual.[74] This strategy does not get rid of the authority question, but it does put it in a larger context. We need to know how and in what respects liturgies lapse into infelicity. Are, for example, non-feminist liturgies and baptisms guilty of "glossing," that is, of using ritual procedures to cover up social problems? Do they commit ritual "violations," actions that are effective but demeaning?

If my budding glossary of ritual infelicities seems cumbersome, there are others in the making. William Seth Adams, for instance, criticizes Episcopalian baptism on two accounts: its ritual incongruence and its ritual incoherence. Both of his judgments are made on the basis of observations and descriptions of that rite's handling of ritual space and action.[75]

The temptation in trying to develop a vocabulary of ritual

infelicity is that it could degenerate into mere academic name-calling. If so, it would, of course, be useless. But if it forced us to be more precise in identifying the level on which criticism of a liturgical rite is being levied, it might actually help the antagonists engage one another more fully and fairly. What worries me is the lack of sustained and direct public debate between male theologians who want to reassert liturgical authority and feminist ones who are marginalized by symposia such as this one because they might challenge or undermine it. What little debate there is, is far too circumlocutious and private.

Whether my terms are the best ones or not, the implication I want to press is this: liturgy's felicitousness does not arise from ecclesiastical, biblical, conciliar, or traditional warrant alone but also on the basis of a rite's ability to meet fundamental human need. Liturgy is as essentially cultural as it is religious. Consequently, it ought to be subjected not just to theological criticism but to ritual, ethical, and others sorts of criticism that proceed on anthropological, ecological, and psychological grounds.

If we were to be successful in reframing the question of ritual authority, our view of initiation, for example, might be different. The symposium organizers wrote in their letter to me, "rites without norms—or rites that are homogenized into a kind of 'generic' condition through over-identification with cross-cultural models (as may have happened when Christians rushed to identify 'baptism' with 'an *initiation rite*')—have a hard time maintaining any *authoritativeness*." Here the general question of ritual authority is focused specifically on baptism.

In my view the attempt to reimagine baptism as an initiation rite has been a largely felicitous step in baptismal history, and the church ought to go further with this experiment, not retrench on it. From the point of view of liturgical erectitude, however, the step is an infelicitous one, making baptism too generic, too cultural. A cross-cultural perspective, however, has helped provide a critical edge for assessing liturgy.

For example, Marjorie Procter-Smith in her critique of Christian baptism lays out several criteria for judging rites: the centrality of women's bodies, naming the sources of oppression, baptism's connectedness with the everyday, dependence on relationships among women, and ritual empowerment.[76] These are dependent in part on cross-cultural research mediated through feminist theological scholarship. Procter-Smith is, at least indirectly, indebted to the notion of initiation or some equivalent, culturally-grounded idea. Her sources are not *only* theological or narrowly Christian but broadly cultural, even cross-cultural. Initiation understood as a bodily, social, and political phenomenon is a product of cross-cultural research. Some of the grounds for liturgical critique, such as those launched by feminist and Marxist critics of so-called "gender ritual," have their roots outside Christian theology.[77] They have been more attuned to ritual infelicities, especially the abuse of ritual authority, than most liturgical theologies have. Both feminist ritualizing (like that of Renata) and feminist liturgical rites (like those proposed by Procter-Smith) are more consistently open to, and dependent upon, cross-cultural research, because they do not construe the authority of ritual as derivative from either its distinctiveness or its exclusivity.

Whatever may be lost by considering baptism an initiation rite, the gain has been considerable. If Christian baptism seems to lose its uniqueness, and therefore authority, by being assimilated to a cross-cultural model, it gains connectedness, not only with women but with other cultures and classes and with human ordinariness. I am not suggesting that some generic initiation rite is necessarily less sexist or more humane than Christian baptism. And I am not arguing for the moral or ritual superiority of other kinds of initiation, but for the value of continuing to imagine baptism pluralistically, as just one (not "the") version of human initiatory activity. Christian baptism, I believe, is more, not less felicitous, if it remains permeable to cross-culturally informed initiation rites—if those who conduct and theologize about baptism do so in the light of non-Christian as well as Christian data.

I do not mean to imply that liturgical theologians need "authoritative" "correction" from anthropologists and historians of religion who work on rites of passage, but rather that mutual critique and collaborative reimagining of ritual processes should be our aim. We in the humanities and social sciences need critique as surely as liturgical theologians need ours. For example, a recurrent assumption of rites of passage theorists is that rites of passage have their proper home in pre-industrial cultures. Victor Turner represents a widespread anthropological view when he says, *"Rites de Passage* are found in all societies but tend to reach their maximal expression in small-scale, relatively stable and cyclical societies, where change is bound up with biological and meteorological rhythms and recurrences rather than with technological innovations."[78] Is this claim true? No anthropologist that I know has presented data that demonstrates that it is the case. Perhaps the problem is rather a failure of the theoretical imagination—this time among secular academics rather than liturgists or liturgiologists. If baptism is, in fact, an initiation rite, is it not evidence that rites of passage continue in industrial cultures? Is not Christian baptism an example of a kind of initiation that continues, recast and reimagined, into industrial and postmodern society? I do not claim that the example of Christian baptism disproves Turner's assumption, only that it makes it questionable.

In *Rites of Passage Theory*, which is not yet published, I am currently struggling with the history of rites of passage theory, which is indebted largely to van Gennep and Turner. Turner's theory of ritual is constructed around the cornerstone of liminality, the second phase in the rites of passage model. But rites of passage theorizing from van Gennep (its originator) to Turner (in whom it culminates) is determined mainly by one kind of rite of passage, namely, initiation; initiation has been regarded as the paradigm for the other rites of passage such as those surrounding birth, marriage, and death.[79] In turn, the examples of initiation are, in almost every instance those of male initiation. So ritual theory itself is not immune from the kinds of critique I have levelled at liturgical theology, because the theorizing itself is contaminated by androcentrism and colonialism.

But so what? What difference does such a conclusion make? It makes little if we imagine that theory has no life beyond the halls of academe. However, I know people who design initiations in three phases—separation, transition, incorporation—the classical threefold pattern formulated by van Gennep. I know feminists ritualizers who set out deliberately to foment liminality, a notion borrowed from Turner, who borrowed it from van Gennep, who borrowed it from . . . . Ritual theory itself is currently inspiring and permeating North

American ritual practices, both ecclesiastical and self-generated. Whether or not van Gennep and Turner would have approved of such a use of their ideas, they (like Jung and Eliade), nevertheless, have fed the initiatory fantasies that have been with us since at least the origins of romance in the Middle Ages and the revival of romanticism in the nineteenth century.

I do not want to privilege ritual studies, religious studies, anthropology, or any other discipline, making it some new arbiter in the clash between ecclesiastical liturgiology and private ritualizing. Each of these is in need of critique. However, liturgical theologians need to stop uncritically appropriating and start questioning their anthropological (largely White male) authorities[80] and begin listening to their female ritual critics.[81] The opening of liturgy and liturgical theology to the cross-cultural resources provided by anthropology and religious studies, though not without its problems, is nevertheless essential to the felicitous functioning of a liturgy that must negotiate its position in what we all hope is a decreasingly androcentric and increasingly pluralistic world. It is also essential for debunking liturgical or theological claims to a false transcendence over culture. When culture is construed as the bipolar opposite of a male-engendered and male-controlled liturgy, it necessarily becomes the overcrowded home of women and "others."

So, what am I actually recommending? I hope for continued, strengthened moral and cultural pressure on Christian liturgies in the direction of a more collaborative, less hierarchical, less androcentric sensibility for handling ritual power. I would like to see a sustained reconsideration of certain key notions—among them: authority, power, order, and tradition. The view of tradition, for example, that identifies its authority with rule-like order or maintains that tradition stands above culture should not be regarded as sacrosanct. There are other ways to understand tradition. It is time we admit that the reigning definitions of such notions are themselves both andro- and ethnocentric and thus in need of theological critique. When I hear calls for liturgical order and pleas for enhanced ritual authority, I cannot help thinking of Huntington and Metcalf's compelling interpretation of Bara funerals. For these Madagascar islanders death is "an overdose of order," thus funerals are necessary injections of chaos to revitalize and rebalance the socially generated cosmos.[82]

The Christian liturgical imagination can no longer afford the luxury of reasserting ritual authority on the basis of rules assumed to be unchanging and universal. Participants can begin to create the conditions for nurturing the liturgical imagination by refusing to reassert the authority of liturgy (or ritual theory) *over* those who participate in it, for the simple reason that many of us who exercise such authority are White middle-class, middle-aged Euroamerican males, who present keynote addresses at symposia like this one. If such a divestment of ritual authority means that one can no longer do the liturgy "by heart" and "without artifice" (two aspirations specified in the symposium proposal) so be it. Let us learn to ritualize our self-consciousness and our lack of authority.

In my view the feminist critique and environmental crisis require of us men who hold various kinds of ritual authority that we drop our preoccupation with ritual *authorization* so that we have the energy to follow the leads of others who know more than we about ritual *generation*. The former is typical of the posture of liturgical erectitude; the latter, of liturgical supinity. The difference between the two emphases is that the authority question (at least as posed for this gathering) starts at the top (the head) rather than the bottom (the roots). The question we should be asking, then, is not what stands above ritual to authorize it, but what lies below it. The best position from which to answer the question is supine. So if I were forced to answer the question, What constitutes ritual authority, without arguing against the question itself, I would have to say something like this: Ritual has (or ought to have) authority only insofar as it is rooted in, generated by, and answerable to its infrastructures—bodily, cultural, ecological, spiritual.

I might have approached the topic of ritual authority in a variety of ways, for example, theoretically or practically, theologically or social scientifically. I have done so ritologically, thereby assuming a position between these two sets of alternatives. My aim in doing so, however, has not been to pretend that I am neutral or to escape critique. I am not neutral, and I am well aware of the dangers of assuming mediating positions in disputes where dividing lines are deeply inscribed.

In the present circumstances my own position is largely that of an advocate of the virtues of liturgical supinity (even though I know I have argued for it with considerable erectitude). I am not recommending it for women, who have known the posture for generations, but for men occupying positions of power and authority. From a supine position, into which many women have been forced both literally and metaphorically (but which I as a man have been able to imagine that I can assume by choice) one has to "overcome from underneath," to borrow a Taoist phrase. One has to employ cultural and religious refuse, that is, the symbols our culture would prefer to bury or forget, recycling and transforming them into tools useful for the liberation of a captive liturgy.

Before I conclude, I must confess to a trick I have been playing. The image of a "supine liturgy" is not my invention. It belongs Aidan Kavanagh, from whom I have pilfered it.[83] I have inverted it, using it in ways quite contrary to his original intentions. Liturgical supinity is not a posture to which he aspires but rather one he fears and deplores. He uses the phrase to characterize the plight of a liturgy that capitulates to middle-class American culture. To quote him, "Liturgy is not [I think he means, "ought not be"] adapted to culture, but culture to the liturgy."[84]

When I first encountered the image, it stopped me flat and stole my breath. It provoked an imagined a scenario: Liturgy was lying on its back, its spine following the curvature of the ground. It was, if you will, in missionary position. I imagined (my imagination being more perverse than Kavanagh's) a very tall, very threatening, not very trustworthy Mr. Culture. He was standing over Supine Liturgy, whose gender I leave to your imagination.

This scenario is one Kavanagh rejects. He would have us reverse the polarities, so I inverted the imagery and ran out another scenario: Now, Liturgy is vertical, male, and standing erect; liturgical authority walks tall. Culture, now obviously female, is supine and vulnerable. To be lying on one's back is dangerous, not to mention bad liturgical style. It is an invitation to abuse.

I do not like either scenario; I mistrust them both. By teasing out the images of erectitude and supinity, I am not suggesting that liturgical issues are really sexual ones. Instead, I am using the sexual images as metaphors for understanding the relations between liturgy and culture. I do mean, however, to imply that gender issues (as distinct from sexual issues) are more fully determinative of both liturgical practice and liturgical theology than most White male theologians readily recognize or openly admit.[85] I am also arguing that the middle class culture before which liturgy is not supposed to be supine includes some of the most articulate, critical, and creative women in the church. Thus, I question both the wisdom and morality of a liturgy-vs.-culture model. I am defending liturgical supinity not because I believe that the church ought to lie prostrate before culture, but because I believe the supine position best symbolizes what men presently prefer to ignore. Men, largely Euroamerican males, have been the inventors of most Christian liturgical traditions, so I believe that we should practice the posture we have assigned women as a way of educating ourselves ritually. We ought not pretend that the Renatas of our time merely invent their rites, while assuming that ours were "somehow given" to us.

American culture can be rapacious. We all know this. I certainly do not want to be seduced, much less raped, by a rapacious American culture. I am wary of it. But I am just as wary of canonized posturing and liturgical displays of the feathers of erectitude. I do not believe that a more prophetic liturgy needs to assume the form of liturgical erectitude or remain impervious to the supine virtues. I believe that Christianity, both Catholic and Protestant, is much in need of liturgical supinity. A more supine liturgy, which I am espousing for White, Euroamerican men, would, of course, be perpetually endangered, a rare species. It would be a liturgy whose authority consists of the act (at once both real and ritualistic) of divesting itself of power. We men who organize and speak at conferences such as this need to meditate upon—or within—the vision of a supine liturgy, one that teases the spines of its practitioners into parallel alignment to, and contact with, the earth.

I conclude, then, by commending the metaphor of supinity to you. If you choose to embody and practice it, it will stretch muscles you did not know you have. And you may be sure that you will be sore the day after.

Part II

Sacred Spaces
and
Things from Afar

Part II

Sacred Spaces
and Things from Afar

INTRODUCTION

PART TWO IS AT ONCE MORE GENERAL AND MORE SPECIFIC THAN part one. It is more general insofar as it is not focused on ecclesiastical liturgy in a particular religious tradition. It is more specific inasmuch as it concentrates on specific ritual components: ritual objects, ritual places, ritual actions.

Chapter four consists of two brief sections, "Portals" and "Processions," each originally an entry in the *Encyclopedia of Religion*. The first, of course, concerns things—doorways, thresholds, and other boundary markers—that divide inside space from outside space. The second part of the chapter is related to the first one inasmuch as a procession is a ritual movement through demarcated space. In both this chapter and the following one I am pursuing topics that were central to my first long-term fieldwork on public ritual and drama in Santa Fe.

In chapter five I argue that a spatial bias governs many histories of religion in North America and that this bias, because it is largely unconscious and unquestioned, embodies sacredly held values. It functions as a "holy" historiography. If one considers regional religious history and geography, say, that of the southwestern United States, where I do fieldwork, it is clear that the typically presupposed perspective of histories of American religion is neither that of the Southwest nor even the center of the country, but rather the northeastern United States. I examine some of the implications of this "standpoint," which is at once geographical, metaphoric, and ideological.

Chapter six is also concerned about ritual and ideology. It looks at the values that govern the way we face sacred objects when we visit museums. Originally, it was a lecture at the Glenbow Museum, which had been the locus of considerable controversy during *The Spirit Sings*, a display on Native Canadian culture. In the chapter I consider two cultural processes, commoditizing and singularizing, that shape the meanings of sacred objects displayed in museum spaces. I propose some ways to minimize ethnocentrism and avoid desecration in the display of such objects.

The final chapter of part three is on masking, a topic related to another chapter on masking in an earlier work, *Beginnings in Ritual Studies*. It treats objects as having "biographies" and constructs a model "life history" of a mask. In addition it compares two kinds of masking sensibility: the biographical (illustrated by a mask of Canadian writer Margaret Laurence) and ritualistic (illustrated by a variety of masks found in North American museums).

4

Processions and Portals[86]

A PROCESSION IS THE LINEARLY ORDERED, SOLEMN MOVEMENT OF a group through chartered space to a known destination to give witness, bear an esteemed object, perform a rite, fulfil a vow, gain merit, or visit a shrine.

Some processions, such as the *Via Dolorosa* procession in modern Jerusalem, constitute major rituals in their own right. Others, for example, the Orthodox "Little Entrance" (in which the Gospel is carried to the front of the sanctuary) or the procession of a bridal party down a church aisle, are only facilitating gestures—formalized comings and goings. The most familiar settings for processions are civil ceremonies (such as coronations, military fanfares, and enthronements) weddings, funerals, initiations, and fertility rites. Major processions seem most widespread in agricultural or urban cultures or those in transition from the one to the other. In hunting, nomadic, and industrial cultures processions are likely to decline in frequency or significance and function only as minor gestural tributaries to other rituals.

The ritual space of a procession is linear. When it is completed by a subsequent recession, one might speak of it as "bilinear." By virtue of its linearity a procession differs from circumambulation. Processual action is not movement *around* a sacred object but *to* a special place. Even when a procession returns to its beginning point, its circuit is not generally continuous. The movement is oriented toward a destination rather than a center. Processants do not occupy centralized sacred space. Instead, they carry their "center" with them. The usual places of honor in hierarchically ordered processions are at the head or end of the line. Whereas circumambulation usually sanctifies or protects the place bounded by its circumference, a procession normally links different spatial orders, for instance, civic and sacred or urban and rural space. The rhythms of processing and recessing establish a corridor between a nucleus of sacred space and adjacent, non-sacred zones or satellite shrines beyond these zones. Distances traversed in processions are usually moderate. One of the longer ones, held during the Greek Eleusinian Festival, was fourteen miles. Others, such as the chorus' entrance (*parados*) and exit (*exodos*) to ancient Greek theater were only a few yards long. *Robigalia*, the ancient Roman procession intended to avert blight and adapted by early Christianity into its Rogation processions, was five miles, a more typical distance.

Walking meditation in Zen Buddhism is called *kinhin*. This practice falls between procession and circumambulation. *Kinhin* is not *to* any place, so it is not strictly a procession. And though its course is usually *around* a meditation hall, there is no centralized object of attention. Instead, practitioners' eyes are on the floor and their attention on the way of walking itself.

The solemn or meditative tone of a procession differentiates it from the expansive, celebrative ethos of a parade or the martial, aggressive one of military marches, picketing, or conquests (such as Don Diego de Vargas' *Entrada* into Santa Fe, New Mexico, in 1692). When Joshua brings down Jerico's walls, he is not processing so much as circumambulating in the service of conquest. Unlike a mere invasion, conquest, now an obsolete military tactic, is akin to ritual because of its obvious stylization and emphasis on symbolic, rather than strategic, ordering.

The usual distinction between processions and parades identifies the former as sacred, the latter as profane. The distinction is minimally useful because processions often try to link these or other classificatory domains. Perhaps we should consider parades and processions as celebrative and solemn versions, respectively, of the same basic type of action. Consequently, speaking of a "religious parade" or "academic procession" is no contradiction in terms. The pace of a procession is typically slower than that of a parade and its rhythms more deliberate than that of ordinary walking (or driving if, say, chariots, pageants, floats, or automobiles are employed to transport participants).

Participation in processions is usually more restricted than in parades. There seems to be a persistent tendency for every procession gradually to relax its exclusivity and become a popular parade in which by-standers can join. Since processing is group movement, it contrasts with race-running, which is ritualized, for example, in the Olympic Games and among some contemporary Pueblos. A race is agonistic, setting one person in competition with another. The object of a standard Euroamerican race is to arrive ordinally (first place, second, third, and so on), not corporately or simultaneously.[87] Perhaps the best term to appropriate if we wish to speak of an "individual procession" is "quest." "Quest," however, is probably better treated as individualized pilgrimage.

Since a procession's destination is known, it is distinct from ritualized hunting, divination-directed migration, religious wandering (of the Hebrews in the desert, for example) and wayfaring (a common practice in medieval China and Japan). Whereas in these perambulatory rituals, becoming disoriented, abiding in unprotected places, and having to invent or discover one's destination are essential, in processions there is no doubt where to begin and end nor little need for concern about personal safety.

Dancing typically has no destination; processing does. Processional dances such as the medieval European Dance of Death or the Hasidic dance with the Torah, are borderline instances. Dance presupposes not only rhythm but, typically, music. When dancing arises in a procession, it tends to become a parade. And when dancing shifts from circularity and symmetry to linearity and asymmetry, the religious climate is likely to shift from prophetic criticism to priestly conservatism.

The space through which a pilgrim passes may be mapped, but, unlike a procession's path, it is not chartered. Pilgrims pass through what Victor Turner calls liminal ("threshold") zones as they go from near to far. Whereas pilgrims tread ways they may not recognize or cross borders that make them subject to foreign authority, processants pass down ways specially cleared, decorated, and authorized for their arrival. At the end of some pilgrimages, for instance, to the shrine of Guadalupe in Mexico City, one may sometimes join a procession as the last leg of a pilgrimage. The chartered quality of procession paths is usually emphasized by the use of stations along the *via sacra*; at these, processants stop, rest, and often perform ancillary rites.

Even priestly processants may have little to say about the intentions of their actions. Processions, unlike initiation rites or sacrifices, evoke little codified commentary, so scholars usually have to infer intentions. The most obvious one is to display what Erving Goffman might have called a "with": these people "go with" that god. By walking with a god, processants gain merit by association and give witness that sacredness is not geographically restricted to one spot but capable of annexing, even if temporarily, other places. Both a territorial imperative and a hierarchy of gods or sacred places is implied in most processions. Being seen, particularly in postures of homage before elevated, but proximate, sacred objects legitimizes bonds and often establishes these sacra as a group's own. Far from having an inversion-effect, as a Mardi Gras Parade might, public processions confirm established hierarchies and sacralize ownership and order. For example, one of the oldest known processions was part of the Great Akitu Festival held in Babylon in honor of Marduk. The first day of the new year was set aside for a solemn procession in which Nabu and other gods (carried in boats), kings, and subjects were seen visiting and paying homage to Marduk in his "chamber of fates." Royalty was allowed to take the hand of the god, as if inviting him down an elaborately paved procession-way, to confirm and renew the divine kingship. At an earlier time Marduk may have been obligated to go in procession to Nabu, illustrating the hierarchical implications of being the object of a procession.

The display of venerated objects, such as the Host during Christian *Corpus Christi* processions or symbols of power, such as weapons in Roman triumphal entries, is a common motive for processing. Lustrations or gestures of purification are sometimes enacted to insure that such objects are not contaminated or regarded as common by over-exposure.

The ritual form most akin to procession is pilgrimage. Though both are styles of symbolic journeying, they differ in essential respects. While pilgrimage is more goal-oriented (the return is usually a come-down), processions may be more focused on a carried object than a goal, and recessing may be as significant as processing. In contrast to pilgrims, processants do not usually eat, sleep, or suffer together—nor endure long periods of solitude. Furthermore, processants are usually the objects of spectating, while such is not the case with pilgrims. For these reasons processions tend more strongly toward social conservatism. Ironically, however, the more popularly successful a procession becomes, the more likely it is to become a ritual of inversion.

Portals

A portal is any gate- or doorway insofar as it elicits ritual actions or becomes a locus of concentrated architectural symbolism. It is a space framed to call attention to spatial transition, so it has characteristics of both path and place.[88] Since a portal often separates a sacred precinct from a profane one or a regulated from an unregulated zone, it is both a termination and beginning point. As a structure that is both inside and outside the same zone, it is a site of considerable ambivalence, attracting dangerous as well as beneficent forces.

The most rudimentary forms of a portal are the cave entrance, stone heap, upright post, and two uprights supporting a lintel. More elaborate ones add not only familiar features such as a threshold, doors, knobs, and hinges but also figures, inscriptions, porches, domical towers, cupolas, niches for statues, and crowning arcades. In some eras portals are so emphasized that they become free-standing monuments, separated from buildings, bridges, or city walls. No longer only markers of paths, they become places in their own right. Three famous examples are the Great Gateway (1630-53 C.E.) to the Taj-Mahal (Agra, India), the pai-lou ("entrance") leading to the Temple of the Sleeping Buddha (near Peking, China), and the Gates of Paradise (1403-24 C.E.) designed by Lorenzo Ghiberti for the Florence Baptistry (c. 5th century C.E.) In cases where a road originates or terminates at a gate, for instance, the Ishtar Gate (Babylon, c. 575 B.C.E.) and its grand procession way or the Jerusalem Lion's Gate (1538-39 A.D.) leading to the *Via Dolorosa*, it seems that in most cases the portal sanctifies the path rather than vice-versa. It is not uncommon for a pilgrim to have to pass through several preliminary gateways on a road leading to a major portal.

The widespread, cross-cultural separation, elaboration, and multiplication of portals suggests that their importance far exceeds their two most obvious functions, that of regulating traffic and providing military defence. Other functions are to commemorate noteworthy events, memorialize cultural heroes and royalty, instruct the faithful, propagandize strangers and outsiders, advertise the nature or use of a building, and dramatize the status of inhabitants.

The bronze doors (1015 C.E.) of the cathedral at Hildesheim, Germany, for example, teach Christian believers to consider Jesus' crucifixion-resurrection as both a parallel and reversal of the disobedience of Adam and Eve by presenting both stories, on the two opposing door-leaves, as a visual *concordantia* of the Old and New Testaments. The best known examples of Roman triumphs such as the arches of Titus (82 C.E.), Trajan (114 C.E.), and Constantine (312 C.E.) commemorate the victories and accomplishments of generals and emperors. Portals such as the Stonehenge monuments (Wiltshire, England) or the Gates of the Sun (c. 1000-1200 C.E., Tiahuanaco, Peru) probably had astrological and initiatory uses.

In both the East and West portals have been the object of intense syncretism. Consequently, historians of art and religion are able to trace a remarkable continuity of style and consistency of symbolism connecting Indian toranas with Chinese pai-lous and Japanese toriis (of which there are twenty different styles). Egyptian pylons and *heb-sed* tents (under which a pharaoh appeared as the god Horus or Ra during a jubilee festival) are historically linked with Greek *prophylaia*, Roman triumphs, and the entrances of synagogues and the cupolas of mosques and churches.

In most cases portal symbolism is distinctly celestial. Besides decorative stars, rosettes, and solar discs, birds and wings appear over portals with considerable frequency; the characters for torii mean "bird" and "to be." Among ancient Hittites and Egyptians a winged solar disc formed the lintel, which was supported by two pillars often personified as guardian spirits. The identification of a lintel with a deity or royalty and of columns with protector spirits or intermediaries is widespread.

In theocratic societies royal dwellings, like the divine kings who inhabited them, were sacred. Portals, since they were one of the architectural features most obvious to a common person, served as a synecdoche for the entire palace, which itself stood for the king, who, himself, incarnated the divine. The court of the sultan in Istanbul, for example, was called "the divine portal." As a result of this tendency, a single pillar or the imprint of a facade on a coin (especially in sixth century Thrace) could stand for the entirety of royal-divine power. The ability of an image of a portal to evoke such authority was probably enhanced by the practice of administering justice at city gates. Only the throne rivals the gateway in its ability to embody the convergence of heavenly and imperial authority. Jesus' claim to be the "door of the sheep" (John 10:7) reaches back to a Mesopotamian sensibility typified by a hymn to King Ur-Nammu (2113-2096 B.C.E.) which addresses him as "Thy gate, thy God."[89] The name "Babylon" itself means "the gate of the gods." The guardianlike pillars of fire and cloud (Exodus 13:21) that lead the Israelites in the desert could be interpreted in relation to the personified door posts, Boaz and Jachin (I Kings 7:21), which flanked Solomon's temple. Pillars, both in their free-standing and supporting forms, frequently undergo stylization into trees or mountains, thus serving as symbolic links between heaven and earth.

Evidence testifying to the importance and meaning of portals is not only architectural but also ritualistic. Large-scale portal rites in the West have been intensely royal. Examples include the Babylonian New Year processions, the Hellenistic Epiphany, Roman Adventus, and Christian Great Entrance (a part of the liturgy of the Mass)—all ceremonies for greeting royalty or divinity. The intentions of participants seem to have been to purify and protect as well as celebrate and elevate. Also, testing and humiliation at gateways is a ritual practice extending from Ishtar's tests at each of the seven portals of the underworld to modern border-crossings.

Small-scale ritual practices at portals are still an active part of folklore. Making offerings, smearing blood on doorposts, burying the dead beneath thresholds, removing shoes, touching pillars, and either jumping, crawling, or being carried over thresholds are common. Lustrations and baths are widespread preparatory rites for passing through portals. Jews touch mezuzahs on the doorposts of their houses; Catholics dip their fingers in holy water and make signs of the cross upon entering churches. From the tradition of carrying brides across thresholds to the shrinking doors of *Alice in Wonderland* and from popular old idioms like "gates of hell" to recent ones like "gates of the dream," popular religion, folklore and fairytales are replete with threshold customs and dangerous doors that miraculously open or that one must not (but surely will) enter.

Not only do portals become detached from buildings and venerated but the portal as a motif becomes metaphorically extended beyond its monumental form. Tombstones are carved in the shape of a doorway, and ossuaries have doorways etched on them, thus associating the dead with the divine. Altars incorporate architectural features of portals; by analogy both table-top and lintel are *cathedra* ("divine seats"). Virtually any vessel of transition such as a mother's body becomes a doorway. The church itself in the Carolingian era (8th-10th centuries C.E.) was regarded as a *porta coeli* ("heavenly portal"). And in modern times the threshold (limen) has provided the key metaphor for the widely utilized theory of ritual developed by Arnold van Gennep in his *The Rites of Passage*.

Finally, there is suggestive evidence that the shaman's experience of a difficult passage across a bridge or through a narrow pass may be a variation on the theme of smiting doors and clashing rocks (e.g., the Symplegades through which Jason and his Argonauts had to pass). The image of the vagina dentata ("toothed vagina") may be another variant. But the portal, unlike the bridge and symbolic vagina, emphasizes royally authorized security rather than shamanistically induced risk.

5

Sacred Space
and the Southwest:
Mapping Histories
of American Religion

Sacrality is, above, all a category of emplacement.
　　　　　　　　　　　　　　　　　—Jonathan Z. Smith[90]

I remember some years ago to have seen a map of Christendom put forth by some protestant Reformation Society in which the catholic countries were painted black, & the protestant countries in a light colour. The black was the Kingdom of the Beast where the children of darkness worship the Virgin Mary: the light were of course the homes of the true Israel, the lands flowing with milk & honey, which having Luther, Calvin, & Cranmer have no need of the Sun or of the Moon to lighten them.
　　—Cardinal Manning, On the Blessed Virgin Mary, an uncatalogued manuscript in the Pitts Theology Library of Emory University, folio 12.

A corner of the map was missing and one of the officials asked how it had come to be damaged. Aggan answered: someone had died who would not easily find his way to heaven, so the owner of the map had cut a piece of it and buried it with the body. With the aid of even a fragment, said Aggan, the dead man would probably find the correct trail. . . ."
　　　　　　　　　　　　　　　　　　　　—Hugh Brody[91]

71

MIRCEA ELIADE, WHO, MORE THAN ANY OTHER SCHOLAR, SHAPED the early formation of religious studies as a discipline, made much of the idea of sacred space and the symbolism of the center, the orienting place from which a people's sacred cosmos is generated. Arnold van Gennep and Victor Turner, both anthropologists, have also strongly influenced our understanding of sacred space, particularly with their notion of liminality, the sacred "threshold" zone that marks boundaries between cultural domains. Nevertheless, all three scholars treated sacred space in ways that were largely metaphoric, having little to do with actual geography or the concrete complexities of the environment. Attention to sacred spaces and environments has been slow in coming to religiology (or, religious studies). Because the sacred has sometimes been imagined in the Euroamerican West as transcending space and time, Western religiologists often lapse into the assumption that religion has little to do with the particularities of the environment. However, under the impact of the environmental crisis, critiques by feminist theologians, and the emergence of ritual studies, sacred space is beginning to be taken with a new seriousness and conceptualized with a concreteness previously absent.[92] Among the results is a growing interest in the regional and local roots of religious practice.

My reflections on the problem of mapping religions in North America started when I began to work as an advisor for a documentary film on local religion and drama called "Gathering Up Again: Fiesta in Santa Fe"[93] and to write a book called *Spirit Catchers: White Lives and Indigenous Religions in the Southwest*. The former required me to ask, "Local in relation to what?" The latter forced me to ask myself, "Southwest of what?" Obviously, the Southwest is southwest only from a point of view located northeast of itself. In New Mexico "south of the border" refers to Mexico. However, the area U.S. citizens designate "the Southwest" is to Mexicans *El Norte* ("the north"). To residents of British Columbia, Washington state is "south of the border." Thinking about the relation between geographical regions and nation-focused histories of religion necessitates paying attention to the ways spatial metaphor, or mapping, functions as an ideological underpinning for histories of religion in North America.

On many anthropological and archaeological maps the southwestern United States is a distinct culture area, though one's definition of the Southwest shifts, depending on the purpose. When considering prehistoric indigenous religions, the Southwest consists of what is now Arizona, New Mexico, the extreme southern portions of Colorado and Utah, and the extreme northern portion of Mexico. If one is referring to the historical period, during which Spanish and Mexicans conquered and settled the Southwest between 1540 and 1821, the Southwestern culture area must include parts of Texas and California because of the strong presence of Hispanic Catholicism in those areas. The Southwest is also a mythic space constructed by the popular Anglo-American imagination. As the imagined home of Indians, conquistadors, and cowboys, and as a mecca for artists, anthropologists, and other tourists from "back" East, it is a stage or arena in which historical characters, mythic forces, and dramatis personae engage in social dramas and historical pageants.

The distinctions among archaeologically, historically, and mythically constructed space may seem absolute to some, but these are only three of the many possible "southwests," depending upon one's purposes and perspective. My aim is make us aware that these are strategies, not facts, and to show how one such mapping strategy has shaped the history of religions in the United States.

But first a word about the mapping the metaphor. The term "map" (Latin: *mappe*) originally meant "tablecloth" or "napkin." A *mappe mundi*, a map of the world, was a flat thing laid out on a table and used to represent features of the earth's surface. Such a "tablecloth of the world" is, of course, a metaphor in a twofold sense. A map both is and is not a tablecloth; a map both is and is not the world. Maps are so useful and the image of a world-in-a-napkin so compelling that the idea of mapping has undergone numerous metaphoric extensions. Outlines, classificatory schemes, organizational charts, lists, and other graphic devices having nothing whatever to do with geographical features of the earth's surface are spoken of as "maps." Even mental representations, mazeways as Anthony Wallace calls them,[94] have become "maps."

Maps render ideologies and sacredly help assumptions with

graphic clarity, a point made with considerable irony by Cardinal Manning in the second epigraph above. A map reflects journeys completed and suggests explorations yet to come. The point of any map, literal or metaphoric, is to facilitate orientation. Religious people try to orient themselves by mapping the world, the body, ritual space, and so on. Students of religion try to orient themselves by mapping traditions onto geographical domains (Hinduism in India, Judaism in Israel, and so on). Presumably, there is some relation between the maps of religious people and the maps of scholars of religion.

Zen masters are fond of reminding their students that the finger which points out the moon is not the moon, and Jonathan Z. Smith tells his students that the map is not the territory.[95] However true such statements are, they are also half truths. Zen masters do not let their initiates get away with thinking the finger is *not* the moon, and Smith wants to convince his readers that ritual is fundamentally a matter of *placement*,[96] for which conceptual maps are determinative. So maps matter. As the third epigraph suggests, for some Native people even a corner of the right map enables the spirits of the dead to find their way home.

Maps—fantastic, mythic, and geographic—dramatize social constructions of, and perspectives on, space and, ultimately, cosmology. Conflicting constructions of space, such as those laid out by Natives, Hispanics, and Anglos in the Southwest determine sacredly envisioned destinies and create centers from which groups engage in critiques of each other's worlds.

"Holy" Historiography

Yi-fu Tuan, a cultural geographer, uses the term "geopiety" to refer to people's reverent bonding and reciprocity with their terrestrial homes.[97] The term as I use it applies to academic culture as well as folk culture. The geopieties of scholars are evident in the few literal geographies of religion there are, for example, Frank Litell's *The Macmillan Atlas History of Christianity*, but geopiety is no less determinative in histories of religion in North America.

Historians' maps are occasionally explicit. More often they are either metaphoric or implicit. Historiography is the study of the ways history is written and, consequently, of the tacit assumptions of historians. Just as religious people make certain spatial assumptions that ground their rites, sacred histories, and cosmologies, so students of religion in America have treasured points of view and spatial metaphors—geopieties— that ground their historiographies, hence, my hyperbolic label, "holy" historiography. This historiography is holy in the sense that sometimes it is held tacitly and persistently and thus not subject to much conscious, critical scrutiny, and in the sense that its spatial orientations enshrine ultimate values that sometimes contradict explicitly stated ideologies.

Not so long ago the discipline known as "American religious history" or "the history of religions in America" was called "church history." As church history it was conceived narrowly in terms of the dominant religion, Christianity. Sometimes it was even more narrowly limited to either Protestantism or Catholicism. In either case church history was too often written as if non-ecclesiastical, non-Christian reality did not exist. Now that scholars write "American religious history," they typically acknowledge the plurality of religious traditions in America. However, even this approach has its blind spots. Many who write such histories do so from the point of view of the east coast and from the point of view of English colonialism and its westward movement.

If one wants to understand the history of religions in the Southwest, there are at least two other major perspectives that must be taken into account. First, there are Native Americans for whom mythic space is sometimes defined by roughly concentric rings, the outermost limit of which is marked by sacred mountains, which are both mythic-ritualistic and geographical. For them the westward movement of Anglo-American history was an invasion, a penetration from the outside in. And second, there are Hispanic Americans for whom destiny moved not only from east to west but also from south to north. So a regional perspective can help correct the overgeneralizations of a national one.

A history of religions is typically written from a standpoint that provides its basic orientation. History, like any other form of narrative, always implies a point of view. But an implied point of view is often more revealing than an overtly stated one, because it is usually less subject to an author's control and manipulation. Claiming that all knowledge is from a "standpoint" is nothing new. Michael Novak popularized the metaphor among religion scholars some years ago in his little "invitation" to religious studies, *Ascent of the Mountain, Flight of the Dove*. For him, however, a standpoint had no fundamental relation to an actual place; it was not a geographical location where one stood viewing the world but a conceptual "position," which was no more bodily than his standpoint was geographical. As important as it is to understand that "point of view" is a metaphor for "presupposition" or "basic value," we must not ignore its geographical and historiographical implications even though they may be tacit.

Though the "holy" historiography is breaking up, there are still remnants of it in use, so it is essential to identify its basic assumptions, for example, the assumption of an east-to-west axis. The dominant historiography usually implies a standpoint located in the northeastern United States. That standpoint functions as a perceptual, orienting center. And, typically, the central standpoint is singular, not plural. There is one center.

From this center destiny, (itself, no doubt, following the frontier hypothesis), rolls westward like a great ball.[98] Historian-narrators—largely White, often Protestant—typically position themselves either alongside or behind this ball, not in front of it.

This east-to-west spatial movement is assumed to coincide with a temporal movement running from the time of the Puritan colonies to that of New Age or new religious movements in California.

Since the great ball of destiny is moving through both space and time, at some point the narrator—not to be left behind what he or she is narrating—shifts points of view from center to circumference. In effect the narrator gains control of both symbolic regions and thus presumes to narrate both mainline religion and its impact on peripheral religion.

Since a metaphoric trick is being played out here, I need to rerun this part of the panorama in slow motion. On the one hand, our historian/narrators see things from the northeast. In their eyes the plains spread out toward the west. California looms large, a kind of golden magnet or target. Pueblos, Navajos, and Hispanic Catholics and others inhabiting the Southwest are somewhere "out there" on the circumference, out there on the desert frontier. The narrator is at the center, the place of a privileged point of view. For a moment it seems that the historian has ceded to those "others" a reservation of sorts. At least they have the hinterland, the periphery.

Then our "holy" history-tellers realize that, as guardians of the center, they are now confined to a single point; the movement of history is leaving them behind. So they shift their spatial point of view. Now, our narrators are at the edge of circle, the circumference. Now they are the container rather than the contained. By reversing the spatial strategy, this sort of narrator becomes a custodian of the all-encompassing circumference, and those "others" become the inhabitants of a small point. Though that point is now in the middle, it is too small to be significant; it may even be defined as nonexistent. The trick then is that our historian lays claim to *both* narrative standpoints, center and circumference, an act of metaphoric omnipresence.

By leaping back and forth from center to circumference, the narrating historian assumes a bird's (or god's) eye view of the whole process. This view from above is conveyed primarily by the rhetorical convention of an omnipresent narrator who is nowhere in particular, everywhere in general. Put in spatial terms, we might call this the assumption of "narratorial generic space." Like writing in an assumed generic gender—neither that of a man nor that of a woman—writing from anywhere or nowhere really amounts to an unconscious strategy for disguising what some experience as epistemological and rhetorical imperialism. Of course, the contradiction between the narrator's omnipresence and his or her location in the east seldom becomes explicit and thus subject to critique.

In some versions of the "holy" historiography another spatial metaphor, a size metaphor, is also at work: some traditions are imagined as greater and some as smaller. The "greater" traditions, for example, Christianity, are treated as universal and referred to as "world" religions—I prefer the term "multi-national." The "smaller" traditions are tribal, local, or regional.[99]

The size metaphor is usually coupled with a deeply rooted directional metaphor. Influence, it is assumed, passes in one direction only: from the big traditions to the little ones. And whatever is local is interpreted as a manifestation of something greater. Local religion is construed as a variation on a theme orchestrated at the national, or some greater, level. Local religion then becomes a "commentary" or "reflection" on national or multinational forms. American religious history is used to account for local religious history, not vice-versa.

One implication of such a mapping of the geography of North American religions is that indigenous religions, for example, are made peripheral; they are off the mainline. They have history—which is to say, exist—only insofar as they are bumped by the great bowling ball of Christian-American destiny as it rolls across the country and down through time. Even in instances where historians choose to recognize that indigenous religions were here first, indigenous histories typically cease to be narrated once the main thread of the narrative is picked up again: first were the Indians, *then* came the Spaniards, *then* came the English, and so on. Once the English and Spaniards are on the stage, the Indians disappear from the story.

An architectural example of the way this spatial metaphor works is reflected in the structure of the new Canadian Museum of Civilization. Its bottom floor contains Native exhibits. The second floor displays "folklore" materials, that is, deposits from recent immigrants, for example, the Chinese. And on the third floor is "history," where the English and French are. Walking into the museum, one enters into a state of nature and ascends through folklore into history. When one gets up to history, Indians are not there. Though the historians at the museum maintain that Indians have history, the proxemics of the museum undermines their claim.[100]

Even when Native people are given primacy of place in histories and museums, the ball of destiny rolls past them as it makes its way into the 20th century. "They" appear spatially static and therefore passive, while "we" appear spatially dynamic and therefore active. "We" are at the center; "they" are on the circumference.

Before proceeding, let me now summarize the key features

of the mapping of religions implied by the dominant, or "holy," historiography:

1. a single center or origin,
2. located in the northeastern United States;
3. a movement of destiny from east to west,
4. coupled with a temporal progression from Puritan colonies to West Coast new religions;
5. an implied omniscient narrator capable of shuttling between the center and the circumference; and
6. a size-as-value metaphor implying that lines of influence run one-way from "great," "mainline," or "world" traditions to "local," "tribal," or "minority" ones.

Some Histories of Religion in America

Since at least 1968, the date of William Clebsch's *From Sacred to Profane America*, there has been a growing effort to achieve what Clebsch called a "polypolitan" view of religions in North America. As opposed to the "holy" historiography, the "polypolitan" historiography aspires to be polycentric and multivocal.

In 1972 Sydney Ahlstrom published his monumental *A Religious History of the American People*. It became the focus of considerable scholarly discussion about a new historiography that goes beyond not only the church history paradigm but beyond Christian history to a pluralistic history of religions in North America. One reason it became central to religious studies was that the book is both a classic representative and an early critic of the "holy" historiography with its implied geopiety. In one sense Ahlstrom's work exemplifies the older historiography, and in another, his call for a more pluralistic history of religions in America helped initiate the turn toward a more inclusive historiography that aspires to pay sustained attention to women, Black people, Native people, and religious groups outside the so-called "mainline."

In 1976, the date of *A Nation of Behavers*, Martin Marty, pursuing this desire for a more pluralistic, less ethno- and religiocentric historiography, became quite explicit about mapping, our topic. The first chapter, called "Mapping Group Identity and Social Location," begins with the claim, "This essay in contemporary history provides a new map of religious America . . ."[101] Among other things, his aim was to put *behavior* on the religion scholar's map, so it was no longer overshadowed by *thought*.

In Marty's book the map metaphor is supplemented by a second spatial metaphor, that of "perspective," which has nothing overtly to do with actual spatial location. Marty hopes to find an adequate perspective from which to explore six general religious "zones." This is a third spatial metaphor—again, having nothing to do with geographic region.[102]

Marty sustains the mapping metaphor throughout his book, using it, for example, to criticize Will Herberg's identification of American religion with Protestantism, Catholicism, and Judaism. He writes, "This [Herberg's] reductionist map was superimposed on the earlier territorial and denominational ones, but soon events would occur, both in religious demography and in the change of the spiritual landscape, that necessitated another map, another layer."[103]

Marty is obviously aware of the problems presented by the idea of a normative, central, or mainline American religion. He takes up the image of a "mainline," not just to utilize it, but to identify its limits so he can attend more fully to non-mainline American religions such as ethnic, or "ethno-," religion.[104] Though Marty thinks his "zones" "account for *all* forms of social religious attachments and expressions" in North America,[105] he is modest and thus expects other maps to be superimposed on his.[106]

In the final analysis, Marty uses the images of map, perspective, zone, and mainline as metaphors. "Map" really amounts to a set of "types," "movements," or "phases." The map metaphor does not spatialize or regionalize his perspective. In fact, he identifies "territorial" maps as a remnant of an older historiography that he wants to leave behind. His analysis has little to do space, locale, or region. As he puts it, these are "'ways' more than 'places.'"[107] By severing maps from places, thereby rendering the former entirely conceptual rather than spatial, Marty jeopardizes his own claim to be studying behavior, because behavior happens in specific places.

One might complain that my objection ignores the fact that the map is not the territory; consequently, an erroneous map is not all that significant an error. However true it is that maps are models, not reality, when we internalize them as cosmologies, they determine how we behave as we negotiate our way through a territory. Maps alter perceptions, thereby behavior, thereby the territory itself. The relationship between territory and map is highly interactive and systemic; a change in one requires a change in the other.

Marty's book is a good, not a bad, example of the newer historiography of religions as it attempts to rectify the abuses of the "holy" historiography. But this new "polypolitan" historiography still clings to remnants of the "holy" historiography insofar as the narrator remains rhetorically omnipresent and his zones, not regionally specific. In my view Marty's good, pluralistic intentions are compromised by the despatialized, disembodied narratorial strategy. One can only imagine—with a certain perverse delight, I admit—how his book would read if it were not only written in Chicago (if that is where he wrote it) but *as if* from Chicago.

There is a tendency in religious studies, particularly in theology and philosophy of religion, to ignore the ground religious people walk on, as if the metaphoric "ground" of their being was somehow independent of the actual land underfoot. A reason sometimes given for this platonic tendency to float above the environment is the view that religion is essentially concerned with mythic, ritualistic, or conceptual space, not actual—which is to say, social or geographical—space. Supposedly taking their clue from religious practitioners, students of religion have sometimes narrated the history of religions in a way that implies that the narrator is an omnipresent one located either nowhere in particular or everywhere in general. Aiming to counteract this tendency, philosophical hermeneutics has reminded us that we approaches texts and other religious phenomena from a "horizon," from a set of presupposed questions and values. But this horizon has seldom been the sort that witnesses sunrises and sunsets. Again, as with "standpoint" and "ground," these fundamentally spatial notions have been rendered as metaphors without ground. There is nothing wrong with them as metaphors; they are quite useful as such. But it is essential to recollect the geographical and environmental bases of the metaphors and thereby take our actual "locatedness" more seriously than we typically do.

Recently, Catherine Albanese, Sam Gill, Robert Michaelsen,

and others have deepened the call for a new approach by insisting on the inclusion of Native religions, not as peripheral objects but as fully historical, fully acting entities. Presently, I know of no serious scholar who denies the need for such inclusivity, though there are few candidates for books in religious studies that have actually achieved it. A major problem that Michaelsen points out is that there is so much data on Native American religions, but there is no compelling perspective.[108] So he proposes one. He calls it "a history of religions done within the framework of *respublica*,[109] by which he means "the underlying legal framework of the United States."

My problem is what such a perspective implies geographically. Put metaphorically, this is still a perspective *from* Washington. The way the metaphor works is insidious, because it militates against Michaelsen's own explicit ideological stance. For example, he treats the American Indian Religious Freedom Act of 1978 as something promulgated by the United States (that is, from Washington), which subsequently has a positive effect at Taos Pueblo, New Mexico, on the Blue Lake controversy. Though I am sure he does not intend to, Michaelsen makes it seem that causes emanate from Washington with effects in Taos. But Taos Pueblos know that Mr. Washington does not move unless someone goes there to push him. I am sure Michaelsen knows this too. But he thinks we should have *one* perspective, so he wants to find *the* proper standpoint for it. To the contrary, I am maintaining that a perspective that is either *from* Washington or from nowhere in particular is a strategy of narratorial omniscience unworthy of a genuinely "polypolitan" historiography. One could put it this way: there is still a latent, mythological "federalism" or "republicanism" in this perspective; it is still a search for overarching oneness and unity. It assumes that "the nation" is the proper unit of consideration. I have no argument against *respublica* as subject matter, but I do as point of view. Catherine Albanese has criticized this nation-state viewpoint as Puritan (therefore ethnocentric) and called for new ways of organizing space and time.[110] And Vine Deloria has criticized civil religion theory, a kind of *respublica* approach, for perpetuating a Christian view of history that sets it against geography.[111] We do well to heed their cautions.

So far I have criticized spatial metaphors implicit in national histories of religion from a regional viewpoint, but regional perspectives are not sacrosanct either. Even the idea of a specific, coherent region, in this case, the Southwest, is a construct that exists in tension with a variety of local geopieties. Even within the Southwest there are a great many maps—some literal, some metaphoric, some mythical—and they represent a set of competing, converging, conflicting geopieties. I do not propose here to try to summarize them adequately but merely to identify a few examples of their mapping strategies that have a potential for grounding critiques of the spatial assumptions of the "holy" and the "polypolitan" historiographies. For example, emergence myths are widespread in the Southwest. One finds them among Pueblos, Hopis, Zunis, and Navajos. The drawing at the beginning of the Navajo Curriculum Center's *Navajo History* illustrates well enough the sense of primal movement from below to above. It depicts the spiralling emergence of Navajo people from below this present world. Though movement upward seems in some respect inevitable or necessary, it is not "progress" as Westerners imagine upward spiraling to suggest. Failure, quarrelling, and sexual impropriety are among the motors of emergence movement. Such emergence, or "going up," myths imply a different set of values from the "going out" metaphors that are at the root of Judaism and Christianity and their secularized, civil-religious offspring.

Another indigenous spatial metaphor is linked to wandering, dispersing, reconverging. Once in this world, so the stories go, emergent people often found themselves wandering, dispersing, engaging in clan formation, and reconverging. In this process certain places, usually mountains, became sacred markers. They marked the ritual extent of a people's world, though not its actual territorial extent. This was not the territory they owned, but the land with which they bonded in forming their corporate identity. Even though a "going out" motif is essential, so is a "returning home" or "coming in" metaphor. The world is not treated as an infinite horizon calling for boundless exploration.

Among religion scholars one of the best known features of indigenous spatial conceptions is that of the sacred center or middle place. Zunis, for instance, refer to themselves as "people of the middle place." Though "place" may be grammatically singular, this centered universe is nevertheless polycentric. On the one hand, there is one emergence place; it is *the* center. On the other, there are many centers, and they are identical with that one. As a diagram and chapter by Alfonso Ortiz illustrates, the Tewa Pueblo spatial universe is roughly concentric but not symmetrical, and there is no simple opposition between center and periphery.[112]

In indigenous worldviews boundaries, however they are conceived, are generally permeable and shifting, or there are no territorial boundaries at all. "As the Navajos saw it, land had no boundaries. The land between the four mountains was a hogan. Navajos lived in it with other peoples and tribes like people living together in a hogan," argue Beck and Walters.[113] Despite the fact of having a world bounded by mountains both sacred and geographic, Native people often conceive of their circumference as open. The sense of territory as carved up like a jig-saw puzzle, was not native to their traditions. This kind of bounded, territorial sense developed largely when treaties had to be negotiated with foreign governments.

A primary difference between Native geopieties and those of Euroamericans was the experience of being penetrated from without, followed by a diaspora from within. Contemporary Native worldviews now include this "historic" redefinition of their sense of space. The sacred circle has been penetrated. Boundaries have been hardened and defended by law or by gun, and the people have migrated from reservations to cities and back again in extended periods of dispersal and reaggregation.

These are only examples, barely sketched, of the kinds of spatialized rethinking that needs to be taken into account if histories of religion are to be genuinely pluralistic in their treatment of sacred spaces, ranging from the local to the cosmological. It is essential to initiate critical reflection on the issue of sacred environments from perspectives other than our own. If one can criticize the way histories of American religion do violence to the Southwest with its regional pieties, then the very notion of southwesterliness must also be subjected to critique from the point of view of indigenous, local geopieties and from the standpoint of Hispanic historiography, something I have not attempted here.[114]

I will conclude by identifying some of the implications that follow if we systematically attend to local and regional geopieties, allowing them to question nationally focused "holy" and "polypolitan" historiographies. We will be prepared to identify implicit standpoints, reflected in spatial metaphors like "map" and "point of view" and thus to hear the historian/narrator's voice, which is probably more indicative of ultimate values than the content of a storyteller's historical or oral narrative. Hearing this positioned voice will makes us more self-aware, recognizing that all historical narratives are positioned and thus mythic. Thus, for example, "Washington" will seem to us no less mythic than the worlds below this one; both are orienting places. Such a recognition can teach us the humility that comes from knowing that maps are plural even within a tradition, not to mention between traditions. A recognized plurality of maps would virtually force scholars to take systematic, theoretical account of the fact that there that are no generic or universal histories—that *all* histories are ethnohistories. One consequence for the writing of religious history, specifically the story of religions in the Americas, would likely be a decision to narrate it by several authors to insure preservation of the plurality of indigenous, regional, and local voices.[115] Such a plurality of voices would, I believe, challenge the tyranny of chronology and introduce less linear strategies for writing history—strategies in which simultaneity is possible, in which several religions and groups occupy the stage at the same time. With no grand climaxes the "star," or heroic, conception of the drama of history would doubtless fall (it is crumbling now), as would the more virulent idea of a "mainline" American religion, from which everything else is a deviation, variation, or local realization. If we, in fact, succeed in taking what one cultural geographer calls a "worm's eye view,"[116] that is, a regional/spatial/land-based view, to supplement the reigning chronological *over*views, we will be well on our way to comprehending the implications of the opening epigraph by Jonathan Z. Smith, who comments, "Sacrality is, above, all a category of emplacement."[117]

6

Sacred Objects
in Museum Spaces[118]

RECENTLY, CONTROVERSIES SURROUNDING THE DISPLAY OF RE-
ligious artifacts in museums have forced museologists, anthropologists, and religion scholars to reflect on the relationship of
the sacred to concrete objects. Religions and cultures vary considerably in what they take to be sacred. The extremes—
cultures in which everything is sacred and cultures in which
nothing is sacred—probably do not exist despite the stereotyped characterizations of so-called "primal" and so-called
"modern" or "secular" cultures. Although one hears people
claim that all things, or no things, are sacred, they usually *act*
as if some things are and some, not. They usually act as if objects that were not sacred can become so, or as if things that
were sacred are no longer so. Consequently, we get further if
we consider a sacred object as a moment in a cultural and historical process rather than as an allusive "thing in itself."

Cultural processes are decisively affected by the spaces in
which they transpire. Sacred objects do not exist in a void. The
spaces, architectural and conceptual, that they inhabit can radically alter, sometimes even determine, their meaning as well
as viewers' comprehension of that meaning. Sacred objects in
synagogues, temples, and churches are one thing; in museums
or art galleries they are another.[119] Even if their "exegetical"
meaning (that is, what people say about them) were to remain

the same, their "positional" meaning (that is, their spatial and/or conceptual relationship with other symbols) is necessarily different.[120] In Western museum and gallery contexts sacred objects present a special problem, one result of which is that we Western viewers are likely to misunderstand, if not actually violate, them. The difficulty arises from fundamental differences between the values and perceptions of Western viewers and those of the traditions and cultures out of which many displayed sacred objects come.

One of the most significant processes affecting sacred objects is that of commoditizing. The secularization of Western culture has been accompanied by the widespread commoditization of religious and culturally treasured objects.[121] A commodity is a product intended principally for exchange.[122] Commoditization is the process by which something not produced for exchange becomes subject to the dynamics of exchange. All cultures—small-scale tribal ones and large-scale industrial ones—utilize commodities. Exchange is a fundamental, and, as far as I know, a universal, human activity. Every culture has its own way of identifying and making things into commodities. It is a necessary process, but one in considerable tension with sacralization as it is understood in the Euroamerican West. Here, sacralizing is sometimes felt to a process that removes an object, space, or activity from the dirty business of money. As an explicit consideration in the midst of sacred activities, concern for or talk about money seems slightly obscene. Yet traffic in sacred objects is never, in fact, removed from economic considerations in the industrial West any more than it is in tribal societies.

Commoditization implies the exchangeability of things. Absolute commoditization (which probably does not exist) would imply that all things are exchangeable; to put it crassly, everything would have its price. Commoditizing an object makes it common. The process depends on being able to reduce two things' values to a common denominator so they can be exchanged. In mainline Western cultures one such common denominator is money. Here, money is much desired but felt to be vaguely polluting. Our pragmatic values lead us to pursue money with an unparalleled vigor, but our romantic and our religious heritages lead us to search for values that cannot be commoditized: the most important things in life are free; you cannot buy love, and so on.

In economic theory the opposite of commoditization is singularization, a process very much tied up with romanticism and aesthetics. When we regard something as singular in this sense of the term, we regard it as non-buyable, as priceless. In our culture you do not sell your mother; you do not sell your children. This fact, or value, is obvious. But we also treat certain symbolic objects as singular. If you are going to sell your mother's wedding ring, which was given to her by her mother, and which she gave to your daughter, you do not tell your mother. Singularizing something takes it out of the market dynamics by treating it as precious, by attributing to it so much worth that it is beyond exchange.

Although museums, when they purchase objects, momentarily commoditize them, they do so "terminally," that is, the purchase terminates the commodity phase of the object. An object in a museum becomes "singular," unique, abstracted from its original context, protected from the market. It becomes precious—in both senses of that word.

In the biography of a Tlingit mask or an image of a Hindu goddess, what kind of moment is it when such a piece lands in a museum? What happens to it as a result of its new environment, this public foster home for material culture,[123] this temple for the booty of civilizations, is complex.[124] It is catalogued, displayed, labelled, singled out, glanced at, and, if fortunate, studied and admired. Surely, it should feel grateful and fortunate. Should it not? Or is this merely what all foster homes think their wards *should* feel like?

In an earlier century the public might have regarded images of other people's gods as idols. Most religion scholars would regard this view as prejudicial—like regarding *other* people's religions as magic. Though some religious fundamentalists still use the term "idol" to refer to statues and masks of deities, most religious liberals and the secularized public would not. They would be more likely to speak of them as "symbols," in which case one looks for "meanings" to which such symbols "point." Or they regard them as "art objects," implying that the proper response is "appreciation" of their formal qualities and workmanship. But both the symbolist strategy and the aesthetic strategy are still very Western. Perhaps they are not as blatantly ethnocentric as self-righteous accusations of idolatry, and they do counteract certain forms of crass commoditization, but they are still very culture-bound, less than sensitive attitudes.

Even though museum objects may have been collected originally out of curiosity or as an act of cultural conquest, museums currently justify their display of sacred objects on the basis of another rationale (or, from the point of view of the conquered, rationalization), namely, to educate the public out of its culture-boundness. But the very act of making relics and such things into scientific-esthetic objects is thoroughly Western. So whatever new information one might gain from museums, their displays are still governed by this agenda, which is peculiarly Euroamerican and which functions, despite intentions to the contrary, as a ritualization of Euroamerican political and social values. The ritual of installing the Hindu goddess Lakshmi, for example, in a museum is a performance of esthetic values, an educational and political ceremony, that fundamentally alters the function of that image.

Museums label artifacts because most viewers are ignorant about them. If we look at the labels in a typical exhibit, we see that many of them refer the images to sacred stories, or what scholars call myths. Referring objects to myths is a way of educating the public, but it is also a practice that occurs in the "home" cultures of most of these objects. So, is not referring sacred objects to cultural myths a way of respecting, if not conserving, their sacrality? I doubt it. In a museum a statue *is said to refer to* a myth: the curators have to tell us that the images refer to myths. By contrast an image in a sanctuary *embodies* a story, reminding devotees of what they already know; it is not merely the occasion on which someone must tell us what we do not know. In its home culture the story was not a little strip of paper under a statue but a cycle of narratives, often widely told and sometimes ritually dramatized. In other words, the mythic story and icon were integrated; here in a Western museum they are not. Because of the connotation the word "myth" has in our culture, our use of it to refer to other people's sacred stories demonstrates our distance from those stories and declares our intention to treat them as them as "objects" of thought, "things" to think about. In ordinary speech we seldom refer to our own stories—the stories we believe—as myths.

So there is no way around it. When the statue of a goddess comes to a museum, she is a stranger in a strange land. This is not home; a museum in the biography of a stone goddess is the archetypal strange land where many trials must be endured. Our proverbial goddess must endure our bored, or if she is lucky, curious and admiring, gaze. In museums we are encouraged to learn the mythological allusions of statues, attend to the magnificent workmanship of reliefs, and imagine the ritual uses of masks. But our goddess will have to forego her milk bath: we may admire her, but we are not devoted to her.

Regardless of curators' and directors' intentions, sacred objects in museums become rarefied by being detached from their everyday cultural contexts, and reified by becoming objects of "curiosity" and "pleasure" that "charm" and "fascinate," to borrow some phrases from a curator writing about sacred objects in the magazine of a well-known Canadian museum.[125] There is considerable dissonance between the educational and aesthetic effects of sacred objects on display and the religio-social functions they served in their original contexts such as symbolizing abstract qualities, expressing belief systems, aiding contemplation, and serving as objects of devotion—all functions identified by the same curator.[126]

The meaning of an object, whether domestic or sacred, is closely tied to its use (this is its functional meaning) and to its place, both physical and conceptual (this is its syntactical meaning). We misunderstand a sacred object if we think its meaning consists solely of its references to myth (its verbal meaning) or to its shape, colour, height, and so on (its formal meaning).

A statue of the Buddha is sacred not only by virtue of the fact that it might resemble the man Gautama, or that its *mudras* (hand gestures) may refer to a specific attitude or event in the life of the Buddha such as his preaching, or that it incorporates the traditional proportions that a statue of Buddha should have, but also that prostrations are done before it. In other words, sacredness is also a function of ritual use, not just of form or of reference.

It is simply not true that a rose is a rose is a rose. A rose on a dinner table under a low light with your wife sitting, hair freshly washed, across from you with a wine glass in her hand is not a Tudor rose, is not a rose growing where your daughter might fall against its thorns (such a rose is merely a weed).

The statues of the gods and Buddhas in a gallery are not "sacred" art but "museum" art, artifacts. The things on sale in the gift shop are "tourist" art, even if they are also "good" art. Art is fundamentally (not accidentally) conditioned by the performances it evokes from us. It is conditioned by our rites, decorum, and other such behavioral formalities—even in North America, where we are not likely to think of our standing in front of masks, pots, and statues as performance at all.

Museum artifacts are singularized, counter-commodities, one might say, in a culture that aspires to secularity. They are not commodities in the sense that they are bought and sold regularly on a open market; they are too "priceless" for that. But when something is priceless, this does not mean that it brings no price. Rather it means it could bring a high price. When we call something "a museum piece," we mean that it is quite valuable. So, functionally considered, when a sacred object becomes a museum artifact, it evokes simultaneously our desire to elevate and isolate it as an art object and our desire to own and control it as a priceless commodity.

Singularizing is the other side of the commoditizing. Cultures with a high degree of commoditizing generate a great nostalgia for singularizing. Witness the "collectibles" our society produces and venerates with quasi-religious nostalgia. The singularized object becomes a kind of zombie. Though religiously dead, it is kept alive. No longer ritually fed pollen, bathed in milk, or offered fruit, it is studied as a specimen and conserved by what the medical profession calls "heroic means" so that its life span is much longer that it would have been in its original context. By singularizing something as a museum artifact or art object, we may have removed it from the dirty business of business, but we have also removed it from the cosmological and ritualistic processes of religion.

Conceptually, I have almost painted myself into a corner. I have characterized the display and viewing of sacred objects in museums as distinctly Western, a culture-bound activity. I have considered two cultural processes, singularizing and commoditizing, and suggested that misunderstanding sacred objects from non-Western cultures is likely. I am on the brink of implying that desecration is inevitable when dealing with traditions that do not share our view that publicly exposing the sacred empowers it. Some very serious questions now loom before us: Should we not shut down museums and avoid going to them? Are not the histories of colonialism and museums so entangled that any attempt to reenvision them really amounts to disguising their role in continued intercultural domination?

Metaphors for the Museum-Bound

Since museums often embody deeply held Western values, even when such display spaces are located in Asia or elsewhere outside the "first" world, there is probably no way to avoid ethnocentrism when displaying sacred objects and visiting museums. The very acts of possessing, conserving, displaying, and viewing them are not universal but culture-specific, so the best we can hope for is to minimalize ethnocentrism and perhaps to avoid obvious desecration. To this end I want to propose three metaphors which, if cultivated, might begin to reshape our sensibilities along alternative lines. I will summarize, then elaborate.

One proposal is that we recover the things-as-persons metaphor as a significant component of our worldview. Such a view is implicit, for example, in Miles Richardson's notion that artifacts are abbreviated acts.[127] Another is that we need to become more aware of museums-as-cathedrals with their own attendant myths, rites, and ethics. The final suggestion is that we learn to construe visits to sacred objects in museums as acts of ritualizing.

The first suggestion, that we recover the metaphor things-as-persons, could enable a better understanding of sacred objects from tribal cultures. Igor Koptyoff provocatively suggests that things, not just persons, have "biographies."[128] He urges us to think about the ideal "career" of an object, say, a painting or a shoe.

For example, the guide to *The Spirit Sings* includes a brief biography of the career of a Athapaskan suit now in the Reiss Museum of Mannheim, West Germany. The author says:

> It was apparently collected by Baron von Wrangell between 1829 and 1834 in Alaska, and sent as a gift to the Russian czar. From Petersburg it went to the Duke of Leuchtenberg, who gave the suit to the King of Bayern. Eventually, after the kings's collection became state property, the suit came to the Museum für Völkerkunde in Munich. Later, it was given to Arthur Speyer, Sr., a German collector, in exchange for other objects. Finally, in 1968, Arthur Speyer, Jr. gave the suit to the Reiss Museum in exchange for a figure from New Guinea.[129]

Julia Harrison, author of this brief account, concludes by observing, "The history of this itinerant piece, and its frequent role as a gift, indicates the high regard in which such objects were held, if one assumes that, among the aristocracy, any object given as a gift implies it is significant and unique."

No doubt this claim is true. But imagine for a moment—for the sake of cultivating our objects-are-people-too metaphor—that this account is a biography. What kind of a biography would it be? I suggest that the nearest analogy is that of the slave or captivity narrative. What is remarkable about the suit is not just its high regard among aristocrats but its sheer disposability. It was not deemed essential either to the life of its owner or to his culture.

In Western cultures our predominant experience of objects is as commodities. Framed as commodity, a thing is a thing and thus it has no rights. Rights pertain largely to persons, not things. Things are objects; and persons are subjects. The biography of the Athapaskan suit is underwritten by that all-pervasive Western subject-object dualism. Consequently, the suit is an object, not an extension of the person who made it. If the object were singular and associated with a charismatic figure (imagine, for example, Hitler's uniform, Abraham Lincoln's cane, or Napoleon's hat) we would likely experience it as more animate; the boundary between person and thing would begin to bleed.

Just as surely as the original making of the suit concretized the worldview of a northern Athapaskan, so its subsequent biography illustrates the worldview of aristocratic central Europeans. A biography of the same suit, had it landed in North America, might have been quite different. In middle class North America it is indecorous to give away a gift you have received. You might do it, but you would try to hide that fact from the original giver. Gifts, like sacred objects, are a problem because the gift, we say, bears the giver ("The gift without the giver is bare"), so giving away a gift runs the risk of being experienced as a symbolic disposal of the giver.

A widely held and deeply valued distinction in Western culture is that which separates persons from things and insists that things are commodities while persons are not. This polarization of commoditized things and individualized persons is, comparatively and historically speaking, anomalous. However, there are interesting exceptions in our own culture that can help us gain perspective on the thing/person dualism. The crassest example of commoditizing people is slavery, which, of course, is a great moral problem (to understate the matter). There are other examples of anomalies in the person/thing classification. How, for example, would we react to the idea of putting a Renoir painting in the garbage? What do we think about the purchase of children by childless couples, the selling of bodily organs, or the abortion of a fetus? Is a fetus a thing or a person? Our struggles with such questions illustrate the difficulty with too absolute a person/thing distinction. Obviously, it is possible to treat persons as things and things as persons. Noticing the anomalies—items that are not classifiable as either person or thing—is a good way to begin reconceptualizing sacred objects.

Sacred objects land in the anomalous zone between the Western categories of thing and person.[130] They are not handleable by this ready-to-hand distinction. Crosses and Buddhas, like blood, Canada, one's honor, public lands, monuments, heirlooms, medieval indulgences, and other such "things," stir us to action if we believe they are being subjected to commoditization. Our deepest ambivalences surround such "things" because they are not just things.

Once we have activated the things-are-people-too metaphor, it is easier to understand how displaying might constitute violation. Would you want your grandmother's Bible on

display? How about your dirty underwear—with your name
beneath it? Or how about your old love letters? Obviously, if
we select our examples provocatively, we may understand the
feeling sometimes expressed by Native North Americans,
namely, that exposure violates; this experience is what the
term "voyeurism" labels.

For Native people sacred pipes are not inanimate objects;
they are vibrant with life; they are animate. At first this attitude sounds strange to non-Native ears. But think of the violation we feel when someone desecrates certain non-persons—
when someone steals from a church, throws away money, or
burns a photograph of an old lover. Though we are not ani-
mists, we do, in fact, act as if certain objects, values, words, or
ideas are violable—as if they contained spirit, condensed life,
or were attached to us like our arms, legs, and children. Construing them metaphorically as animate, as persons, helps us
understand the reactions of "other" people whose things we
display.

My second suggestion is that we recognize the religious or
quasi-religious functions of museums. Some museum directors have already done so. For example, George MacDonald in
a brochure describing the Canadian Museum of Civilization
(CMC) speaks of the building and its Grand Hall in tones bor-
dering on religious enthusiasm: "The hall is an open cathe-
dral-like space featuring a dramatic backdrop almost three sto-
reys high, evocative of a Pacific rain forest. Six totem poles . . .
stand sentinel, mutely speaking of kinship, spiritual values,
and relationships to nature." In the same brochure the director
speaks of the CMC as "a treasure house for cultural objects
which possess power as enduring standards, icons, and reality
anchors."

Such religious rhetoric might be used merely for the purpose of constructing hyperboles that boost our sense of accom-
plishment. But employed more self-critically, it also might
provoke museums into recognizing that they cannot hide behind the ideologies of neutrality, scientific objectivity, univer-
salism, and humanism. Rather they must, as the CMC is commissioned to do, assume a posture of advocacy, of actively
working to change unjust or ethnocentric attitudes. Even if we
insist that museum-as-cathedral is only an overblown meta-

phor (and thus we can maintain that museums are also museums and cathedrals, cathedrals), the metaphor still should be taken seriously (though not literally). The metaphor implies that museums are quasi-religious institutions with their own ethics, myths, and rituals. The act of defining and housing cultural treasures, parallels that of formulating canons and identifying works as classics.

Thus, a museum's interests are vested. Museums like to view themselves as neutral mediators between contesting parties, and sometimes they in fact are. But the metaphor, "museum as cathedral" reminds us that they are just as often one of the contesting parties, legislating things into reality and conferring status on them. Recognition of this function among some museum administrators can lead to a more self-critical posture which we, the viewing, visiting public, should applaud and support.

A third, final metaphor worth considering is that of the museum visit as ritual. Previously, I have suggested that we use the gerund "ritualizing" to refer to the act of cultivating emergent ritual (as distinct from "rite," which I use to denote already defined, culturally recognized enactments).[131] By recommending a ritual practice I enter treacherous territory. Having gone from analyzing to prescribing is dangerous enough, but now I am advocating ritual practices in museum spaces. Some will argue that my position is religious. Perhaps it is, but it is not religious in any denominational sense; it is not the position of a theologian who speaks as an insider from within a specific tradition.[132] Though I make no pretence that my position is scientific, and though I admit that I intend to foster a reverent attitude, I nevertheless intend my position to be open for debate on the usual grounds assumed by discussions in the humanities and social sciences.

To continue, I suggest that we go beyond mere appreciation of the artistic qualities of sacred objects in museum spaces to the practice of contemplative ritualizing, by which I mean activities that soften the boundaries between viewing subjects and spectated-upon objects. Two features of such ritualizing are synesthesia and religious ordinariness.

Contemplative ritualizing often accompanies synesthesia, the cross-tabulation of senses that occurs when they "talk" to one another. Imagine, for example, greeting objects with senses other than sight—not that sight is inherently irreligious (it in fact has a long religious history) but that the sight-obsessed tend to distance themselves from what they see. What would happen if we were to cultivate synesthesia in a museum—if instead of trying to see the Buddha on the pedestal, we practiced hearing the Buddha instead?

Of course, it would be a violation of the liturgical decorum of museums to fondle the statues, so in front of most of them we would just have to stand there contemplating that stone image—both we and it looking quite ordinary. For the most part our fellow museum-goers will never see us as we touch him with our eyes, kiss him with our ears, and see him with our hands. Synesthesia is most likely when we are allowed tactile encounter with at least a few objects with more than one sense. Some museums, for instance, one at the University of British Columbia, already have a class objects called "touchables." People can actually use them. In the Ritual Studies Lab at Wilfrid Laurier University we have developed ritualized practices with objects, involving the tactile, kinaesthetic, olfactory, and gustatory senses.[133] These senses (along with the obviously overworked auditory and visual ones) involve participants more radically. Thus, they are more likely to rekindle ritual awareness among sensorily-distanced Western "audiences."

A second persistent feature of contemplative ritual is its refusal to dichotomize the extraordinary and the ordinary. Emphasizing the centrality of metaphor to religion, Lynda Sexson says in *Ordinarily Sacred*, "the extraordinary is the ordinary celebrated." "Why," she asks, "do children collect feathers, hide gold paper, delicately perch a marble in the arms of an unresisting house plant, or stick shells under their beds or stones into their mattresses? The 'junk' that is precious to children—and to adults—is precisely the stuff of the sacred."[134]

Our culture produces a lot of junk, so we might imagine that we are well prepared for the "ordinarily sacred." But we are not. Sexson is talking about treasuring, the act of valuing what has been discarded or overlooked. Since ours is a supposed to be a materialistic culture, we may imagine that we already have a good sense for things, but we do not. In a materialistic culture objects are largely either disposable or priceless. They are either so far below us (as commodities or junk) or so far above us (as cultural treasures or priceless art objects) that we have little inclination to contemplate them. Either we buy them, use them, and dispose of them, or we cannot buy them, so we admire them for a split second in a museum and then pass on to another for the sake of collecting viewing experiences. In either scenario we do not contemplate them.

What am I implying? That we should feed Native North American masks, do *puja* in front of images from India, and prostrations before the Buddhas?[135] Imagine the security problems if we all tried on the Noh mask, or the acid stains if we all touched Kali's breast. And, God forbid, think of the disease control problems if we all kissed the Bodhisattva Kwan-Yin's foot. Since neatness, cleanliness, and orderliness are sacred values ritually performed in Western museums, one can imagine how seriously my polymorphously perverse suggestion of resensualizing our relationship with objects would to be taken if we were to use worship as our model. So, no, I am not calling for worship but for contemplation; they are quite different ritual processes.[136] A contemplative posture is not necessarily an approving one, nor does it imply the superiority, moral or spiritual, of object to viewer. Contemplation is not worship but rather dwelling in the possibility that what one imagines is out there (in the display case) is also in here (in the heart), and vice-versa. Consequently, I would still argue for a contemplative stance even if the encountered museum object were not a sedentary Buddha at the Glenbow Museum in Calgary but a stained Aztec bowl in the Denver Museum of Natural history, a vessel that once held the sacrificed hearts of human beings.

To conclude, I am arguing that a museum may be most fruitfully imagined, as a "trap for contemplation," to use Denis de Rougemont's words,[137] rather than as a cathedral, a quasi-ecclesiastical institution in which people "worship." So imagined, we would begin our practice at home, in the junkyard, or at the recycling depot, not at church, synagogue, or temple. We would reconsider ordinary objects—spend time with industrial discards, displaced objects at home, things happened upon in the streets.[138]

Imagine that you have played with some useless junk in the sandbox of your mind (or soul or heart or whatever empty space you can find) and that you learn through hours of practice to fondle an old spoon, for example, until you lose track of subject and object, thing and person, touching and seeing.[139] Then you will be on the edge of contemplation, a practice possible in museum spaces—one less likely to eventuate in the desecration attendant upon voyeuristic appreciation and more likely to open the Western eye to what is at the heart of non-Western sacred things.

7

The Life History
of a Mask[140]

AFRICAN MASKS AND INUIT MASKS ARE EXAMPLES OF THE KIND
of masks that usually fill large-format, coffee-table books and
draw people to museum exhibits. They are also the kind presupposed by most theories of masking. Such masks are "other"; they are not products of Euroamerican culture, which is
the predominant source of collecting, classifying, and theorizing about masks.

The most widespread assumption about such masks is that
the proper context to be invoked for their interpretation is that
of performance, ritualistic or theatrical. Theories of masking[141]
that assume a performative context, however, run into difficulty when confronted with a mask like that of the prominent Canadian writer, Margaret Laurence, because it is not a mask for
either theater or ritual. It is, for lack of a better word, a biographical mask. We see it and wonder about its relation to the
life of the novelist. It would strike us as absurd to link this
mask to Laurence's ritual tradition, that of weekly worship in
the United Church of Canada. In contrast to Inuit and Gyodo
masks this is a mask of a person, knowable in the flesh, and
living when it was made. This mask is not that of a dramatic
character or a ritually defined spirit, animal, or god.

Figure 1: Margaret Laurence holding her mask, accompanied by artist Connie Gallotti. (Photo by Connie Gallotti)

One way to get a perspective on the differences between a biographical mask and a ritual mask is to consider the typical life history of each. Igor Koptyoff has suggested that things, not just persons, have life histories.[142] He urges us to think about the ideal "careers" of objects as they go through the stages of their life. Here is one simple way to schematize such a scenario:

SEVEN MOMENTS IN THE LIFE HISTORY OF A MASK

The Typology ⟶	Ritual Mask	Biographical Mask
The Scenario ↓		
1. Making	Ritualized art/craft	Non-ritualized art/craft
2. Wearing	Worn in ritualistic-dramatic performance	Not worn except in the making
3. Encountering	Encountering a deity or spirit. The essential moment in the life history of a ritual mask	Encountering a symbol that refers to something else and whose meaning is elsewhere
4. Removing	A secretive moment or an exercise in disenchantment	Part of the making; an experience of momentary freedom or a metaphoric "birth" experience
5. Exchanging	If sacred, sometimes desecrates. If tourist art, produces income	Buying and selling are acceptable, except in the minds of friends or family
6. Displaying	Not done separately from the masker and the performance	An invitation to contemplation and/or study. The essential moment in the life history of an aesthetically or educationally framed mask
7. Destroying	Allowed to deteriorate or destroyed ceremonially	Preserved, not destroyed

This chart is a device to enable one to think cross-culturally and comparatively about multiple phases in the life history of two different types of masks. I will not comment in detail on any one phase, because it is the overall process that is important. A truly comprehensive theory must take account of all of the moments and not limit itself to any one of them.

In the left column are typical phases in a model life history for a mask. I have identified seven. There could be other phases, and there could be fewer or more of them.

In addition to the seven phases of masking, the chart also schematizes two types of performance and their affiliated types of masks, ritualistic and biographical. One could add other performative types, theatrical, for instance. Or one could subdivide ritual and biographical masks, which would nuance and complicate the scheme, thus helping to avoid overgeneralizations. Further, any specific mask in its lifetime might migrate across types, because the definitions of the types are not determined so much by formal characteristics as by their performative uses, social functions, and cultural contexts. So the scheme is not sacrosanct; it is a generalization, a simplification of the actual empirical complexity of masks and masking sensibilities. In this instance I have eliminated theatrical masks because the specific performative circumstance I want to consider is that of the museum and art gallery, not the stage.

In the center column we follow a ritual mask through the schematized biography. In the right column we follow a biographical mask through the same scenario. The aim is to compare two different masking sensibilities on the basis of a common continuum. I use the term "masking sensibility" when I want to indicate the whole complex that includes mask, masker, and masking in the plurality of their social settings.

Making a Mask

The first stage is that of making a mask. Margaret Laurence's mask is one of a set of twenty-six masks of famous Canadians called simply Cultural Connections. The set, which includes figures such as writer Timothy Findley, singer Joni Mitchell, radio personality Peter Gzosky, and scientist David Suzuki, was made by Connie Gallotti, who lives in Toronto, where she facilitates art and healing groups for survivors of sexual assault. When the artist made Laurence's mask, she herself wore a mask during some phases of the process. Seeing such a process, visitors from other cultures might have wondered whether the artist was protecting herself ritually from the power of the mask being constructed. Westerners would probably have guessed easily that the artist's mask was her way of protecting her health from harsh chemicals. The rationale was technological, not symbolic.

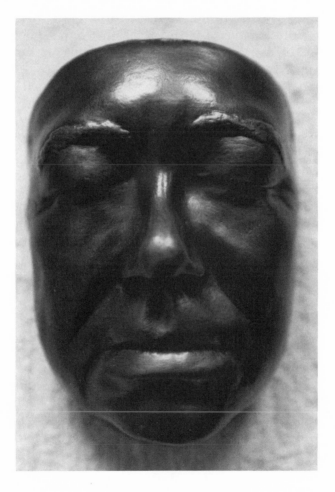

Figure 2: Final, bronze version of the mask of Margaret Laurence made by Connie Gallotti. (Photo by Ron Grimes)

There were sub-phases within the process of making Cultural Connections: applying plaster-impregnated gauze to a subject's face, casting, firing, sculpting, and so on. The final result was a bronze casting.

For ritual contexts the first moment, that of mask making, is not well documented by scholars. Neither the theories nor the documentary photos take much account of it. In the history of scholarship on masking we have been shown blanks being cut from a tree, a tree that has given birth to several masks, or, eye holes being burned. But for the most part ethnographers have left the making of masks to the occasional how-to book, as if only dramatic artists interested in duplicating or replicating the technique were interested in it.

Sometimes the making phase is ritualized, hedged with taboos, framed with chanting, praying, and purification. Sometimes it is not. The making of Margaret Laurence's mask was not ritualized, that is, not formalized or stylized, nor was it understood to be a religious activity. Gallotti, the primary maker of the mask, is not a member of any religious group. In newspaper interviews she sometimes spoke of mask making as ritual, but only when referring to her workshops, not when talking about Cultural Connections. When speaking of her project, she treated it in practical terms as a technique. The rhetoric she employed was what one would expect when discussing an art or craft rather a spiritual practice.

Wearing a Mask

Theories of masking pay more attention to the next moment, that of wearing a mask. Expressivist theories, those that study the relationship between mask and wearer, concentrate on this phase.[143] But it is still rare for masking documentation to include wearers along with their masks. Photo journalists and ethnographers occasionally show us a person wearing a mask, as, for example, in a Nigerian Edo festival. Such photos sometimes appear in studies of ritual and festivity but seldom in the study of masks.

Theories of masking that focus on transformation sometimes fail to distinguish the impact of masking on an audience from the impact on a wearer. For example, when Laughlin and Young-Laughlin propose their provocative thesis that masks transform the brain, they do not specify whose brain, that of the wearer or that of the participant audience.[144] However, it seems that when Mircea Eliade speaks of masks as "instruments of ecstasy," he is probably thinking of the wearer as the ecstatic one, though one cannot be certain.[145] We are familiar with the claim that in some cultures a wearer becomes a god. The masker does not just symbolize a spiritual power but actually becomes it. Those who have studied the Zuni Shalako rite regularly report such a transformation. But those of us who make Halloween masks with our children do not enter ecstatic states when we put on our witch and vampire masks. So we must take care not to overgeneralize about the effects of wearing a mask and to specify who is transformed and in what respects.

Some treatments of masking emphasize the enhanced authority of mask-wearers. In the early part of this century, for example, there was a theory which held that wearing masks was the privilege of males. According to this view masks were the primary device by which men convinced women and children that men were gods and thereby gained power over women in the primal patriarchy.

Whether or not there is any truth to this theory, wearing a biographical mask is quite another matter. In Gallotti's project the phases of making and wearing the mask are the same thing; phases one and two collapse. The only time the twenty-six Canadian heroes wore their masks was during the making of them. Clearly, they did not achieve power by wearing masks. Rather, they were chosen to be subjects of mask making because they had, and therefore were symbols of, cultural power. Their masks were the result, not the cause, of their power.

Laurence said she found that having the mask made on her face evoked her experience of giving birth in Africa. If her mask conferred power at all, it was the power to undergo, not "power over." Laurence's experience epitomizes a theme common to having a mask made on one's face, namely, the evocation of birth. Gallotti encouraged her subjects to put a candle behind their plaster masks or to dress them up and spend an evening contemplating them. In some instances this ritualized practice—this closet performance of the self, by the self, for the self—led to a kind of self-recognition or revelation. But the effectiveness of this performance depended on *not* wearing the mask. It arose from contemplating a "transition object," a thing simultaneously the self and not the self.[146]

Much more study needs to be done of the ways maskers relate to their masks. The range of possibilities is considerable. Japanese Noh performers, for example, sit in front of a mirror contemplating their masks before they go onstage. Hopis feed theirs ritually. And we need to understand such performances with or on masks in relation to what Erving Goffman called "face work," the performative transformation of faces themselves into masks to avoid "the state of ritual disequilibrium or disgrace."[147]

Some maskers claim that wearing a mask is an experience of freedom: one has a different identity and can hide one's personal feelings. Others claim the experience of wearing a mask is one of bondage: one feels unimportant, a mere channel for forces greater and more important. In the latter case one acts out of obligation, not out of a desire for, or a feeling of, power.

What a masker experiences is not what a viewer experiences. After all, the inside of a mask—which is the only part of it the wearer sees while performing—is radically different from the outside. And an audience responds to the outside, not the inside. So wearers have to internalize what an audience sees, thus being forced into reflexivity with regard to their masks. They are almost forced to recognize the constructedness of their power.

A recurrent theme in masking theory is that masks allow wearers to act out of their unconscious, thus making the repressed public. But expressivist theories that interpret masks in relation to wearers' feelings and values have their limits. Not all masks are "of" the wearer. Masking is not always a personally expressive activity in which people wear masks of themselves. It may be a culturally reflexive activity in which the collective unconscious—that is, the ambivalences and contradictions latent in a culture—are acted out. In ritual contexts masked acting is seldom a matter of performing an individual's repressions. So only in biographically preoccupied North America is psychoanalytic interpretation likely to hit the mark.

Encountering a Mask

Now we consider the act of encountering a mask. In this phase a ritual and a biographical mask differ radically, because we must take into account primary and second contexts. In a ritual context a ritual mask is typically encountered on a person; in a museum or art gallery, both secondary contexts, a ritual mask is encountered without its animator. In our biographical example Laurence's mask is encountered on an acrylic stand. There is no animator; this is its primary, which is to say intended, context. In ritual circumstances, mask plus performer plus audience equals a deity (spirit or other such being). In the biographical case mask minus performer plus audience equals a symbol. In the usual view a symbol points elsewhere. Like the tomb of the Gospels, it is empty, and viewers are forced to look elsewhere for the reality the mask disguises. The person is gone, and we are left with a mere shell, a mere persona, a mere empty mask.

But these two different dynamics (mask as embodiment of deity, mask as empty shell) are matters of culturally determined perception.[148] Everything depends on how a mask is received, interpreted, and encountered. So any theory of masking has to take seriously the audience, congregation, tribe, chorus, musicians, and others, who themselves may be masked. There are many kinds of audiences, thus many ways of encountering masks. There are initiated and uninitiated audiences, elders and children, participating insiders and observing outsiders, to name but a few.

Although we routinely speak of sacred objects and include some masks in this category, we need to notice that the distinction between sacred and secular has little to do with formal characteristics of objects themselves and much more to do with the ways audiences encounter and interpret masked performers. Sacredness and secularity are determined by the social interaction itself.

Theorists typically assume the paradigm context for a mask is that of the viewed performance, either ritualistic or dramatic. In our North American example, that of Margaret Laurence's mask, the mask is typically encountered, not only without a wearer, but also without a viewer—at least in the literal sense. Cultural Connections was produced for a blind and sight-impaired audience. The masks are now on permanent loan to the W. Ross McDonald School in Brantford, Ontario. Students do not see the masks dancing on anyone's face. They do not hear the sound of drums in the background. They have not been initiated formally into cosmologies as preparation for encountering these masks. Rather, they feel them, reading them as they might read a Braille text. They imagine the faces of those whose voices they have read in books or heard on recordings, radio, or television. They read whatever biographical traces are etched into the masks and thus circumvent the taboo that prevents their touching actual faces. The masks are not important for their color but for their shape, size, weight, and texture. Kids get to scratch Native artist Doug Maracle's thick beard, stroke David Suzuki's wispy one, or speculate about what is being held back by Murray McLauchlan's tight lips.

Typical biographical masks in the West have as their primary contexts museums, art galleries, and historic shrines, not schools for the blind. So this exceptional set of masks reminds us that the sensorium organization we usually presuppose is specific to a social class, the sighted. Even though we may sometimes treat sculpture as touchable, we assume that the proper audience relation to a mask is that of seeing it. Because blind children are allowed to touch the masks, they are, in effect, invited symbolically to violate a taboo that inhibits tactility between strangers. In a gallery or museum even Laurence's mask, not to mention her actual face, would be off limits to the hands, so these contexts are almost as appropriated, or secondary, as they are for ritual masks.

Most theories of masks are functional ones. That is, they concern the relation between masker or mask, on the one hand, and audience, on the other hand. These theories focus on the long-term effect this relation has on the society which is its context. So it is essential that we keep the audience in the picture even though photo documentation and museum displays do not typically include primary audiences with the masks they display. In performative circumstances such as that of ritual, audiences may, in fact, be the real animators of masks and maskers. The widespread North American view of audiences as passive receivers is conditioned by culture-bound experiences in theaters, churches, and synagogues and may not at all indicate the real source of initiative and performative energy in other cultures.

The usual conclusions about what masks do for the societies that constitute their audience is that they summarize cultural information, transmit traditions, consolidate authority, and provide entertainment and escape. The problem with such generalizations is that they apply to every other item of material culture as well. They are generic; most of them are not specific to masks. Statues, paintings, chalices, fetish bundles, and a hundred other things evoke ambivalence, represent transformation, effect bodies and brains, transmit tradition, and so on. The question needing answering are: How do masks as such function? What is unique about the way they work?

Removing a Mask

The fourth phase, that of removing a mask, is implicitly an iconoclastic moment; "unmasking" is a Euroamerican metaphor for debunking. CBC Television's "The Journal" told us after the stand-off at Oka, Quebec, that it would take us behind the Mohawk warriors' mask. In its 1991 calendar, illustrated with masks, the Canadian Museum of Civilization aspired to go "beyond the mask." Westerners tend to mistrust masks and want to rip them off the faces of wearers, or at least peer behind them.

The moment of removal is sometimes one of high reflexivity, of heightened self-consciousness. Removing a mask raises the question of our identification with it and our difference from it. The "self" Margaret Laurence held in her hands was at once herself and radically other. Often unprompted, the experience of removing a mask in one of Gallotti's workshops evoked spontaneous, strong reactions. Having weathered the ordeal and holding their masks in hand, people sometimes wept. They did so, not from pain, but from a shock of recognition. Their masks represented a self both intimate and strange, both themselves and not themselves. For many it was a mysterious moment—one that led some people to refer to the whole process as a ritual.

In other cultures masks are sometimes removed in secret

and hidden until the next performance. Among Hopis and Navajos, for instance, unmasking can constitute a demystifying
moment—one that is initially shattering—one that parallels,
but is far more devastating than, that of learning that Santa
Claus is just your grandmother or uncle wearing a mask. Navajo children sometimes get to look momentarily through the
eye holes of a freshly removed mask. After a performance that
impresses them with the supernatural reality of masked dancers, they get to try out the mask themselves and experience the
ordinariness of the most mystified aspect of the ritual event.

If theorists are going to speak of masking as a transformative process, we cannot attend only to the transformation of a
person into a spirit or ancestor. We must attend to the re-
transformation of that spirit or ancestor back into a human being and pay attention to the circumstances that surround the
removal of a mask.

Some masks advertise their transparency and call attention
to—rather than disguise—the fact that there is a wearer underneath. This is the case with the Olmec and the Mayan "x-ray"
convention, which displays both the mask and the masker's
face so that in profile both are visible simultaneously. Japanese Noh drama masks are sometimes designed with very narrow sides to call attention to, rather than hide, what is behind
them. Jowls of old male actors hanging out around the edges
of small, delicate female masks are considered aesthetically
powerful because of the visual paradox set up.

So masks, even while worn, can anticipate their removal
and call attention to their transparency. Many of us recall the
famous photograph of Jacqueline Kennedy behind her veil at
her husband's funeral. The veil kept us out but simultaneously
invited us to take note of the interior dimensions of a national
drama. So we should resist the tendency to think of masks
only as hiding faces. Some attempt to hide the fact that they
hide anything. Makeup is an even more obvious example than
the veil.

Exchanging a Mask

The next phase is that of exchanging a mask, by which I mean
selling, trading, or giving it away. This moment is part of my

model, because it anticipates a mask's journey from primary to secondary context, from the Pacific, Asia, or Africa to a Western museum, a sequence typical of many of the masks we North Americans encounter. It is not hard to understand why some masks, like jade Mayan funeral masks or Japanese Gyo-do masks, become extremely expensive collector's items. Masks are not just tools used in performances, they are objects of desire and admiration. They condense economic, not just ethical or religious, values.

The exchange phase applies as well to the moment when a Western artist sells or otherwise loses control of the mask she has made. So far I have talked as if there were only one, original mask of Margaret Laurence, but there are several. With Laurence's death the several versions of her mask acquired a new, increased value. The artist had to struggle with this fact. She insists Margaret's mask is not for sale. She hopes to convince the National Archive to accept the plaster original. She will not sell it; the Macdonald School would not sell its bronze copy. And Laurence's children, though disinclined to keep Margaret's mask at home, would not be likely to remove their bronze copy from the Margaret Laurence Memorial Home in Neepawa, Manitoba. One might touch it by making a pilgrimage to Neepawa, but buying it is out of the question. The artist, who became a friend of Laurence as she was dying, would regard it as an act of desecration if the mask were to go on the market, bringing higher and higher prices with each subsequent sale. In the artist's view sale of the mask would violate the bond that the act of mask making precipitated. The mask functions for the artist as a relic mediating the presence and absence of the deceased novelist and friend.

If the sale of a mask made by a woman in supposedly secular Canada could evoke such a reaction, we do not need to wonder when people in other cultures complain about the expropriation and display of their masks and raise the issue of repatriation of sacred objects. By purchasing masks of other people, buyers gain symbolic control over aspects of other peoples' cultures. There is nothing absolute about the sacred/secular distinction. A secular biographical mask may be sacred to the artist who made it or to the children whose mother it represents, while it is secular to the casual passerby in an art gallery. A sacred ritual mask from Native America may become secularized by its display in a museum, but an ordinary object from Native America may become sacralized by its elevation to the status of museum piece.

One ought not romanticize masks or other sacred objects. In some cultures they are sometimes commissioned, bought, and sold without jeopardizing their sacrality. Economics as such does not pollute. So the morality of exchange depends upon specific historical and intercultural circumstances. Whatever the circumstances, it is just as important to think of a mask as a symbol of purchasing power as it is to consider it an embodiment of sacred power.[149]

Anticipation of the market can influence the makers and wearers of masks just as it can any other object. When this anticipation begins to determine the intention of the maker-artist and to dictate the form of the product, it becomes tourist art regardless of whether it is good or bad art. There is no reason a mask cannot be both tourist art and sacred art. Memorabilia from religious shrines and pilgrimage sites regularly fall into both categories.

Displaying a Mask

Closely connected with that phase in a mask's life when it is bought and sold is the next one, the moment in which it is displayed and thus becomes an artifact (a representation of another culture to be studied) or an art object (the subject matter of contemplation). Whereas an art dealer or exporter is the primary actor on the mask in the previous phase, in this one curators, students, scholars, and connoisseurs are the actors.

Scholars classify mouth shapes, styles, and every other imaginable feature of a mask. Curators collect walls and cases full of other people's surrogate faces. Masks were probably treated as ethnological artifacts before they became of interest as art objects. As artifacts they are subjected to quantification, curation, classification, and analysis. Masks are examples of what anthropologists call "material culture." In effect, masks as artifacts function for us as condensations of other peoples' cultures. Specific masks become examples that evoke someone else's cosmology. As artifacts, indigenous North American or

Japanese masks, for example, do not first of all evoke divine beings or recall specific ceremonies. They symbolize "Indianness" or "Japaneseness"; they condense otherness. They are important for the impression they convey, not for what they refer to.

However much a mask displayed as an artifact may have been once used to concretize divine presence, now it only refers to that presence. It says more about absence than it does about presence. There is nothing more ghostly than a large mask collection in a museum. The casual viewer may fancy that such ghostliness is a result of the makers' and users' intentions, but it is really a result of the commoditizing and artifactualizing processes that result from masks' migrations across cultural boundaries.

In the case of a biographical mask the moment of display is its essential one: it is made to be displayed, not worn in performance. Margaret Laurence's mask is no exception. In Cultural Connections it is labelled in typescript for the sighted and in Braille for the blind. A label is a sure sign of the didactic, educational dimension of Connie Gallotti's project, just as it is in a museum. This setup encourages a hands-on encounter. But such an encounter has to be seen as expressive of a particular, post-1960s ideology characteristic of Gallotti's project as well as some of the high-interaction displays at the Canadian Museum of Civilization. In many cultures one would not touch a mask, nor would it need a label.

There is, of course a difference between blind Canadian children who fondle Margaret Laurence's bronze mask and sighted people who long to be able to handle Zuni Shalako masks or Navajo *jish* bundles. Handling Navajo fetish bundles would make them more palatable, more consumable, thus, in Navajo terms, more dead or more polluted. In some instances to handle—or even to view—such objects in a museum is to engage in the form of cultural performance we call desecration. When a blind child contemplates Margaret's mask, it is made more alive.

Destroying a Mask

Some would say that ritual masks are destroyed the moment they are bought and sold. However true such a view may be metaphorically or spiritually, it is not so physically, so we need to distinguish possible desecration from the actual disintegration or destruction of a mask. In some traditions destruction or deterioration is understood as a mode of sacralization, a proper and fitting end to the life cycle of a mask. Henry Pernet, one of the few theorists who pays attention to the beginning and ending of masks, summarizes one of the most widespread reasons people offer for destroying a mask or allowing it to deteriorate:

> Often the making of the mask is in itself a ritual, which reproduces the various phases of the creation of the archetypal mask. Therefore, it is vitally important that the following cycle start anew at the beginning, that is, with the making of the mask. This is probably the reason why masks can be destroyed or left to rot without regret at the end of a cycle.[150]

The destruction of masks in nonliterate cultures may occur for other reasons as well. For example, destroying may release spirits originally infused into a mask. On the other hand, destruction or negligence can amount to an assault upon either the powers a mask represents or the owner who uses it.

In North America we are typically repulsed at the idea of destroying masks. We can imagine two reasons for destroying or abandoning a mask: (1) an incurable artistic error during construction might require the destruction of a flawed mask, or (2) one might destroy an original mask mold to prevent the production or further copies. Gallotti's attitude is typical. She wants Laurence's mask to be preserved; the mold is an "original." Gallotti hopes to have it conserved by the National Archive; she cares about its fate. Her attitude reflects the national attitude: the Canadian Museum of Civilization, for instance, installs special glass to prevent sun deterioration of its West Coast totem poles, masks, and other artifacts. The preservation ethic is central to artists and museums in part because it is central to North American values. Preserving masks rather than destroying them is our way of symbolizing their value. In the mainline West masks are valuable investments financially and culturally. History and culture somehow reside in them; the "somehow" tips us off to the tacit metaphysics, the "secular sacred," that permeates much of the North American attitude toward masks and other ritually significant objects.

The preserved mask is different from the dead mask. Because objects like masks are never really alive for most Euroamericans, they can never really be dead either. They can only be preserved. In other cultures masks and other sacred objects may be alive or dead. Navajo singers, for example, destroy sand paintings after completing the healing rites they support, and Yaquis destroy *chapayeka* masks after their use. In some cultures it is essential to allow masks to deteriorate naturally and die, to give them decent burials, or to repaint and rebuild them.

Recently, the destruction of art has become a legitimate feature in contemporary performance art. Such destruction often has an iconoclastic tone to it; it deliberately violates the widespread taboo against ruining things of value. Even when an artist destroys an original mold, it is usually to protect the value of castings made from the mold. So in both cases—destruction in performance art, destruction of artistic originals—the preservation ethic is still determinative. The Westerner's denial of death extends far beyond embalmed human bodies into the realm of material objects.

From Aesthetic Contemplation to Ritual Performance

With the death of a mask, we complete the life history. Implicitly, I have argued a theoretical point by working through a scenario—from making, wearing, and encountering a mask through removing, exchanging, displaying, and destroying it. This succession of moments, labelled metaphorically a "life history," has served as an axis along which to plot out a comparison between two kinds of masking that I have called "biographical" and "ritualistic." Considering masks in the context of the masking process is more useful than formalist studies of masks that isolate them as objects or functionalist studies that treat them as reflections of social structures, because doing so enables one to study masks in the plurality of their cross-cultural contexts rather than being confined a single "home" culture and because it reminds us that masks, like persons and institutions, undergo change.

The effect of using both the typology (the horizontal axis of the chart) and the scenario (the vertical axis on the chart) may not be to relieve us of our ethnocentrism—the scheme is still Western, still scholarly—but it does call systematic attention to the fact that masks are not mere static objects. They themselves are in process, even though they may appear to be frozen in time and space in museums and art galleries. Their meanings change as their positions and contexts change.

Both the scenario and typology are generalizations, but the biography-ritual distinction is the more generalized, thus the most in need of further qualification. I could have chosen a biographical mask from another culture and a ritual mask from this culture, but the difficulty of finding many such examples confirms my belief that the typology, if it is not turned into a dualism, is defensible.

I have used the distinction between ritual and biography to define two different masking sensibilities. In effect I have construed them as polarities: Ritual is collective; biography, individualistic. Ritual is transpersonal; biography, personal. Ritual is performed; biography, written (or, in this case, objectified as a work of art). Ritual is acted out therefore embodied; biography, essentially verbal, therefore relatively disembodied, and so on. Though biography is in some sense performed and collective, we have to stretch our understanding of performance to make this connection. Though ritual may be individualistic, it is not generally so. The distinction between ritualistic and biographical stands up then, but it is by no means absolute.

The biographical sensibility, though not exclusively Western, is largely so; the literature on written biography amply illustrates this claim. I have let biographical masks and contemplative attitudes symbolize the Euroamerican West and performatively employed ritual masks suggest other cultural traditions.

Westerners' relations to masks are largely divorced from ritual performance. Even Western theater cannot be described as a predominately masked tradition, though masked theater still has a place in the West. Though Western literary and visual artists paint us as socially masked, and "mask" is an important metaphor in the Western understanding of selfhood and social roles, we imagine ourselves masked more often than we actually don masks. "They" use them ritually and therefore believe in them. "We" appreciate and collect them and therefore do not believe in them.

Though making the link between cultural traditions and corresponding masking sensibilities is useful, pushing the typology much further produces stereotypes: ritual is precritical therefore primitive; biography is critical, therefore modern or Western, and so on. Here we must draw the line, because other cultures have no monopoly on the primitive, and we have no monopoly on criticism; nor does ritualizing preclude critical thought. So the polar typology must not become a dualism; the latter implies the absence of mediating types. Several dualisms—sacred/secular, ritualistic/nonritualistic, Western/non-Western—strongly influence how we understand the masking process, especially in situations where one of "their" masks lands in one of "our" museums. If we treat masks in terms of the phases of their life history, we are more likely to become culture-specific and less likely to fall into stereotypes when employing the typology.

Like most people who introduce polarities, I want both to use and to transcend or qualify this one. Though I have associated contemplation with the displayed, biographically interpreted mask, the association is just that; it is not a logical necessity nor a universal. And neither contemplation nor biographical masks are confined to Euroamerican cultures. In numerous traditions contemplation may feed ritual performance; masks may be both displayed and contemplated. They can be appreciated for their artistry, color, and suggestiveness in the same moment that they are used in ritual performance to concretize spirits and ancestors. Ritual contexts do not obviate aesthetic appreciation; in fact, a ritual sensibility may presuppose an aesthetic one. I do not want to imply that other cultures care nothing about beautiful objects or that participants in those culture do not remark on their pleasure at some magnificent work. They do. But when a tribal mask lands in an art gallery, it becomes *primarily* an art object which is, subject, if it is lucky, to contemplation. If not, then it can become a mere decorative item in, say, a lawyer's office. As such, it only creates "atmosphere" and is unlikely to become an object of contemplation.

Just as ritual performance may presuppose aesthetic contemplation, so aesthetic contemplation may proceed toward, or on the basis of, ritualizing. There were persistent tendencies toward it in almost every phase of the process of producing and displaying Margaret Laurence's mask. The latent tendencies became manifest upon Laurence's death: the mask was increasingly experienced and interpreted as ancestral. Some who viewed it would not touch it though invited to do so. Enshrinement of the object became inevitable.

So the typology, like all typologies, blurs at its boundaries. Like all polarities, it begins to evoke some third, mediating category, which in this case may well be that of theatrical masking, a genre of performance bracketed early in this discussion. A study of theatrical masking, along with the dramatistic metaphors it sometimes evokes, would enable us to see museum visits as a peculiar species of theater and to see biography as a peculiar species of performance.

So far I have used Margaret's Laurence's mask not as an object of contemplation but as an occasion for reflection. As a metaphoric ancestor, her shade would be restless if I stopped here however. Both my scheme and her mask seem to require a moment in which we actually exercise the contemplation I schematize.

When I pause before her mask, I am struck by the sheer ordinariness of it. Laurence could be our aunt. Or mother. Or grandmother. She does not look like a famous Canadian author. (What do authors look like anyway?) There is a great deal of power in the photo of the mask despite (or because of) the ordinariness of it.

This is not a mask *of* a man or *on* a man—the predominant case if we examine biographical masks cross-culturally. It is of a woman by a woman. And it does not function to conceal—as Eliade claims men's masks do—but to reveal.[151] We do not wonder what is behind it. Margaret Laurence does not have her glasses on. Her face is more, not less, accessible here than her usual public, bespectacled face. Eliade insists ritual nakedness is necessary for "woman" to achieve sacral power. In this mask Laurence is accessible without being naked. Here is a very womanly, powerful, non-naked mask that challenges the validity of Eliade's theory.

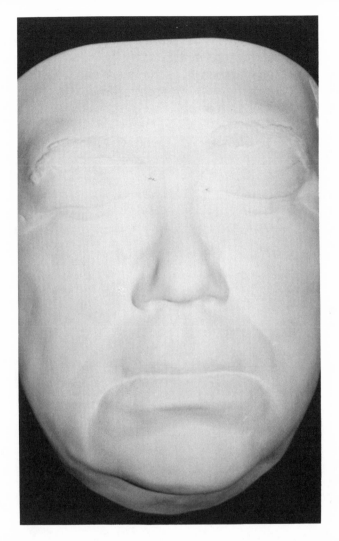

Figure 3: The preliminary plaster version of Margaret Laurence's mask made by Connie Gallotti. (Photo by Connie Gallotti)

The eyes are closed. We can hardly avoid thinking of this as a death mask, though it was actually a life mask. Laurence died in 1987, not long after its making. Its coldness to the touch reinforces our sense that death lurks about the mask, giving it a transcendent quality in spite of its ordinariness and our avowed secularity. The death we see in (or project onto) this mask is not "other," not brought by some demonic force from some other world. It is in the mask itself. Here the living woman and the dying woman are the same; death is not a serpent, not a man, not a demon.

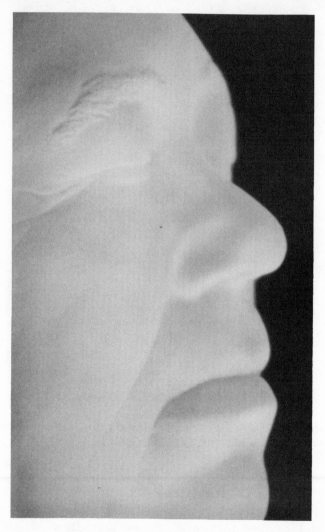

Figure 4: A profile view of the plaster version of Margaret Laurence's mask made by Connie Gallotti. (Photo by Connie Gallotti)

This face is not pure, demure, coy—it is not the mask of Eve-like femininity, not that of a "lady" offering us the fruitful parts of her anatomy but that of a woman offering us her grounded attention. Her face is specific, marked by age and heaviness. It is not erotic, but it is still sensuous. We might want to confide in this face, but it would resist distanced, pornographic gazes such as those invited by a number of religiously inspired, Western depictions of women.[152] Laurence cooperates with our contemplation of her face but not with our voyeurism.

Contemplation is sustained, sympathetic, reverent attention. It is what occurs when we take time to dwell. In the face of such attentiveness even a biographically framed mask has the possibility of becoming an actor, not merely the acted upon. As an acting subject, it promises, or threatens to become, animate, and, if animate, then alive though dead, and ritualistic though biographical.

We the sighted are prone to imagine that contemplation is a kind of seeing. Western mysticism, in which the idea of contemplation is rooted, is shot through with visual metaphors. But touching Margaret Laurence's mask reminds us that for Westerners the fingers, not the eyes—tactility, not vision—may be the real window to the soul. It is conventional in the West to hold that soul is immaterial and that all we ever meet in someone else is persona (Latin for "mask"). If we imagine this to be the case, perhaps we should make a pilgrimage to Neepawa, Manitoba, Laurence's ancestral home, close our eyes (or put them in our finger tips) and, with a hand on her mask, decide for ourselves whether what we have in hand is persona or soul. To do so is to pass from aesthetic contemplation to ritual performance.

Part III

Fictive Ritual

Part III

Fictive Ritual[153]

INTRODUCTION

IN *BREAKING THE FALL* ROBERT DETWEILER, OFFERS A DEFINITION
for what it means to read literary texts religiously:

> A religious reading of literary texts nowadays thus would be
> one in which a reader understands herself as part of a commu-
> nity engaged in simultaneously recognizing, criticizing and re-
> shaping the myths and rituals it lives by.

> One trait of a religious reading is that it joins the play of story
> and ritual in an atmosphere of festival.

> A religious reading could seek to regain the group-celebratory
> nature of story enactment by transferring it to the reading expe-
> rience.[154]

I can think of no better way this to describe what I do in
part three, although I speak of it as "reading ritually." As long
as one understands by the term "religion" something as broad
as Detweiler implies by his characterization, mine are certainly religious readings. There is no necessary contradiction (or
identity) between reading religiously and reading ritually.

The chapters that make up part three constitute a ragged
edge of my research and writing. I hesitate to refer to it as my
"growing edge," because I started on them a dozen years ago
and was unable to finish them until recently, that is, until the

completion of *Marrying and Burying*, an autobiographical book on rites of passage. I attribute my inability to finish *Fictive Ritual* to its exploration of topics profoundly entangled in my own life: ritualization, imagination, and male identity. In the process of writing on ritual in literary works I discovered a subtext that eventually worked its way to the surface, namely, the peculiar twist that a Euroamerican male author's imagination sometimes gives to ritual processes.

I did not initially select the literary works studied here because of their treatment of male ritualization, but the theme began to emerge in a way that was too strong to avoid even though it remains subordinate to that of ritual. With one exception all of the works considered here were written by men, and even the one exception, though *by* a woman, is *about* ritualization among men. Often the sort of ritual that appears in these works is merely fantasized, out of control, violent, or self-preoccupied. What manifests itself is a sometimes embarrassing portrait, especially if one looks into these works of literature as into a fun-house mirror.

Part three consists of previously unpublished works that were originally intended to be parts of an experimental project called *Fictive Ritual*. The chapters are about ritual dimensions of literary works, specifically fiction, drama, and autobiography. They are not standard literary-critical essays in which one offers close readings of a text, surveys the relevant secondary literature, and then distinguishes one's own critical interpretations from those of other scholars. The only one that comes close is the chapter on Flannery O'Connor's *The Violent Bear It Away*.

I do not mean to suggest that in these pieces I give up the critical or interpretive tasks but rather that I work to integrate them with that of storytelling. Thus, as readers move from the beginning toward the end of part three, they will find that the boundary between telling, interpreting, and evaluating begins to dissolve. In the beginning of each chapter I assume the posture of a storyteller rather than that of a literary critic. I am less interested in accuracy—the reproduction of some previous version—than in telling a good story. I teach a course called "Stories and the Sacred" and am aware that there is much more to a novel, play, or autobiography than its story.

Some of my examples here—those whose emphasis is not on narrative—force me to recognize the limits of a storytelling tack, but I pursue it as far as I can in order better to comprehend the relationship between ritual and narrative. When I originally read and studied these works, I did so in the light of the new criticism; I attempted to read them in their own right and for their own sake. However, I later re-read them using reader criticism in order more fully to comprehend their ritual dynamics.

I tell the stories in a way that does not assume readers know the works, although all of them except *Dom Casmurro* are well known in religion-and-literature circles. Unlike literary critics who wish to assume that readers have read the works under consideration, and that their stories therefore do not need retelling, I assume the need to narrate because I propose to treat these texts *as if* they were myths, narratives somehow related to rites. Even though I know that novels are not myths, and even though I am certain that all myths do not lead to ritual, I employ this hermeneutic, hoping to learn something about ritual that I cannot learn in any other way. The sort of ritual that these works "teach" me about is, of course, not liturgy but fictive ritual, ritual as imagined, constructed, made up.

The first three chapters are more conventional that the final ones. Two are on novels (Flannery O'Connor's, *The Violent Bear It Away* and Saul Bellow's *Henderson the Rain King*); one is on a play (Jean Genet's, *The Blacks*). In these chapters, *after* a brief retelling of the story, I reflect *upon* ritualized elements in the work, sometimes using methods or ideas borrowed from either ritual theory or literary theory. The last three chapters are less conventional. One is on an autobiography (Jean-Paul Sartre's *The Words*); one is on a work of fiction (Machado de Assis' *Dom Casmurro*), and the other (Søren Kierkegaard's *Repetition*) is unclassifiable. In these chapters, *during* the telling of the story, I attempt to reflect *within* its the ambience.

Because of their experimental nature, the last three chapters need fuller explanation. They share a common strategy inspired by reader criticism, a method that parallels the so-called "reflexive turn" in anthropology. Both methods, one formulated for literary texts, the other for cultural performances, insist that meaning is transactional. It is an event that transpires *between* reader and text, performer and observer. It does not reside in the text, author's imagination, or reader's mind. Using this approach, I begin to soften the line between narrating and reflecting. I begin to interact with the stories as I retell them. Not only do I refuse to confine myself to literary-critical interpretation, I transform what I tell. I make the stories mine. I interject, argue with characters, anticipate turns in the narrative, and poke at the boundary between storytelling and scholarly interpretation until it bleeds. The way becomes labyrinthine as I play with, and within, the literary works whose visions of ritual I covet and whose perversions I hope to avoid. I retell stories to provide context. Just as I would not study an observed rite without attending to its social context, so I prefer not to meditate on fictive ritualizing without providing some context, because contextualization is a means of chastening the theories and assumptions a reader brings to a text.

Bruce Lincoln suggests that footnoting is a kind of scholarly ritual.[155] Not only does footnoting carry on the work of establishing a canon, it is a means of blazing a trail through a dark wood in case others wish to follow. So for scholars who wish to wend their way back from my retellings to the root texts, I have liberally scattered notes. Their very existence, however, is ironic, even ludicrous, in portions that aim at telling rather than reading. So I imagine them as bread crumbs from the trembling hand of a Hansel bent on protecting his sister.

Steven Mailloux has summarized the approaches of prominent reader-response theorists such as Wolfgang Iser and Stanley Fish.[156] Minimally, reader criticism requires a descriptive analysis of the flow of successive reading activities. This means that time, and sometimes a specifically narrative sense of it, are part of the interpretive style itself. James Resseguie notes:

> Whereas most traditional holistic interpretations of texts neglect the sequential interpretations and effects upon the reader in favor of the final holistic interpretation, reader-response critics believe that the series of interpretations and effects which lead up to the final synthesis are also important and have value . . .[157]

In the last two chapters, by following the pattern of anticipation and retrospection, the cycle of expectation and fulfilment (or disappointment), I hope to work on, and then through, the manifest content of the books to the baseline of their ritualization, which, in the case of Kierkegaard's *Repetition* is not so much *in* the text as *beneath* it.

The tacit argument of part three is simple. It is that fictive worlds are sanctuaries in which one can fruitfully reimagine ritual. Just as a ritually defined arena can serve to keep ordinary existence at bay by putting action, as it were, in quotation marks ("dying" ritually is not the same as dying in an auto accident), so fiction can bracket off ritual from the imperative to embody and enact, which rites normally entail. The relative disengagement provided by fiction can either become a disease, a way of hiding and refusing responsibility, or it can substantially renew that from which it is tactically and momentarily disengaged. Although I have sometimes argued for the virtues of theorizing on the basis of practice, an incessant obligation to practice or perform (such as a monk, priest, rabbi, or pastor must feel weekly if not daily) can dull the imagination. So it is essential to consider both the advantages and liabilities of meditating on fictively-framed ritual.

Most of us are able to recognize that a fiction, though it is something made or made up, has a certain facticity about it. It is likewise true that all facts, including religious ones, have a certain fictionality about them. Ritual partakes of both qualities. It is at once made up and real. A ritual is fictive insofar as we are aware of its constructed qualities, "factive," we might say, insofar as it is felt to be derived from tradition or revelation. People engage in ritualizing with varying degrees of awareness of its fictionality. Barbara Myerhoff has put it well:

> All rituals are paradoxical and dangerous enterprises, the traditional and improvised, the sacred and secular. Paradoxical because rituals are conspicuously artificial and theatrical, yet designed to suggest the inevitability and absolute truth of their messages. Dangerous because, when we are not convinced by a ritual we may become aware of ourselves as having made them up, thence on to the paralyzing realization that we have made up all our truths; [that] our ceremonies, our most precious conceptions and convictions—all are mere invention, not inevitable understandings about the world at all but the results of mortals' imaginings.[158]

Some of the ritual that one encounters in literature is "ritualization," which is to say, it is preconscious or tacit—not recognized as ritual by the character or author engaging in it. Searching for tacit ritualization, we can lose our bearings. We can be tempted to make ritual into a hermeneutical principle or a metaphor for the cosmos, as has been done with language. (Everything, including ritual, has been treated metaphorically "as language.") One gains little by countering that everything is ritual, unless we continue to remember the explicit, non-fictive rites that root our metaphoric predications.

Erving Goffman and Edward T. Hall have written a great deal about "invisible," "ordinary," or "interaction" ritual in daily life. As the introduction to Goffman's *Frame Analysis* illustrates, this strategy easily lapses into irony. Hypothesizing an invisible ritual, like Freud's positing hidden meanings for slips of the tongue, can imply a superior point of view. This "superiority," though, is really "inferior," because it is a perspective from below, not above. Goffman's students analyze the contents of trash cans and study the junk in back alleys; Freud's poke around in the subconscious, the garbage can of the ego.

As soon as we introduce the notion of tacit ritual not recognized by the one performing it, we enter a whirlpool. We cross over into the strange nether regions between theory and mythmaking if we claim to notice ritual in actions that others deny are so intended. Either we are perceptive indeed or we are peering at the world through a metaphor that belongs more to "us" than "them." We risk interpretive imperialism. We introduce a dangerous split between those who know and those who do not.

The tacit ritual of a work of fiction does not quite "exist," which is why I speak of it as fictive. There will be some who consider it quixotic to attempt anything more than considering ritual as a theme (among a hundred others such as love and death in the American novel). I will not argue with the accusation that in looking for tacit ritualization I go beyond scholarship into mythmaking. If I were to do so, I would counter that all scholarship, implicitly or explicitly, generates or arises from mythic premises, by which I mean master images, root metaphors, and master narratives. Reading ritually may or may not be a desirable activity, but until we perceive its presence, we are in no position either to foster or criticize it.

Ritual in Literary Criticism

The rhetoric of ritual began to make its way into modern literary criticism during the early part of this century. Robert Segal has chronicled the history of anthropological thinking about ritual's relation to myth, and Richard Hardin has shown how the idea of ritual promulgated by anthropologists permeated literary criticism.[159] Even though anthropologists such as Clyde Kluckhohn and classicists such as G.S. Kirk have generally discredited the so-called Cambridge School's speculations about the origin of ritual and questioned ritual's necessary interdependence with myth, the study of ritual's relation to literature continues, though on premises other than their supposed common origins. Earlier theorists such as Northrop Frye or Kenneth Burke and later ones such as J. Hillis Miller and literary students of Victor Turner have explored literature's formal and structural analogies to ritual.[160] Often they or their followers have posited functional equivalences between ritual and other cultural phenomena. For example, Barbara Myerhoff and Deena Metzger treat journals as the equivalent, if not the actual offspring, of rites of passage.[161] The limitation of this kind of treatment is that it misses the ritual dimensions of the works themselves and that it sometimes ignores or minimizes the actual rhetoric and content of literary works.

In my estimation far more attention needs to be paid to the ways ritual is imagined both in specific works of literature and in popular culture generally; also we need to attend to theories that enable scholars to shuttle between the study of ritual and literary criticism. Some examples of this kind of work, which is all too rare, are Victor Turner's anthropological study of Icelandic sagas, Barbara Babcock's treatment of the "carnivalization" of the novel, Edward Vargo's analysis of ritual in the novels of John Updike, and Sophia Morgan's study of reflexivity in two examples of Hispanic "meta-literature." These examples illustrate the convergence of symbolic anthropology, ritual studies, and literary criticism (especially of the rhetorical and reader-oriented variety).

How are we to make sense of ritual in literature? Are metaphors survivals of a bygone, ritually-saturated era? Are they incipient symbolic acts, latent scenarios waiting to dictate our actions? Or are they merely literary jewels enshrined in formally self-contained, imaginative worlds? Using the standard literary critical strategies summarized by Giles Gunn in his introduction to *Literature and Religion*, one could suggest several approaches to fictive ritual in literature:

(1) the expressive: the ritualization of the writing process itself, for instance, Kierkegaard's writing as a way of carrying on a courtship ceremony;

(2) the functional: ritualization of readers' responses to literature, for example, a Jew's religious obligation to study the Torah, or Quixote's enacting knightly romance;

(3) the mimetic: ritual as depicted or alluded to in fiction; ritual as subject matter;

(4) the formal: ritual-like features of fiction such as repetition and rhythm (for instance, the seasonal rhythms in some of T.S. Eliot's poems and plays); and

(5) the archetypal: a reader's perception of a character, action, or work as a repetition or variant of other characters, actions, or works.

The first two, since they involve overt actions, reading and writing, would lead us in the direction of performance theory. Mimetic criticism would produce various "images of" (which may differ considerably from "images in") ritual. And a formalist strategy could take us a long way toward uncovering tacit ritual processes buried in the mythos, or plot structure, of works of fiction. I will be assuming all of these perspectives, though without naming them as such.

Readers may wish to know how I locate my approach in relation to other literary critics who have paid attention to ritual. So I shall articulate it briefly in dialogue with two theorist-critics, Northrop Frye and J. Hillis Miller, an earlier archetypalist and a more recent deconstructionist.

To invoke and extend one of Northrop Frye's metaphors from *Anatomy of Criticism*, a work of fiction can be read either "centripetally" or "centrifugally," that is, inward toward its own center or outward toward its circumference. Centripetally read, a work is treated as a self-contained world. Centrifugally read, it reaches out toward other works of literature and beyond—into non-literary aspects of readers' lives. At its circumference, it rubs tangentially against other works by the same author or those of others, until ultimately it encompasses the whole of one's reading experience. Expanded by such a reading, a work does not merely *reflect* the world of everyday life but *contains* it.

Some works bear this centrifugally amplified reading better than others. Those that do we sometimes come to regard as sacred. If not that, then mythic. And if not that, then mythlike. Critics who read mythically do not necessarily wait for works written by authors who intend to write myths. Nor does an author's having a mythic intention, which contemporary readers would be tempted to interpret as a pretension, necessarily result in its functioning as a culture's account of itself.

A question of continuing importance is how far we readers ought go with the act of reading centrifugally. The penultimate limit, at which thematic connections are made between works of literature, Frye calls "archetypal." The outermost circle in which the world is "contained" rather than "container," is the kind of reading Frye calls "anagogical." But what should we call it if a reader leaps beyond reading into action in such a way that action is thereby "textualized?" In effect, this sort of reading—in which fiction is read outward toward action and for which Frye has no name or category—breaks the circumference of the literary circle.

Kenneth Burke goes further than Frye in his willingness to consider a literary text as a social scenario—as incipient, or symbolic, action.[162] In addition to the literary criticism of literature, he develops a dramatic and rhetorical criticism of it. Obviously, one way we move from a text to action is by performing it in a theater. In a theater, though, the action itself is in the "subjunctive"; it is "bracketed." Another way to move from a text to action is by enacting it as ritual. In ritual, action is not so much subjunctive as paradigmatic. It attempts to prescribe rather to query "what if?"

Rhetorical strategies read literature as a paradigm for action. Read rhetorically, a work of fiction provides us with images, maxims, sometimes even rules, which we imitate morally rather than theatrically. Insofar as we readers expect

literature to be edifying—to enable us to think more profoundly, feel more deeply, or behave more ethically, we are engaging in one kind of rhetorical criticism.

Rhetorical criticism borders on ritual criticism. Both Frye
and Burke anticipate a ritual criticism, but neither, in my estimation, develops one. They use the rhetoric of ritual, but their
rhetoric lacks consolidation as well as substantial connection
with ritual theory. One of Frye's most explicit statements
about ritual is this:

> From such a point of view, the narrative aspect of literature is a
> recurrent act of symbolic communication; in other words a ritu-
> al. Narrative is studied by the archetypal critic as ritual or imi-
> tation of human action as a whole, and not simply as a *mimesis
> praxeos* or imitation of an action. Similarly, in archetypal criti-
> cism the significant content is the conflict of desire and reality
> which has for its basis the work of the dream. Ritual and
> dream, therefore, are the narrative and significant content re-
> spectively of literature in its archetypal aspect. The archetypal
> analysis of the plot of a novel or play would deal with it in
> terms of the generic, recurring, or conventional actions which
> show analogies to ritual: the weddings, funerals, intellectual
> and social initiations, executions or mock executions, the chas-
> ing away of the scapegoat villain, and so on.[163]

Fortunately, Frye does not define ritual only as a response
to cyclical rhythms and recurrent situations such as birth,
death, equinoxes, and solstices. He is aware that this view,
given free reign, would reduce ritual to unconscious or auto-
matic repetition. Ritual has its dialectical dynamic as well:
"Ritual is not only a recurrent act, but an act expressive of a
dialectic of desire and repugnance: desire for fertility or victory, repugnance to drought or to enemies."[164]

Although Frye anticipates the crossing over of narrative
into action, he pulls up short, choosing to remain within the
circle of literary theory and criticism. He is not interested, he
says, in the ritual origins of literature, only in ritual insofar as
it is the content of literature.[165]

I come to the interface between stories and enactments from
another direction, ritual studies. My approach to narrative is
not part of a systematic anatomy of literary criticism, as Frye's
is, but the outcome of a view of ritual studies that insists on

the formative and essential nature of imagining ritual and on the importance of imagining ritually. Frye's stance locates him between literature and its literary interpretation; mine places me between narrative and ritual action. However, a ritual reading of literature is not exempt from having to make sound interpretations. Even as simple an operation as deciding that a character is treating her house as a "sanctuary" or going on a "quest," is a literary, not a religious, judgment.

Frye's view implies that narrative is the aspect of literature to which interpreters must turn if they want to grasp literature's ritual qualities. Even though I agree in some respects, I do not equate archetypal and ritual criticism. Archetypal criticism takes place within the world of literature. Ritual criticism, besides inquiring about the actions of characters, also examines what happens at the junctures between reader and text as well as writer and text. Ritual criticism and archetypal criticism overlap insofar as they attend to the sequence of actions in a narrative, but ritual criticism goes on to treat the attendant actions of reading and writing.

Frye's understanding of ritual, because it is based on literary criticism, of necessity casts ritual in a derivative role. Archetypally read, literature is myth, and it "contains" ritual. The sort of ritual that concerned Frye, in his theories at least, is imagined in the words of poets and novelists or acted out by dramatists. Frye does not claim that rituals-in-narrative are religious, nor does he claim his act of interpreting them is theological. However, when he declares that the corpus of modern literature is a "secular scripture," he has implicitly passed beyond purely literary criticism into cultural, if not religious, criticism.[166] My way of teasing out the implications of his hints and asides is to argue that if literature is a scripture or myth, then reading it is a ritual of sorts. The question is, What sort?

J. Hillis Miller is another literary critic and theorist who is helpful in trying to discern connections between ritual and literature. Though Frye's approach is archetypalist and Miller's deconstructionist, both reveal a considerable debt to new criticism and agree that texts ought not be reduced to something else. Their essential difference, as Miller sees it, lies in Frye's assumption that the complete reading of a work can be done in the context of "a total simultaneous integrating recall of all the details of the text in question."[167] The notion of recall is crucial. Frye's archetypalism depends on recollection. An archetype is a recurring image in literature, so one must remember its earlier instances in order to see its later ones as variants of the archetype. A reader only constructs a genre or recognizes "the whole body of literature" by building up such ideas from repeated acts of reading that are subsequently recollected.

Miller's disagreement arises because he notices the ways repetition in literature can lead readers to forget. If popular archetypalism is a way of reading that can lead to a "cult of similarity," popular deconstructionism leads to a "cult of difference." Frye and Miller respectively avoid these extremes despite their strongly contrasting positions.

Even though Miller brings to his texts an extra-literary distinction between two kinds of repetition—the "Platonic" grounded and the "Nietzschean" ungrounded—he, like Frye, chooses not to transgress the bounds of the literary universe, even though he says a competent reader does:

> I have just said a novel deals with relations among people, while a few paragraphs ago I was emphasizing the way it is made of words. These are two surfaces of the same continuum, and the competent reader of a novel moves easily back and forth between attention to complexities of verbal texture and thinking of the characters as if they were real people among whom there are relations of one sort or another.[168]

Despite their differences Miller and Frye both posit a vital connection between fiction and action. I assume they would agree that the act of reading is what constitutes that connection. But readers read differently. As Miller notes:

> If I say, "The novel is a representation of human reality in words," that definition contains the possibility of three different kinds of discourse about fiction, each of which has its validity or necessity, none of which can be kept wholly separate from the others. If I emphasize "human reality" in the definition, then I shall be likely to ignore the fact that I know the fiction is only a fiction, willingly suspend my disbelief, speak of the characters as if they were "real people," and work out the "meaning" of their story in terms of ethical values, judgments of good and bad, happy and unhappy, and so on. If I emphasize "representation" in the definition, I shall focus on the con-

ventions of storytelling in a given case as vehicles of meaning. From this focus there may be developed a full-fledged "phenomenological" criticism of fiction. This will concern itself with the assumptions the novelist makes about the kind of consciousness of himself and of others the narrator has or the characters have, or with the temporal structures of consciousness the novel expresses, or with the elaborated emotional responses the story as a sequence of represented events arouses in the reader. Finally, if I remember that a novel is a representation of human reality "in words," I may focus on local features of style, the "rhetoric of fiction," taking "rhetoric" not as modes of persuasion but in its other meaning as the discipline of the workings of tropes in the most inclusive sense of the word: all the turnings of language away from straightforward referential meaning.[169]

Both the continuities and differences between Miller and Frye emerge in this passage. They agree on the priority of attending to literature primarily as made of words, even though they know it is also about, or even creates, human reality. They disagree insofar as Frye reads toward greater and greater unity of literary experience whereas Miller emphasizes its heterogeneity. For Miller "Platonic" repetition takes all concrete instances of literature to be grounded in an overriding unity or archetypal model.[170] Each realization "participates" in this archetype. In the discontinuous version of repetition, the Nietzschean mode, a second instance only *seems* to repeat a first one. The second appears to be a sort of ghostly double of the first even though there are basic differences. In the grounded model knowledge is experienced as commemorative; in the ungrounded, as fictive.

Miller contends that each kind of repetition in literature calls up the other, so he avoids setting up a dualism between construction and deconstruction in criticism. Deconstruction is an attempt to bypass either/or strategies, as well as both/and ones, by showing how "a narrative creates both the intuition of unitary origin and the clues, in the unresolvable heterogeneity of the narration, to the fact that the origin may be an effect of language, not some preexisting site or some 'place' in or out of the world."[171]

Far from taking the presence of symbols to imply an underlying, organic unity, Miller illustrates how they can be emblems for a lack of ground. A novel, he shows, can display oneness and twoness, continuity and difference, on a single surface. Miller's argument implies that a reader ought not assume, as E.K. Brown does, that "Undoubtedly repetitions make for unity . . . ."[172] Repetition, Miller shows, can subvert order and organic form.

This conclusion is of immense importance to ritual studies, since the same assumption is usually made about repetition in ritual, namely, that it reinforces social order, leads to moral and psychological stability, and indicates the presence of unitary, cohesive structures. I hope to show the contrary, namely, that ritual imagined fully and critically can subvert the status quo, dissolving structures into processes, and that it can either renew or entrap.

Though I have defined my literary critical position in relation to two well-known theorists, it still may not be clear exactly what one looks for in reading works ritually. These are some of factors I consider insofar as they indicate ritual's "presence" in fiction:

(1) The *repetition* factor: the regularized recurrence of incidents in a plot structure; or the perception of recurrence either by a narrator or character. Sometimes this kind of ritualization takes the form of one event's being interpreted as a "version," "type," or "figure" of some preceding one.

(2) The *inevitability* factor: like heavily controlled civil ceremonies, a sequence of actions can seem structured or scored by sources beyond the reach of decision and will; the plot behaves as if it had a will of its own independent of the characters or even the narrator.

(3) The *stylization* factor: like liturgical rites, actions can be elevated to the status of gestures; they seem to *mean* more than they *do*; they elevate the ordinary toward transcendent limits.

(4) The *ludic* factor (the opposite of #2 above): like the liminal phase of a rite of passage, some plot structures cut causal linkage, thus allowing things to invert. Then inversion itself is handled in a tone reminiscent of rites of celebration.

(5) The *template* factor: like commemorative rites, events in a story can become "generative" of other events, functioning as a template or criterion; such events are singular, hinge occur-

rences that stamp their mark on subsequent or extra-literary ones. Since we will be especially alert to the ritualization of reading in the chapters that follow, we might notice variations of this paradigmatic function. A story becomes "templated," and thus ritualized, when readers begin

(a) imagining the author to be an oracle or diviner whom they consult;

(b) meditating on a book's revelation, awaiting its healing, or expecting to be inspired;

(c) envisioning one story as uniting with other stories until a kind of monomyth, scripture, or encyclopedic cluster forms among the totality of readings, and then considering this the single most comprehensive story (the story of stories);

(d) searching for archetypes, that is, modulated, recurring images;

(e) identifying generative metaphors and imagining the whole as having been born of these elemental metaphoric predications;

(f) identifying with the characters and aspiring to act like them;

(g) amplifying the story by dreaming about it or imagining it in other ways;

(h) re-reading it; treating it as classical, canonical, or required reading; using it as an ethical norm or literary paradigm;

(i) defending it; endeavoring to control what kinds of critical attention are paid to it;

(j) associating with others who regard it as the reader does;

(k) treating the book itself with extra care, for example, by keeping it in a special place or having it bound in expensive materials;

(l) avoiding actions that do not accord with values or episodes of the story;

(m) allowing the story to judge, convict, or weigh readers in the balance; treating a narrative as a trial or test;

(n) re-enacting the story or taking it as a charter for action.

Literary critics, particularly those steeped in new criticism, will be appalled at such anticipated entanglement with texts. They will worry, fearing that reading ritually falls short of detailed attention to a text's verbal structure and yet goes considerably beyond it by employing stories as reasons for acting. I agree with Wayne Booth, who argues that stories are no better or worse than other reasons for acting. The trick, he says, is matching literary "arguments" to appropriate conclusions, a skill that Don Quixote never developed. But this difficulty is itself no good reason for holding works of fiction completely at bay from lived life. Booth puts it well:

> Plato warned against dramatizing heroes who embody false values; he knew that when we have fallen in love with a character, we tend (by a kind of ethical proof) to believe what he believes, to fear what he fears, and desire what he desires. There has been a lot of critical talk in modern times arguing that to allow this effect is naive, but I doubt that anyone who reads seriously ever escapes it for long, whether in reading "true" works like histories or fictional works. And I know that my students and I discover again and again that we have succumbed to it, and gladly. Like Don Quixote imitating chivalric tasks and Emma Bovary imitating romantic heroines and my freshmen imitating Holden Caulfield and Siddhartha and Yossarian, I find myself trying on for size the attitudes urged upon me by Tolstoy and George Eliot and Faulkner and Bellow, and though my malleability decreases as I grow older, it is only when I haven't been *into* a book that I come out without being changed.[173]

8

Anagogy and Ritualization:[174] Baptism in Flannery O'Connor's *The Violent Bear It Away*

OLD TARWATER HAD SAVED FRANCIS TARWATER FROM RAYBER, the boy's uncle. The uncle had once come out to the farm at Powderhead, Tennessee, with a social worker to retrieve Francis after Old Tarwater had kidnapped and baptized the boy. The old prophet had taken a shotgun to this school-teaching uncle. Uncle Rayber had fled back to town and married the social worker, who bore him an idiot child named Bishop, whom Old Tarwater insisted must be baptized, if not by himself, then by the young Tarwater.

Long ago, the old man claimed, he had baptized the school teacher when he was seven, but his redemption had lasted only a while. And what infuriated Old Tarwater most was that his nephew had grown up and analyzed him in a teacher's magazine. The teacher had written, "His fixation on being called by the Lord had its origin in insecurity. He needed the assurance of a call, and so he called himself."[175] Enraged, the old man had repeatedly warned Francis that if the boy were ever around Rayber, he would be in danger of becoming just a piece of information in his head or a note on some chart.

Rayber had informed his prophet uncle that there was no savior but himself and no salvation except human effort. So the prophet had stolen Francis from Rayber's custody, leaving a note behind that read, "THE PROPHET I RAISE UP OUT OF THIS BOY WILL BURN YOUR EYES CLEAN." When Old Tarwater rehearsed this tale for young Tarwater, he would add, "It was me could act . . ., not him. He could never take action. He could only get everything inside his head and grind it to nothing. But I acted. And because I acted, you sit here in freedom . . . in the freedom of the Lord Jesus Christ."[176]

Young Tarwater admired his elder's craftiness but resented having his freedom connected to the Bread of Life. He was not hungry for it and was suspicious that his great uncle's madness came from it and might be passed on to him. The boy was angry but, he imagined, free. Despite the boy's view of himself, the prophet's words were beginning to course in his bloodstream and had begun to move "secretly toward some goal of their own," the narrator tells us.[177] Rayber's father had rescued him, but no one had re-claimed Francis.

When Old Tarwater dies, the boy hitchhikes into town, finds his Uncle Rayber's house, and arrives unsure whether he is entering a trap, not knowing whether he is most in danger from his uncle's rationalism or his great uncle's prophetic compulsion to baptize. Rayber begins trying to make a useful young man out of Tarwater, while Tarwater, as soon as he sees Bishop, Rayber's idiot child, wants nothing to do with him. Yet he is tempted to enact the one rite a prophet must perform:

> Tarwater clenched his fists. He stood like one condemned, waiting at the spot of execution. Then the revelation came, silent, implacable, direct as a bullet. He did not look into the eyes of any fiery beast or see a burning bush. He only knew, with a certainty sunk in despair, that he was expected to baptize the child he saw and begin the life his great-uncle had prepared him for. He knew that he was called to be a prophet and that the ways of his prophecy would not be remarkable. His black pupils, glassy and still, reflected depth on depth his own stricken image of himself, trudging into the distance in the bleeding

stinking mad shadow of Jesus, until at last he received his reward, a broken fish, a multiplied loaf. The Lord out of dust had created him blood and nerve and mind, had made him to bleed and weep and think, and set him in a world of loss and fire to baptize one idiot child that He need not have created in the first place and to cry out a gospel just as foolish. He tried to shout, "NO!" but it was like trying to shout in his sleep. The sound was saturated in silence, lost.[178]

Wrapped in a mantle of isolation, Tarwater grows sullen, and his uncle, ridden with guilt for not having rescued the boy earlier, falls all over himself playing father and savior. His nephew cuts him short, "I ain't ast for no father. I am out of the womb of a whore. I was born in a wreck."[179] "I am free," he hisses. To Rayber the crazy prophet is even more present in this young Tarwater than when the old man himself had lived with the school teacher, so he soon tires of trying to educate his nephew.

Rayber does not believe he himself is made in God's image, though he is sure Bishop is. Bishop never speaks. In his father's view he is a question mark, an X symbolizing the hideousness of fate.[180] Occasionally, the father feels a surge of something like love; it throws him on the ground in "an act of idiot praise." Otherwise, he is a paragon of liberal rationality, who, knowing that madness and fanaticism are in his blood, has laced himself tightly with discipline and non-participatory observation.

Rayber thinks he must teach Tarwater to look Bishop in the eye and confess that the urge to baptize is pathological, so he devises a plan to take the boys on a fishing trip—an excuse to get Tarwater back to Powderhead for a confrontation. They go to a lodge not far from Old Tarwater's place. Young Tarwater's desire to baptize begins to turn into a hunger. He eats voraciously before they go boating. His uncle plays therapist, hoping to save the boy from the old man's ghost. Tarwater says he don't talk no words, he does 'em, and he accuses Rayber of being unable to act. The schoolteacher counters by saying that he had at least resisted Old Tarwater. My guts, Rayber boasts, are in my head. He lectures the boy about the unconscious, but Tarwater ain't worried about what his "underhead" is doing, even if his uncle thinks he can read him like a book. Eventually, Rayber confesses that he once tried to drown his idiot child. Tarwater vomits, re-establishing his voracious emptiness, and jumps overboard, swimming ashore; this is one child who's not going to be "cursed with believing."[181]

Later, Tarwater proves he can act, and Rayber, that he can only observe. The uncle sees the nephew row Bishop out in the boat. He watches Tarwater hold Bishop under the water until there are no more signs of struggle. Rayber collapses and realizes he feels no pain. His own stability had depended on Bishop; now "the whole world would become his idiot child."[182]

This baptism by water is just the first. This is a Flannery O'Connor story, so, of course, it must be followed by another violent one. Matthew 11:12 says, "From the days of John the Baptist until now, the Kingdom of Heaven suffereth violence, and the violent bear it away." From this passage O'Connor takes the title of her book, *The Violent Bear It Away*.

Tarwater hitchhikes back to Powderhead and is sexually abused on the way. A truck driver who gives him a ride is sleepy and incapable of comprehending the boy's confession, "I baptized him. It was an accident. I didn't mean to. The words just come out of themselves but it don't mean nothing. You can't be born again. I only meant to drown him."[183]

What the boy finds back home is the grave of his great uncle, who has been buried by a black man with the sign of the Savior at his head. "The boy . . . leaned forward, aware that [his hunger] was the same as the old man's and that nothing on earth would fill him. His hunger was so great that he could have eaten all the loaves and fishes after they were multiplied."[184] Now his hunger rises to become a tide that sweeps him up and sets his burning feet in the direction that beckons every prophet: the city. He leaves, the woods burning behind him.

Anagogy

A reader is likely to have two kinds of impulses toward Francis Tarwater after reading *The Violent Bear It Away*. A psychological one is to try explaining his motivations; a moral one is to imagine oneself protecting the boy. But the author prevents us from choosing either response. If we do either—put Tarwater on the couch or play parent toward him—we can only do so in the role of Rayber the antagonist. O'Connor forces her reader to search for an alternative posture regarding the boy, particularly his act of murder-baptism.

The central gesture of *The Violent Bear It Away* is baptism and its related imagery of water and fire.[185] Eucharistic imagery, especially that of bread, is present but not dominant to the same degree. If readers merely reject the baptism-drowning, they are in trouble, because O'Connor anticipates this response and forces those who choose it to identify with Rayber. On the other hand, if readers merely accept the gesture, they are complicit with a homicide, no matter how much it may resemble a ritual sacrifice. If we say yes to the baptism we imply our approval of murder—and rape as well, if we view the final conflagration as a baptism by fire. If we say no, we join Rayber in trying to corral irrational forces in our heads; we engage in reductionism regarding what is most essential to the faith and practice of the Tarwaters.

Readers are forced to search for a third alternative that transcends both yes and no, both moral judgmentalism and psychological naiveté. Two complementary points of view—anagogical and ritological—can help us explore an alternative view of baptism, the story's central gesture.

Commenting on her own work, O'Connor reflects:

> I often ask myself what makes a story work, and what makes it hold up as a story, and I have decided that it is probably some action, some gesture of a character that is unlike any other in the story, one which indicates where the real heart of the stories lie. This would have to be an action or a gesture which was both totally right and totally unexpected; it would have to be one that was both in character and beyond character; it would have to suggest both the world and eternity. The action or gesture I'm talking about would have to be on the anagogical level, that is, the level which has to do with the Divine life and our participation in it. It would be a gesture that transcended any neat allegory that might have been intended or by pat moral categories a reader could make. It would be a gesture which somehow made contact with mystery.[186]

Francis's baptism of Bishop almost fits O'Connor's own definition of anagogy. The drowning is the hinge of the narrative, pointing to the paradox that lies at the heart of the story, namely, that baptism is both a symbolic act of violence and a gesture of grace insofar as it exposes the harsh truth of things. Tarwater's baptism of Bishop is so completely in character that it seems inevitable and ritual-like. We can see it coming pages before it happens. Though the drowning is a dramatic shock, it makes—unfortunately—perfect sense. Certainly, it transcends any moral categories, pat or otherwise, that might inform a reader's judgment.

However, if we follow O'Connor's description of anagogy, one tough question remains: whether the mystery that engulfs the reader is divine or demonic, whether it evokes eternity or merely the depths of uncontained, irrational forces leading to degradation and derangement. O'Connor explicitly connects anagogy and the grotesqueries of the Protestant, Bible Belt South.[187] As a Catholic novelist she believes she has to follow the spirit into strange places, and anagogical symbols with their grace-bearing, all-encompassing tendencies best convey and evoke spirit that accepts the unacceptable, including what most of us regard as demonic or violent.

Horton Davies has examined the idea of anagogy as O'Connor explains it in *Manners and Mystery*,[188] but he avoids the hard question and does not adequately explain or illustrate her use of anagogy. When he tries to show how the idea is worked out in her fiction, he simply hunts for examples of five literary devices (which he calls anagogical signals): the incompleteness of her characters as suggested by physiological characteristics (for example, Hulga's wooden leg in "Good Country People,")[189] the use of animal metaphors (for example, "a bull-like old man") to suggest atavism, so-called liturgical colors (for instance, Mrs. Chestney's purple hat in "Everything that Rises . . ."), the symbol of the sun in several stories, and the formulaic use of the phrase "as if." His treatment of *The Violent Bear It Away* consists of (1) a claim that we cannot understand Tarwater's hunger without recognizing that Christ is the bread of life and (2) a recognition that the sun that emerges at the baptismal fountain probably has christological significance.

However true it may be that Francis's hunger is connected with Christ as bread of life and that the sun symbolizes Christ, these have little bearing on anagogy. An anagogical symbol is not just any symbol, even a recurrent one (which we best regard as archetypal); it is a symbol that "contains." It encompasses other symbols. As important as they are, neither the sun nor bread plays such a role in *The Violent Bear It Away*. The gesture of baptizing both contains and determines the other symbols, hence its anagogical status.[190]

The story precipitates a thorny question: By what criteria do we recognize an anagogical gesture and differentiate it from a symptom? Many readers, I suspect, are tempted to follow Rayber uncritically in regarding the urge to baptize as a compulsion. Some may not like Rayber and find his faith in education and rationality misplaced and contradicted by his own actions. But disgust with him does not lead us to trust the Tarwaters more. A liberal reader is more prone to identify with Rayber's sentiments than those of the two Tarwater prophets.

But the author presses us in the opposite direction. She wants us to take the action of baptizing seriously, not demean it as mere compulsion. She places it at the center of the novel and exaggerates it, hoping to jolt the reader into a recognition of the gesture's significance. O'Connor declares that her own sentiments lie with the two Tarwaters and that she had to spend seven years trying to keep Rayber from just being a stereotype.[191]

Anagogical symbolization is one device O'Connor uses to jolt us off the track of moralizing, psychologizing, and playing social worker. Tarwater is a character not a literal boy, and we are readers not social workers or converts in this character's world. Literalizing this story by treating it as if it were a mirror image of the world—the religious world of the South— would be a great mistake. Rather it is a purposeful transformation of what a reader might consider a "normal" baptism. O'Connor says,

> When I write a novel in which the central action is a baptism, I am very well aware that for a majority of my readers, baptism is a meaningless rite, and so in my novel I have to see that this baptism carries enough awe and mystery to jar the reader into some kind of emotional recognition of its significance. To this end I have to bend the whole novel—its language, its structure,

its action. I have to make the reader feel, in his bones if nowhere else, that something is going on here that counts. Distortion in this case is an instrument; exaggeration has a purpose,
and the whole structure of the story or novel has been made
what it is because of belief. This is not the kind of distortion
that destroys; it is the kind that reveals, or should reveal.[192]

Obviously, O'Connor does not put her exaggeration in the
service of pious Christian apologetics. She has not painted a
pretty picture of baptism, hoping to tempt readers into conver-
sion. But neither is it an enlightenment attack on Southern pie-
tism. The story is written in a manner that anticipates a reader's attempt to indulge in psychological reductionism; it puts
"liberal" reactions in the mouth of the antagonist, Rayber.
O'Connor has little interest in psychological realism. In this respect she differs radically from those modern writers for
whom exterior action is only a means to gain access to interi-
ority, the location of the really real. For O'Connor motivation
is not directly accessible. It is mysterious, reversing itself as if
another person were inside a character. So she calls attention
to the efficacy of symbolic action, the meaning of which is not
reducible to psychology. The difference between her treatment
of symbolic action and that of many other modern writers is
considerable. She does not believe that pathology is the only
thing revealed by Tarwater's baptism. If the reader reads as
she wishes, revelation in the religious sense of the term occurs,
that is, one experiences simultaneous judgment and grace
while doing it. This is what it means to say that anagogy has
to do with the divine life and our participation in it.

If we can get beyond regarding the baptismal gesture as
only a pathological symptom, we are free to ask what an action on the anagogical level is. Anagogy has re-entered the vocabulary of modern literary criticism, most notably in the
work of Northrop Frye. Flannery O'Connor's use of it is probably not gleaned directly from Frye but from Catholic medieval sources. The scholastics, as early as John Cassian's *Colla-
tiones* (ca. 370-435 A.D.), distinguished four levels of meaning
in a text: the literal, allegorical, moral, and anagogical. Nicho-
las of Lyre summarized these four levels in a popular lyric:
"The literal teaches history, your belief is allegory; Moral is
what you do, where you go is anagogy." Anagogy was consid-

ered the most sublime hermeneutical category; it was the "heavenly" level.

Today we would be more likely to speak of it as "mythical" or "cosmological." When O'Connor speaks of a gesture as "anagogical," she means that its mystery is irreducible and that it requires an exaggerated, hyperbolic form of expression.[193] It is unlike any other and cannot be explained away by sociological or psychological reductions, or even literary ones for that matter.

An anagogical action is one that does not need to be authorized precisely because it carries authority in its very doing. In *The Violent Bear It Away* baptism has its own authority not borrowed either from the words characters say about it or the authorities that might have commissioned its performance. Insofar as the rite comes into is own, it achieves a renewed necessity. Insofar as it is compelled by Old Tarwater or resisted by Rayber, it turns violently in a circle.

Frye's discussion in *Anatomy of Criticism*[194] of anagogy is fuller than O'Connor's. If we follow his reformulation, an anagogical action operates like a monad, a window on the universe. Symbols in their anagogical phase are "apocalyptic"; they have reached their imaginative limits. The whole of things becomes condensed into a single action. The world no longer contains a gesture, rather a gesture contains the world.

Discussions of anagogy often lead to ritual, and Frye's is no exception. Ritual, he observes, has a tendency to become encyclopedic. Fiction that becomes involved with anagogical actions begins to imitate human action as if it were total ritual. In literature of this sort, total social action coincides with total individual thought, that is, ritual is conjoined with dream. Ritual action informed by symbols of anagogical status and power become praxis, creative or originating action. The form of literature most influenced by anagogy is the scripture or apocalyptic revelation, and any literature functioning paradigmatically will be interpreted as a microcosm of all literature. Frye notes:

> The anagogic view of criticism thus leads to the conceptions of literature as existing in its own universe, no longer a commentary on life or reality, but containing life and reality in a system of verbal relationships. From this point of view the critic can no longer think of literature as a tiny palace of art looking out

upon an inconceivably gigantic "life." "Life" for him has become the seed-plot of literature, a vast mass of potential literary
forms, only a few of which will grow up into the greater world
of the literary universe.[195]

Tarwater's gesture, perverse though it may be, is a gesture
that contains the world—his world with all its contradictions. No matter what the gesture, any condensation of the
polyphony of actions into one super-action leads to religion.
An anagogical gesture is not just one action among others,
not even the best. Rather, it is the one action capable of being inclusive of all others.

Since an anagogical action is potentially identical with every other action, it is implicitly metaphoric. In *The Violent Bear
It Away* all of Tarwater's actions are metaphorically "baptismal." The logic is that of Paul's when he says, "I die daily."
For him being crucified is identical with every act of daily life.
To view the whole of one's life as a sacrifice or sacrament is to
employ one action as if it contained all others.

An anagogical symbol, if it is successful in containing the
broken pieces of a world, generates a cosmos, a system in
which symbiotic interdependence is characteristic of the
whole. Such a symbol does the work suggested by the etymol-
ogy of the term symbol: to piece together (as when shards of a
broken pot are re-assembled.) *Anagoge* was originally a Greek
word meaning "to elevate" or "to reveal a mystery." If we allow O'Connor's actual practice to qualify and inform our interpretation of her more theoretical statement cited earlier, we
have to say that for her anagogy elevates by conjoining opposites. Anagogy does not merely transfer what is below to a position above. Instead, it makes a whole of what is above and
what is below. But in so doing, the tensions between opposites
are retained, not dissolved.[196]

Gerhart and Russell define metaphor as a way of introduc-
ing curvature, or distortion, into a world of meanings in such
a way that an "ontological flash" is possible between two distinct fields.[197] In the case of schizophrenics the metaphors, because they cannot be recognized as such, fail to link up dispar-
ate domains of their existence in any such revelatory moment.
Instead, the rules of their world become tangled. The rules

that govern the ways we bind together our sub-worlds into a more or less unified cosmos are seldom conscious to us; they are not "thoughts." Consequently, they are almost impossible to change directly or wilfully.

Tarwater's baptism-drowning is a gestural metaphor which, on the one hand, one must interpret as obsessive-compulsive and, on the other, as anagogical. Those who see the action of drowning Bishop as obsessive probably make their judgment on moral grounds, but even morally, can we be so sure that Tarwater did the wrong thing? Was it murder? Could it have been euthanasia? No court is convened in the story. If there had been a court, it probably would not have cared. So in whose judgment is Tarwater a murderer—God's, Rayber's, ours?[198] I cannot resolve the question. I do not think O'Connor resolves it. The point is simply to note that the gesture is, as she argues, "both totally right and totally unexpected"; "right" here means appropriate to the character and story; it has nothing to do with moral judgment. What a work of fiction can present that is not easily perceived in the social world is an action that is so fully contextualized that it makes perfect sense in a character's world.

Ritualization

It is not enough to consider baptism in *The Violent Bear It Away* as an anagogical symbol. That the symbol is anagogical tells us something important about its scope and status but nothing about its medium, namely action. Gothic cathedrals were anagogical; they sculpturally and iconically contained other symbols and thus comprised a cosmos. But an architectural symbol functions differently from a gestural one. Whereas one can enter and exit a cathedral, one *embodies* a ritual symbol. So the nature of ritual symbolization requires more care than it is usually given.

Few critics and interpreters have bothered to notice, much less understand, the role of ritual in the religion of poor whites living in the deep South of the United States. O'Connor, a Catholic living in Bible-belt Georgia, was in a unique position to contemplate non-mainline, "prophetic" Christianity.

In religious studies treating prophetic and priestly actions as opposites is a commonplace, particularly among Protestant theologians. The result of this split is to sever ritual (associated with the former) from social criticism (associated with the latter). But O'Connor exposes the inadequacy of the typology by telling the story of a boy whose ritualized baptizing is also a way of expressing prophetic judgment.

Though there are exceptions, scholars have not widely studied or appreciated the functions of ritual in Southern religion, in literature generally, or in O'Connor's writings specifically.[199] Driskell and Brittain[200] and Warnke[201] use the rhetoric of ritual in discussing O'Connor's work, referring to its employment of "ritualistic resolution through violence" and "ritual cleansing," but neither defines or explores the concept. In "Ritual and Violence in Flannery O'Connor" J. Oates Smith [Joyce Carol Oates?] uses the notion of ritual to organize and focus her approach to O'Connor. She examines what she calls variously the "ceremonial, formal structure", the "ritualistic formality", or the "ceremonial, almost ritualistic devices" of the novel.[202] The ritual of the novel amounts to the fact that the fates of characters are predictable; they can "only act out their roles."[203] In her view such a structure requires "a classic predestination", a hotly contested issue.[204]

Whereas "Smith" is interested in the rituals of the author, I am focusing on the ritualization of Francis, one of the characters. Thus, what she means by ritual is not what I mean. A more fully elaborated understanding of ritual is required. For instance, Jonathan Z. Smith's definition of ritual is helpful, since he calls attention to ritual's manner of containing actions that would otherwise be dangerous:

> I would suggest that, among other things, ritual represents the creation of a controlled environment where the variables, (that is, the accidents) of ordinary life have been displaced precisely because they are felt to be so overwhelmingly present and powerful. Ritual is a means of performing the way things ought to be in such a way that this ritualized perfection is recollected in the ordinary, uncontrolled, course of things.
>
> It provides the means for demonstrating that we know what ought to have been done. But, by the fact that it is ritual action rather than everyday action, it demonstrates that we know "what is the case." It provides an occasion for reflection and ra-

tionalization on the fact that what ought to have been done was not done. From such a perspective, ritual is not best understood as congruent with something else: a magical imitation of desired ends; a translation of emotions; a symbolic acting out of ideas; a dramatization of a text. Ritual gains its force where incongruency is perceived.[205]

By Smith's definition Tarwater's baptism of Bishop is not a quite a ritual; it is neither perfected nor controlled. Rather it is rampant and uncontrolled from the characters' point of view, controlled to the point of being predestined from that of some readers. The baptismal-homicidal act is not quite ritual, but neither is it free of ritual. It may be a poor baptism or an unauthorized one, but it is still a baptism of sorts. But what sort? Even a failed rite is still a rite; so is a compulsively performed one; so is a violent one.

Of baptism Volney Gay, a Freudian psychologist of religion and ritual studies scholar, writes:

> Baptism clearly involves both the aggressive action of drowning the child who is loved and hated and the loving action of rescuing it from the physical danger represented by the water, from the symbolic danger of being without a name or place within the human universe as mapped out by the church, and from the interpersonal danger of remaining bound to the narcissistic spheres of its parents.[206]

Gay's interpretation assumes the church's way of baptizing, not Tarwater's. But it helps us recognize the symbolic violence implicit in the conventional rite, and thus makes Tarwater's variant somewhat less idiosyncratic and aberrant. For the perceptive eye the shadow of a ritual is cast as much by the rite itself as by the aberrant person who performs it. Flannery O'Connor's letters show how keenly aware she was of Freudian psychology and how eager she was to avoid its explanatory myths. Gay's study goes a long way toward correcting the view that Freud considered ritual pathological. Freud, he insists, did not consider ritual actions to be dysfunctional. On the contrary, argues Gay, ritualization is problem-solving behavior. Because rituals offer stereotyped solutions, they conserve energy in the psyche's economy. The danger of this "upward" path is that individual explorations and solutions are not likely. The ritual way, Gay argues, "cannot promote radical critiques of either the prior or contemporary states of adaptedness."[207]

Tarwater's baptism of Bishop is, I think, a radical critique of both his seniors' uneasy accommodations to their environments. His enactment rescues both Bishop and himself from the narcissism of the two uncles, but the rescue lays the groundwork for further entrapment. This seems to me the dilemma of every ritual, traditional or aberrant. Perhaps Gay is right in maintaining that ritual cannot promote radical critiques. Nevertheless, ritual is, in this instance, an implicit critique; the critique is suspended in solution.

Ritual may seem safe, but it is not, especially if it is uncontained. "Rites" are contained; "ritualization processes" are not. Rites, such as ordinary weddings, funerals, and baptisms, are differentiated from everyday interaction and recognized as legitimate types of symbolic action. Ritualization, on the other hand, is what happens when ordinary interaction constellates into nascent ritualizing or when rites overflow their socially defined boundaries. Because ritualization is comparatively undifferentiated, it is always possible to debate whether it is best named "ritual" at all. Some prefer to regard it as pathology; others, creativity.

A religious, or liturgical, rite such as baptism is an attempt to contain gesturally and posturally those symbols that contain us, hence the inevitability of paradox. No matter what the content of such a rite, the very dynamic of actors attempting to contain what contains them is bent with torque, hence the ambivalence and doubling characteristic of all powerful rites.[208]

Considering Tarwater's baptizing in this light enables us to comment on it as ritual without resorting to moral or psychological judgmentalism. We can avoid a fruitless debate over false alternatives: ritual gesture vs. pathological symptom. The action is ritualized, without question. But it is liturgy only in nascent form; it transpires without a controlled environment. The environment is not a made-up one but an overwhelmingly present and powerful one. So the baptism does not "perform the way things ought to be in conscious tension with the way they are." Rather it performs them the way they are in the uncontrolled, "outside" world. Tarwater does not have a ritual community or invent a ritually constituted world that is "large" enough to contain the real one. As a result, it spills over and the water baptism is followed by one of fire.

What his rite does well is to identify a social incongruency and act it out with fidelity. Since there is no ritually contained context for it—since it is an "unlabelled metaphor," to use Gregory Bateson's term—it begins to spread like a fire.[209] Its enactment does not serve as an occasion for reflection by the characters in the story. Rather, for Tarwater reflection has been displaced by vocation. Now he must become a prophet and re-enter the city.

Perhaps no ritual ever does more than aspire to the enactment of a controlled environment capable of containing the world anagogically. Even worlds fictionally imagined and ritually controlled are imperfect. Compared to "the" world, the worlds of fictive ritual may be total, complete, or controlled, but since our imaginations are less than perfect, even our fictions need redemption. So writers and readers are not entirely unlike Tarwater. Sometimes the stories we read and write, like the performances we enact, run away with us. We are not always able to distinguish repetitions that redeem from those that feed vicious cycles.

The Violent Bear It Away illustrates two principles: (1) that the avoidance of ritual can become ritual avoidance and (2) that whatever we flee pursues us. Both principles are true of most rites, making them on a deep level latently subversive. All rituals are, in profound respects, reversals. The trick is how to locate the reversal, or, having located it, to change its direction. Tarwater cannot sacrifice either the old prophetic religion or modern rationalist critiques of it. Neither can he go home, except to burn and to be burned.

Ritual action, we might say, is curved. And this curvature of action insures that whatever we think we are leaving behind, we are about to confront. Likewise, whatever we think we are containing we are also releasing. So ritual gestures operate like cemeteries and filing cabinets. In them we dispose of what cannot be lived with immediately in ordinary life, but that disposal is not simple or literal, because the act of disposing is also one of preservation.

A rite is implicitly a critical, ambivalently embodied gesture. Ritual is crisis held in suspension. In this respect all ritual, not just Tarwater's, is symptomatic. To put it this way is quite different from saying that ritual action is pathological. Rites are Pandora's boxes; open them up and out fly not only virtues and health, but vices and illness as well. Even the purest of ritual intentions cannot produce an action without presenting some danger of contamination.

Consequently, the novel's progression from baptism by water to baptism by fire is an anagogically revealing, albeit illegitimate, form of baptism symbolism.[210] There is nothing in the Christian baptismal symbols themselves—only in the moral prescriptions surrounding them—that precludes Tarwater's version of them. Acting out is his way of critically appropriating some old symbols. The reason this threatens us is that it reminds us that what we have taken to be laws, rules, or rubrics are only culturally sanctioned associations.

What ritualization (symbolic action constellated without established boundaries) allows that liturgy (symbolic action constellated within established boundaries) does not is the acting out of the private associations and fantasies of participants. If we knew what participants actually imagined during the eucharist and baptism, I suspect we would be astonished at their richness, comedy, and violence.

If we had read of Bishop's death in a newspaper, we would probably have quite a different judgment of the story's significance. Our moral considerations would dominate our ritological ones. But this story is not a newspaper report, it is a work of fiction, so my treatment of Tarwater's action is inseparable from its fictional context. It may be symbolically appropriate for a character to drown-baptize his uncle's retarded, speechless son. It would be horrendous for a person to do the same thing. Is it not acceptable for a priest to put a ritualist to "death" by immersing the person in water? Is it not all right to enact cannibalism by eating "body" and drinking "blood?" A ritual definition of a situation, like a fictional one, makes moral questions secondary.

Liturgical rites, such as baptism, must constantly reinvent the grounds of their necessity. We short circuit the search for compelling grounds by laying down ethical criteria too soon. Since fiction is not as prone to moral self-censorship as religion is, it provides a framework for imagining actions to their remote ends. If it is immoral for the Tarwaters in our local hometowns to drown the Bishops, it is also immoral for the elders in our lives to hide the fictive qualities of ritual behind its revealed ones. If Tarwater is acting out a compulsion, it is not just because his "underhead" or the devil is making him do it. It is also because the stranger's voice sounds sometimes like that of the uncles who exercise authority over his life. For too long we have pretended that the necessity for ritual comes from the authorities that transmit it.

What Flannery O'Connor's novel does for baptism is to render it urgent. I do not say desirable but urgent. There are enough champions of baptism's cleansing power, but most modern readers do not sense its killing power. In many healing traditions the medicine that heals also kills. O'Connor shows us action in a state of acute emergency and yet she forces us to ask whether the state of being liberated from such a ritual process is any more liberating than the state of being immersed in it.

Ritualization is how we enact unresolvable ambivalence.[211] It is what we do when nothing can be done, how we act when our only choice is inaction. The temptation of a verbose culture is to soften this paradox by offering didactic or theological comments that purport to resolve it. But a ritual action must carry its meaning inside itself. It has to express meaning within action, or inaction, without inserting abstract statements of meaning in the middle of the rite. A rite's values cannot be appended in the form of commentary or added as explanatory accompaniment without causing the actions themselves to fail to do their job of holding things in suspension. Ritual meaning must have weight, extension, and duration. It cannot be just another item in Rayber's, or some other scholar's, head.

It is sometimes useful to treat a ritual as if it has an intentionality of its own apart from the conscious intentions of ritualists. One can imagine this intentionality as belonging, say, to a stranger, the devil, or the unconscious. But it is useful to imagine a formal intention that belongs to the action itself. The sequence of actions in a work of fiction are what Aristotle would have called its *mythos*. The intention of the mythos, or plot, is its climax or conclusion. And this intention supersedes that of the characters, who only partly see where things are leading. So even if a ritualized action is consciously initiated and deliberately designed, it is part of a larger framework of rhythms and gestures. Ritual is always a sub-pattern, and its inclusion in a greater one, that of a mythos or cosmos, means that rationally calculated or morally chosen actions do not by themselves determine the outcome, though they may influence it. Not all ritual actions are so tightly constructed that their order precludes the intrusion of mythic patterns and cosmic powers. A divination rite, for instance, mediates the rhythms of ritualists and those of the cosmos. A fertility rite may have its dates and actions partially dictated by larger natural rhythms.

The popular Protestant view is that prophetic action and priestly ritualism are opposed in principle to one another. Prophetic action is supposed to take the form of a divinely and morally motivated proclamation. It is "punctual," like Old Tarwater's accusations: it breaks into the middle of things. Our story, however, takes another view. It depicts ritualized prophesying, (which seems quite appropriate for a Catholic writer in the South). What we are shown is not an action motivated by a divine finger punching holes in the sky or a prophet's head, but one that is transmitted as a heritage. Tarwater receives his prophetic vocation from his great uncle, and he receives it despite, not because of, his intentions.

Of course a Baptist, or even a Catholic, could object: "None of this could happen if baptisms were left in church with those called and commissioned to perform them. The abuse of baptism comes about only in deviant individuals or in fiction."

My reply would be that ritual actions tend to evoke their own reversal. And if ritual systems do not provide an internal mode of criticism-in-action (as opposed to verbal criticism of the same) an external one will emerge. In Western Christian cultures, the arts, notably fiction and drama, have generally performed this function. Nascent ritual actions constitute an "acting out" (in the psychological sense) of the hidden scenarios of a culture. But having become established, that same ritual no longer acts out (like an adolescent), but rather prescribes, action (like a parent). The problem with prescriptions for action is that their heteronomy removes them increasingly from the actions they would shape. So fictive rituals begin to grow in the cracks between ritual paradigms and non-ritual actions. And often the actions of fictive rituals are deviant, or they invert the rituals of which they are critiques.

No group of symbolic actions ever comprises a complete, self-consistent system. This is why the term "symbol system" as a synonym for "ritual" can be misleading. Rituals are not systematic actions that parallel systematic theologies. Rituals only develop in those spots where systematic interconnections have been unable to develop. A rite is not constructed on the basis of a system but on the presupposition of its absence. Therefore, we should expect it to hold contradictions in suspension. Rituals enshrine the promise of, and desire for, resolution. A ritual is a temporary resolution, but eventually this state of suspension itself becomes a problem. The cure becomes part of the disease. And some individual is now likely to imagine a ritual aberration that in effect dissolves the suspension. To do so a ritualist acts out the contradiction rather than the resolution-by-suspension. If a ritual's shaky foundations are never exposed, we lose track of what its symbols are supposed to be mediating; we are left permanently on hold.

As a Catholic O'Connor would no more separate nature and grace than an ecological anthropologist would separate person and environment. But as a Catholic she would press us one step further—into allowing the ritual, grotesque though it may be, to judge us. If in the beginning Powderhead, Tennessee, was a kind of Eden and the city a hell, in the end the flames suggest an apocalyptic reversal, making the country a kind of hell. As Tarwater turns his face to the city it is toward us that he is coming to announce judgment and bring baptismal fire.

9

Fictive Character
and Paradigmatic Deeds:
Saul Bellow's
Henderson the Rain King

FIFTY-FIVE YEAR OLD EUGENE HENDERSON, WHO IS SIX FEET FOUR, weighs two hundred thirty pounds and, according to Lily his second wife, is "unkillable," does not follow through with his threat to commit suicide in Chartres cathedral. Replete with lines from Christian prayers and hymns, he decides to raise pigs. When Nicky Goldstein, an old Jewish war buddy, says he is going to raise mink, Henderson loses track of his vocation. The ironic gesture presages the culmination of Henderson's quest. What does he really want? "I want! I want!" he repeats throughout the book. The verb never has a direct object. One day he commits a funerary gesture: he finds a dead old lady and puts a "Do Not Disturb" sign on her body.

Not knowing what he wants, Henderson leaves his pigs and family to go on a quest to discover an action that will mark his transformation from a Becomer to a Be-er. "Every man born," he says more than once, "has to carry his life to a certain depth—or else!"[212] Where else but Africa would an American male go to accomplish the magnum opus of taking on Being?

This is the right place to make his life illustrate something. This is a primordial space, he imagines, one that will take him beyond maps. He wants to penetrate beyond geography, because geography is "one of those bossy ideas according to which, if you locate a place, there's nothing more to be said about it."[213]

In Africa Henderson is befriended by a Black Methodist guide, Romilayu, who repeatedly falls on his knees in prayer and eventually leads Henderson to the Arnewi and the Wariri. When he arrives, he is as American as Henry Ford. He feels he has entered the past, where "there is no history or junk like that."[214] This Africa is "the original place." Yet it is some place new.

Henderson is soon making a boorish fool of himself by setting the bushes on fire to help the Arnewi, whom he fancies need help with a lion that is bothering them. The real reason for their fears is that, upon sight of a stranger's face, they are supposed to confess their misdeeds to cows. The prince of the tribe informs Henderson, in English, that the tribe has already been discovered. Prince Itelo, in fact, is educated.

Arnewi culture is based on cows. Their language has fifty terms for them. But presently, the cows are dying because frogs are proliferating in their drinking pond. And the tribespeople will not kill the frogs. Our picaresque parashaman, who wishes he were a doctor like Schweitzer, ("Healers are sacred")[215] comes to the rescue armed with prophecies from Daniel about being driven among the beasts of the field. He tries to convince the tribespeople to kill the frogs or to let the cows drink, but the Arnewi insist they must not take animals from drinking water nor let cows drink from it. Henderson argues that if it comes a choice between a ritual custom and living, one should choose living—if for no other reason than to live to make other customs.[216] Still, they refuse, so he begins to devise a plan to do the deed for them. Mr. Missionary, though by no means Christian, will save these poor Africans. His painfully intense concentration on the practical task is both admirable and terrifying. It will become his grand gesture. It will be "the hour that bursts the spirit's sleep."[217]

Meanwhile, Henderson accepts Itelo's invitation to wrestle and beats this Arnewi champion, who ceremoniously places the American's big foot on his head crying, "I know you." This victory brings Henderson to the attention of Queen Willatale, one of the Women of Bittahness. Henderson thinks these women profoundly happy, not bitter at all. Itelo tells him that Women of Bittahness are both masculine and feminine at the same time. Willatale is called both father and mother by children. In Henderson's estimation she is the epitome of wisdom. He believes she can show him the source, the cipher, the mystery; she could tell him the truth about himself and straighten him out.

When Queen Willatale observes that the world is strange to him because he is still a child, he bubbles with assent. Then he begins to sing from Handel's *Messiah*: "He was despised and rejected, a man of sorrows and acquainted with grief. . . ." Willatale declares that Henderson has *Grun-tu-molani*; he is a man who craves life. He is ecstatic, certain for the moment that "God does not shoot dice with our souls."[218] Inspired now, he invents a bomb to blast the frogs out of the cistern to show his gratitude.

Of course, his Big Deed is a disaster. Our demolitions expert, armed with slightly rusty military know-how, blows a retaining wall out of the cistern; water and dismembered frogs fly everywhere. What else can we expect from a good-intentioned, former combat officer to whom the croaking of frogs sounds like the "Agnus Dei?" What should we expect from one who declares, "I am Man—I myself, singular as it may look. Man. And man has many times tricked life when life thought it had him trapped."[219]

Henderson, because he wins the wrestling match with the prince, is allowed to flee, leaving behind a stunned tribe, herds of thirsty cows, a destroyed well, and a tangled mass of frog parts. If readers are not dangling from the trees laughing, they are surely left weeping like the Arnewi.

Soon Henderson arrives among the Wariri, whom Romilayu says are children of darkness. This time our "hero" is not met with inexplicable crying but with guns. He is thrown, along with his Methodist sidekick, into a hut containing a corpse. He imagines the dead one says to him, "Here, man, is your being, which you think so terrific."[220] Later that night Henderson dumps the corpse in a gully, asking its forgiveness. He does not

learn until near the end of the novel that the corpse is the former rain king. Nor does he yet know that he will be made a rain
king. So, of course, he does not view this corpse as a symbol of
himself, as we do if we trek through this novel a second time.

The next day Henderson is given a royal welcome by Dahfu, the king, his amazons, and the tribespeople. Dahfu, who almost failed medical school and whose body and mind are so
elegantly tuned that our pith-helmeted friend is in awe, quickly befriends Henderson, considering him a "monument" of a
man. Henderson is soon drawn to Dahfu's side in an intra-
tribal struggle between the king and chief priest. Dahfu's kingship will not be fully consolidated until he can capture a
marked lion that has been made ritually (and therefore, really)
identical with Gmilo, the former king, Dahfu's father. Dahfu
has instead captured Atti, a female lion and keeps her in a den
as his tutor. The priest and people regard her as a witch and
suspect the king-elect will not be able to legitimize his reign.

Water, it seems, is also a problem among the Wariri as it
was among the Arnewi. A myth has it that the two tribes were
once one. The two present kings were classmates and remain
friends, so Henderson hopes Dahfu does not hear of his earlier
botch. Whereas the Arnewi seemed as docile and gentle as
their cattle, the Wariri play games with the skulls of former
dignitaries, and they sacrifice cattle. The Wariri word for the
Arnewi means "unlucky."

The Wariri are performing a rain-making ceremony. The
American has read *Scientific American* and knows all about
rain problems. Dahfu takes up Henderson's wager that it
won't rain. Of course it does when Henderson succeeds in lift-
ing the fat statue of Mummah, goddess of the clouds and fertility. Henderson's ardent desire "to work his stitch into the
design of destiny"[221] is finally realized. He lifts the statue, and
it rains. Our "hero" becomes a ritual functionary. He hears his
calling to the vocation of rain king from the silent face of the
Bunham, the priest and enemy of Dahfu. Henderson imagines
he hears these words:

> Listen! Harken unto me, you shmohawk! You are blind. The
> footsteps were accidental and yet the destiny could be no other.
> So no do not soften, oh no, brother, intensify rather what you
> are. This is the one and only ticket—intensify. Should you be

overcome, you slob, should you lie in your own fat blood senseless, unconscious of nature whose gift you have betrayed, the world will soon take back what the world unsuccessfully sent forth. Each peculiarity is only one impulse of a series from the very heart of things—that old heart of things. The purpose will appear at last though maybe not to you.[222]

Now that Eugene Henderson has become Sungo, the rain king, he has all sorts of resistance to being "in the bosom of the people." The old individualist cannot bear tribalism. The people use him to help cleanse ponds and wells, provide stagnant water for fertility purposes, and perform all sorts of ceremonial tasks. Soon he is utterly worn out. Bruised and muddy, the man who treated everything in the world as if it were medicine now *is* medicine for the people.[223]

From call to fall is a short course. Now that the people have stripped him naked, listen to him:

> Here comes Henderson of the U.S.A.—Captain Henderson, Purple Heart, veteran of North Africa, Sicily, Monte Casino, etc., a giant shadow, a man of flesh and blood, a restless seeker, pitiful and rude, a stubborn old lush with broken bridgework, threatening death and suicide. Oh, you rulers of heaven! Oh, you dooming powers! Oh, I will black out! I will crash into death, and they will throw me on the dung heap, and the vultures will play house in my paunch. And with all my heart I yelled, 'Mercy, have mercy!' And after that I yelled, 'No, justice! And after that I changed my mind and cried, No, no, truth, truth' And then, 'Thy will be done! Not my will, but Thy will!' This pitiful rude man, this poor stumbling bully, lifting up his call to heaven for truth. Do you hear that?[224]

Henderson, in the green bloomers that costume an official rain king, has long philosophical discussions with the almost-king of the tribe. The two men come to love and respect one another. One day Dahfu introduces Henderson to Atti, his lioness, and begins giving the rain king instruction in lionlikeness. In the lion's den Dahfu insists that hanging from the underside of a lioness will force the present onto a man, thereby teaching him a new habit of being. Nothing like hanging from a lion's belly to teach our Henderson how to distinguish what is inherent from what is made and to follow the former.

Despite his trembling, and against the warning of those

parts of his anatomy that shrink from Atti's muzzle, Henderson learns to roar. But repeatedly in his attempt to identify selfhood with lionhood he finds himself left with a remainder, a human remainder. Admiration for the king's lionlikeness notwithstanding, Henderson objects: if the lion doesn't imitate him, why should he imitate the lion? Words keep creeping into his roaring—words like "Hoooolp!" "Moooorcy!" "Secooooooooo" and De profoooooooodis."[225] (All this is a little too much, I admit. But what can we expect from a would-be pig farmer who has already failed at cows and frogs and now tries a lioness who may be a witch?)

Dahfu enters the jungle intending to capture Gmilo, the lion which is his father and who alone can legitimate his kingship. If Dahfu captures Gmilo, he may reign until he begins to fail, at which time he will be strangled and ritually made into a lion for his successor to capture. Henderson accompanies him, knowing he himself will never be able to become a lion. The king, whose wisdom and competence usually show up his friend's clumsiness, falls atop the wrong lion and is ripped open to meet his death. Unlike Henderson, Dahfu has not lost his chance to go beyond "creature-blessing" to "project number two—the second blessing."

This is not a happy place to end my telling. Too much is left unanswered: Why, when Henderson grabs his return flight to LaGuardia, is he carrying with him a lion cub stolen from the tribe? Why have the tribespeople not named it "Dahfu?" Why isn't Henderson angry with his friend, whose very death was a trick? After all, Dahfu knew that a rain king must succeed any hereditary king who fails to capture the lion that fathered him? After all, had Henderson not escaped with the aid of Romilayu, he would have been forced to hunt the cub when it was two or three years old.

Henderson has as hard a time finding rubrics to "classify" (his term) Dahfu, his friend, as he did in trying to make sense of the wrestling match that Prince Itelo expected of him as a stranger. And how shall we classify Henderson when he steps off the plane claiming he is going to medical school after having lived in the wilderness with his cub and fed on locusts like the Baptist?

Paradigmatic Acts and the Ritual Formation of Character

Henderson says people will forgive us many crazy deeds as long as we have no theory about them. King Dahfu had a theory. The result was that his rivals and the wrong lion got him. So I begin to theorize with trepidation. Now that our hero is initiated, probably I should heed his wisdom and rest content with storytelling, but I follow his example rather than his advice, for in the end Henderson too had a theory:

> Oh, you can't get away from rhythm, Romilayu. . . . You just can't get away from it. The left hand shakes with the right hand, the inhale follows the exhale, the systole talks back to the diastole, the hands play patty-cake, and the feet dance with each other. And the seasons. And the stars, and all of that. And the tides, and all that junk. You've got to live at peace with it, because if it's going to worry you, you'll lose. You can't win against it. It keeps on and on and on. Hell, we'll never get away from rhythm, Romilayu, I wish my dead days would quit bothering me and leave me alone. The bad stuff keeps coming back, and it's the worst rhythm there is. The repetition of a man's bad self, that's the worst suffering that has ever been known. But you can't get away from regularity. But the king said I should change. I shouldn't be an agony type. Or a Lazarus type. The grass should be my cousins.[226]

This rhythm, this regularity, this systole and diastole, this seasonality is the stuff of ritual. Rites arise out such muck, the bad stuff that keeps coming back. At yet we hope rites protect us against the worst suffering we've ever known. How strange.

A commonly held view of ritual is that it is paradigmatic. The source of this claim is usually Mircea Eliade. Eliade writes very little specifically about ritual. He is more concerned with myth. Most of what he has to say about ritual makes it derivative of myth. This part of his theory has little current credibility. Nevertheless, the language of paradigms remains influential in ritual studies. When Eliade speaks of myth as paradigmatic, he usually means that it recapitulates the beginnings of things. In the origins of things reside the paradigms, the powerfully generative archetypes. So to return to them is to experience renewal. Henderson's returns—a mythic return to Africa, a literal one to the United States—are less than renewing.

Inspired by Eliade, theorists of religion continue to build the notion of paradigmatic force into their definitions, descriptions, and theories of ritual. Evan Zuesse, for instance, says, "Ritual is the paradigmatic way of the body knowing itself to be in the world."[227] And Richard Pilgrim defines ritual as "a specific and usually repeated complex 'language' of paradigmatic word and gesture.[228] Unfortunately, those who speak of ritual as paradigmatic seldom tell us much about how paradigms actually work.

Henderson the Rain King confronts us with two quite different sorts of paradigms. Henderson's actions imply one kind, and what I have quoted above as his "theory" suggests another. And the two are in conflict. Henderson's central act, his leaving home for a far-away place, is fraught with the belief that the only authentic, or paradigmatic, action consists of a great deed enacted during a heroic quest. Such a deed must be both culturally significant (for instance, it should save a tribe) and personally expressive (that is, it must not be generic, it must be uniquely one's own). Henderson aspires to such a deed but fails to achieve it. When he comes home ready to enter medical school, he still seems driven by the desire to accomplish Big Deeds. What does he plan to do—return to Africa as a medical missionary?

The other sort of paradigm, which Henderson sometimes recognizes, oftentimes forgets, is neither personal nor culturally productive. It is "the rhythm." It is the sort of action that a person cannot author but can only recognize by yielding to it or attempting to align himself with it. In Henderson's (or is it Bellow's?) myth this paradigmatic rhythm is not metaphorically back at the beginning. Rather it is here, now. Further, it is not necessarily good or generative. It can overtake the best laid plans of a man.

The formation of character occurs as grist between these two great mills, which, for short, we might label "the deed" and "the rhythm." By "the deed" I mean the necessity to forge one's own personal vocation, make one's mark on the world, perform something worthy of a good tombstone epitaph. And by "the rhythm" I mean the necessity to dance in eddies not of one's own making.

Henderson, brimming with American male activism, decides he must make an overt contribution to the culture of two African tribes. If he cannot do this, he wants at least to perform deeds that "illustrate something."[229] If he cannot be a culture-bringing hero, he at least wants to be a figurehead, a personage, a real character, a man who condenses action into being. He fantasizes that he has lived through and worn out the calling distinctive to American males: to act decisively, to achieve. He aspires to be. But to get from Doing to Being, a mere mortal male has to *do*. This doing-toward-being (I apologize for sounding so much like Heidegger) has a proper name: The Quest. Quests are journeys in search of paradigmatic deeds.

If we men ask ourselves who we are as we approach holy ground aspiring to paradigmatic deeds, don't we have to admit that we are Hendersons? One reason for telling his story is to play with the possibility that we are Hendersons all. But I suppose trying to get you to play Henderson is like Dahfu's trying to get Henderson to assume the posture of a lion: The pigs, cows, frogs and such "human remainders" get in the way. They get in the way because they so fully embody the rhythm that Henderson so fears.

Henderson—wealthy, ivy-league educated, and a former military captain decorated with a Purple Heart—is a "civilized" man before he goes to Africa. When a native prince wants to wrestle this stranger as a way of coming to know him, Henderson is unable to make sense of the event. He knows only what he learned at Camp Blanding: to kill, snap bones, and gouge out eyes. His "classification problem" is rooted in an unimaginative reduction of ultimate deeds, which rites are supposed to be, to murder or suicide. "Truth comes in blows,"[230] he exclaims, but he has a difficult time knowing the difference between playful ones and martial ones. Henderson does not become a hero in the glamorous way of movies or the bigger-than-life traditions of myth. Rather he is a buffoon, a picaresque, soppy-hearted anti-hero whose Quixote-like violence and extreme gestures strike a reader sharply on the funnybone.

I have identified two differing notions of the paradigmatic: the heroic deed and the recurrent rhythm. There is a third way to understand ritual as paradigm. Ritual is paradigmatic insofar as it exercises the capacity to sculpt reality outside the ritual arena itself. We might call this its capacity for formation. But what is it that is formed? Throughout Western intellectual and religious history a multitude of answers have been given to the question—character, spirit, soul, body, and social values among them. Here I will consider only one, character, though I suspect that pursuing any one can lead to all the others.

Character is a useful notion in a discussion of fictive ritual, because it suggests both the made-up qualities of literature and the moral, normative ones nurtured by ritual: character is both constructed and ultimately real. We should exploit this ambiguity. "Character" suggests a role in a drama or novel, as well as religious-moral fiber. Ritual's capacity to exercise formative power in sculpting character is a not unlike the formative influence exercised by literature and theater. Both ritual and literature are character-forming fictions.

Sometimes we use "character" and "role" interchangeably. Both terms are used in sociology as well as in the study of drama. Dramatistic methods use them both ways at once and thereby imply that too neat a distinction between fiction and social life is misguided. Social scientists such as Victor Turner and Erving Goffman have shown how fruitful it is to treat social interaction as if it were drama (that is, dramatistically).

Ethicists are more prone to speak of "character" than "role." Though the distinction in usage is not absolute, "character" suggests something one is or has, while "role" is something one fills or plays. We talk about "playing a character," never "playing character," which would amount to hypocrisy or dissimulation. Ethically considered, one *has* character. Dramatically, one *plays* a character. To boast that I fully coincide with my character is a fiction. Such a claim says either too little or too much. Human beings undergo character dissolution, and they act out of character by failing to be what they aspire to be, so to insist that one is identical with one's character is to inflate oneself into the normative status of an archetype or allegory. I am both more and less than this—less because I regularly fail, more because I am multifaceted, not reducible to morality and religiosity any more than to sociology or psychology.

Character is inextricably bound to the fictive, and the fictive permeates everyday life as surely as it does the literature we label "fiction." Henderson is not only a fictional character, he is driven by a fiction. This is both his glory and the bane of his existence. Though you and I are not characters in novels, in this respect we are no different from him. Some might object: A reader is a reader; a ritualist, a ritualist; and a character, a character. So why bother approaching ritual by way of a fictive individual rather than a real group? One reason is that rites are themselves a kind of fiction, and some fictions are a sort of ritual.

I ritualize my relation to *Henderson* by returning to it, as to home. Like my self or my family members, Henderson is sometimes an embarrassment to me, but we are made of the same stuff, he and I, like it or not. He exercises influence on my character, even if he only provides a good bad example not to follow.

In identifying with, aspiring to, or allowing ourselves to be judged by the characters enacted in ritual and narrated in fiction, character is built. Morally considered, character is formed as people embody their myths, enter fictive words long enough to be shaped by them, engage in ritualistic performances, or do good deeds. Character is formed when one connects images, stories, or the principles embedded in them with action. Insofar as we attempt to live up to (or live down) a story we consider normative, we are building character. But since we sometimes cannot live up to our stories—they may be bigger than we—the relation between story and self is fragile. A self has character in the way an actor embodies *a* character. The identification is never complete; the one is always on the way to coinciding with the other. So one's character (since it is, in part, an ideal) is as subjunctive as a character on a stage.

It should be obvious by now that "fictive," does not necessarily mean "false," "negative," or "unreal," but means "meta-real," "reality-inducing," "world-making." The meta-reality of fiction exercises paradigmatic force by forming character. But character is not just what we *really* are; it is also what we aspire to be. We both judge and are judged by character. In this respect moral character and fictional characters are the same: we both make them up and are measured by them.

I have identified three ways of understanding the paradigmatic function of cultural forms such as ritual: (1) as any "big" or definitive deed that serves as a fulcrum or model; (2) as any transpersonal rhythm that exceeds individual ability to decide, will, and act; (3) as the capacity of humanly constructed cultural forms such as ritual or fiction to form character. Then I explored the moral-dramatistic notion of character, articulating several of its connotations: (1) the ethical: "Henderson has little character"; (2) the psychological: "He reveals his true character by blowing up the pond"; (3) the literary or dramatic: "Henderson is a character in Bellow's novel."

I conclude by adding a final facet of character that brings us full circle and reminds us of who we are, namely, readers or hearers of a story: (4) the paradigmatic: "Old Henderson is quite a character." If we remind ourselves that Henderson is just a character in a story, we disidentify: he is there, we are here. But when we embrace him as our "old" buddy, quite a character, we place ourselves in a family portrait alongside him. The old bastard standing there, full of himself (how else would he have gotten so big?) freshly off the plane from Africa, is our brother. Old Henderson is like the rest of us who are in quest of big or ritual deeds—only more so. He is what we might be if our latent tendencies were more overtly realized, if we acted them out by going to Africa instead of reading books about characters who do so on our behalf. Old Henderson is something of a caricature, and caricatures are reductions. Old Henderson would be *only* a caricature if he would let us get away with reducing him to the gesture of putting a "Do Not Disturb" sign on Miss Lenox's corpse or blowing up the pond. But he resists. Though he is a homeless bungler, the man *really is* in search of his soul. Part tourist, part missionary, part parashaman, he begins to define us by insinuating himself into our actions. In this sense he is not only a "real character" but a *real* character. He acts upon us, teases us, lures us. We return to him. We return looking for ways to accomplish the Big Deed, hoping to fall into being, knowing that it is better to fail here than in Africa, where the Hendersons of the First World have run rampant for quite some time now.

10

Ritual Contradiction and Ceremonial Irony: Jean Genet's *The Blacks: A Clown Show*

A WHITE WOMAN HAS BEEN KILLED; OR WAS SHE ALREADY DEAD? A Black man named Deodatus Village has done it; or does the White jury only imagine that he did? The White woman, a tramp smelling of wine and urine, was strangled; or was she stabbed? The Black man loved her; or did he hate her? The catafalque onstage contains her corpse; or is it that of an old down-and-out vaudeville singer? Perhaps that of a milkman, a seamstress, a four-year old on his way home with a bottle of milk—or even a dog or a doll? Is there a corpse at all?

The dead White woman's name was Marie. That must have been her name, because her ill mother was crying out her name from an attic bed, hollering for aspirin and sugared almonds and announcing that it was time for prayers. That was when the Black man did what he did to this magistrate's beautiful daughter. He raped her. Or did she seduce him?

Whatever happened, it is now being re-enacted for a jury so its perpetrators' condemnation will be warranted. However, the ultimate gesture, as in Greek tragedy, takes place behind a screen.[231] Is this decorum a mere clown show for the sake of the White audience? Or a cover-up for subversive activities going on off-stage?

The Blacks are re-enacting the crime for the sake of the court played by Black actors sitting on an elevated platform and wearing White masks. A White man wrote this play for Black actors playing before a White audience.

As Deodatus Village's re-enactment transpires, a trial and execution of one of their own, a traitor, is being conducted off-stage by the Blacks. Diouf, an Uncle-Tom cleric, is sent behind the on-stage screen where Deodatus Village is re-enacting the crime. Diouf, a Black man, is dressed to play the White woman whom Village is supposed to be raping and killing.

The dead Diouf now appears in a mask that symbolizes both his death and entry into the White world. Blacks die by ascending into the White world; Whites, by descending into the Black one. Having been taken by Village's desire and now with child by him, Diouf is unable to stop playing his role even though the other players now remove their masks. A Black-become-White, a living-man-become-dead-woman, he gives birth to dolls.

The White court played by Black actors, some of whom have figured out that they are presiding at a masque of their own funeral, descend from their platform. They come onstage drunk and walking backwards to their executions.

The Blacks, claiming there really was no corpse at all, and therefore that there has been no murder, have been condemned anyway, so now their judges must be put to death. But how do Blacks kill Whites when Whites, as the pallor of their skin indicates, are dead already? Why make a corpse of a corpse?

Felicity, who is a priestess presiding over the executions, offers an incantation:

FELICITY: Behold our gestures. Though now they're merely the mutilated arms of our ravaged rites, bogged down in weariness and time, before long you'll be stretching lopped-off stumps to heaven and to us. . . .

THE QUEEN (to the Court): What should I answer?

FELICITY: Look! Look, Madam. Here it comes, the darkness you were clamoring for, and her sons as well. They're her escort of crimes. To you, Black was the color of priests and under-takers and orphans. But everything is changing. Whatever is gentle and kind and good and tender will be Black. Milk will be Black, sugar, rice, the sky, doves, hope, will be Black. So will the opera to which we shall go, Blacks that we are, in Black Rolls Royces to hail Black kings, to hear brass bands beneath chandeliers of Black crystal. . . .[232]

Before the Whites can be put to death, the ceremony is inter-rupted by news that the ultimate offstage deed has been com-mitted. So the Whites momentarily remove their masks, re-vealing their Black faces. Then they don them again to finish the ceremony.

The Whites insist on showing discipline, making declara-tions, going to death voluntarily, and other face-saving de-vices. Eventually, all the Whites are shot with a silent revol-ver, the missionary screaming that he has been both castrated and canonized.[233]

The play ends where it began, and where it will begin again tomorrow night: with the Blacks standing around the catafalque and with the opening measures of Mozart's *Don Giovanni* playing.

Ritualizing the Contradictions

The plot of *The Blacks* has to be pieced together out of ambigu-ous, if not contradictory, fragments. According to the charac-ters, the story is a diversion tactic; the audience is led to sus-pect that the most important events are going on offstage. Of every action, Genet forces his audience to ask, Is this really happening? Are we being shown what always happens be-tween Blacks and Whites? Is the performance merely what someone thinks we want to see? Do these actions cover-up more important ones? Does sacrality belong to Whites or to Blacks—to ritual killing or to the refusal to sacrifice?

Genet's play is a "clown show," a combination of inverted liturgy, minstrel show, trial, smoke screen, and Parisian folly. So its storyline only partly conveys what is going on. The ac-tion is rife with symbols and low on chronological develop-ment. The characters refer to the performance variously as a ceremonial, recital, rite, and funeral.[234] As in most of Genet's other plays this one is reflexive and circular. Not only is it about Blacks and Whites but it reflects on ritualistic-dramatic conventions themselves, especially the interaction of audiences and actors, which is a division made coextensive with the White/Black one.

No contemporary playwright used ritual forms and themes more perceptively and persistently than Jean Genet. Although his criminal activities stigmatized him as a prince of the underworld, he earned an international reputation. No modern playwright has a more keenly developed sense of ceremony than he. When referring to him as "St. Genet," Jean-Paul Sartre was not making ironic observations about Genet's moral life but alluding to his predilection for repetition, incantatory language, multi-layered symbolism, and other such devices that typically characterize ritual.[235]

Genet's dramatic style is not just ritualistic in general but specifically liturgical. By this I do not mean "having to do with the Mass" or "Christian" but "religious." *The Blacks*, like many other of Genet's plays, is religious in a profane way. The values and symbols in them are those of the underworld, not those of an upper, heavenly one. His plays are distinctly other-worldly, but "other" does not mean "supernatural" so much as "infracultural," "other then respectable" or "other than the world of his audience." Genet uses liturgical language, conventionally expected to confirm the social status quo, in order to throw it into question.

A widely held anthropological view of ritual, including religious ritual, is that contradictions are at its core. Such contradictions are social rather than purely logical; they concern the rifts, injustices, and inconsistencies of social structures. One variation of this view is that ritual covers up contradictions, protecting ritualists from being aware of them and functioning as the "opiate" that Marx complained was at the heart of religion. The other version of the theory maintains that ritual deliberately "suspends" social contradictions, holding them "in solution" as it were, so that participants can contemplate them as the building blocks of their society. In performing them, they have the option of changing them.

A whole series of polarities develops in the play: Black/White, upper platform/lower stage, onstage/offstage, playacting/the ultimate act, actors/audience, truth/illusion. Polarities are nothing new to either ritual or theater. What is unique is the radicality of Genet's enactment of them. They are not just static or merely antagonistic opposites. Each nourishes and consumes the other. Each contains the other. And each sucks the blood of the other. The opposites thrive on antagonism, and this contest (or *agon*), not some supernatural or social reality beyond it, is the creator of Genet's world.

Antonin Artaud who, like Genet, conceived an essentially dramatic-ritualistic world, wrote:

> Our petrified idea of theater is connected with our petrified idea of a culture without shadows, where, no matter which ways it turns, our mind (*esprit*) encounters only emptiness, though space is full.

> But the true theater, because it moves and makes use of living instruments, continues to stir up shadows where life has never ceased to grope its way. The actor does not make the same gestures twice, but he makes gestures, he moves; and although he brutalizes forms, nevertheless behind them and through their destruction he rejoins that which outlives forms and produces their continuation.[236]

Following Artaud and Genet, one might imagine ceremony and drama as each other's "double." Theater, through its fictionality, sometimes spawns an "other" reality not quite containable in standard Western dramatic forms. And ceremony, typically grounded in what is serious, ultimate, and inescapable, finds itself drawn in the direction of play-acting and fiction. Like Blacks and Whites, theatrical and ritualistic sensibilities continually oppose and coincide. In this respect theaters are the shadow of churches and synagogues, and drama is the shadow of liturgy. Christian institutions in the West imagine themselves as doing good by "spreading" the Gospel. Artaud imagines theater as "spreading," but he has another metaphor in mind:

> For if the theater is like the plague, it is not only because it affects important collectivities and upsets them in an identical way. In the theater as in the plague there is something both victorious and vengeful: we are aware that the spontaneous conflagration which the plague lights wherever it passes is nothing else than an immense liquidation.

The plague takes images that are dormant, a latent disorder, and suddenly extends them into the most extreme gestures; the theater also takes gestures and pushes them as far as they will go: like the plague it reforges the chain between what is and what is not, between the virtuality of the possible and what already exists in materialized nature. It recovers the notion of symbols and archetypes which act like silent blows, rests, leaps of the heart, summons of the lymph, inflammatory images thrust into our abruptly wakened heads. The theater restores all our dormant conflicts and all their powers, and gives these powers names we hail as symbols: and behold! before our eyes is fought a battle of symbols, one charging against another in an impossible melee; for there can be theater only from the moment when the impossible really begins and when the poetry which occurs on the stage sustains and superheats the realized symbols.

These symbols, the sign of the powers previously held in servitude and unavailable to reality, burst forth in the guise of incredible images which give freedom of the city and of existence to acts that are by nature hostile to the life of societies.[237]

Genet's plays work like a plague. They shadow the "white" reality of the respectable "upper" world. They do so by employing polarities, oppositions, and contradictions. In *The Blacks* Genet uses contradictions both to hide and to reveal. One such contradiction is that between the sacred and the profane. One the one hand, he glosses over the differences between the two domains, making sacred and profane identical. On the other, he reveals and cultivates their differences. He uses the sacred liturgical forms to negotiate what appears to be a profane topic: interracial conflict. The topic is profane, however, only in the etymological sense (*pro fanum*: "before the temple," "in front of the sacred precincts"). Profanity is not mere secularity, since secularity does not depend on the sacred by inverting or denying it. Secularity is indifference to the sacred. Genet is anything but indifferent; his dramatic ceremonies operate by sacred negation. For him the profane is sacred.

Preceding the *dramatis personae* Genet appends two notes that condense the central theme of *The Blacks*:

One evening an actor asked me to write a play for an all-Black cast. But what exactly is a Black? First of all, what's his color?[238]

This play, written, I repeat, by a White man, is intended for a White audience, but if, which is unlikely, it is ever performed before a Black audience, then a White person, male or female, should be invited every evening. The organizer of the show should welcome him formally, dress him in ceremonial costume and lead him to his seat, preferably in the front row of the orchestra. The actors will play for him. A spotlight should be focused on this symbolic White throughout the performance.

But what if no White person accepted? Then let White masks be distributed to the Black spectators as they enter the theater. And if the Blacks refuse the masks, then let a dummy be used.[239]

The performance is less a story about a murder or rape than a recycling and bodying forth of the contradictions that drive Black/White relations. It traps Blacks into performing and Whites into spectating, thereby calling into radical question this social division of labor. Actors are watched and thereby violated. Audience members are verbally assaulted and their authority undermined. This dynamic is not merely a theme presented onstage but is a transaction actually occurring between the audience and the actors. As each group suffers its entrapment, it is enabled to contemplate the possibility of breaking out of the trap and simultaneously forced to face the possibility that this role-trap may be an ultimate feature of their social existence.

The Blacks mirrors and transforms an actual social drama rooted in a stubborn contradiction: the we/they dualism. Its attempt to solidify and undermine this contradiction hinges on the question, "What exactly is a Black? First of all what's his color?" Genet lures us into asking a loop of imponderable, but essential, questions: Is negritude a skin color? An attitude? A cultural heritage? What is whiteness? If a Black can play, or pass as, a White, can a White become a Black?

Genet treats reality itself as if it were constituted by the interplay of seeing and being seen, or between play acting and literal action. In *The Blacks* and other works by Genet, the cosmos, with its opposed dramatic "heterocosm," is theatrical-ceremonial. His characters play, mask, and repeat themselves into being. He takes ritual-drama to be not just an occasion alongside others, an event one attends and likes or dislikes. Rather it is the fundamental way of relating self and other. In this theatrical-ceremonial world each character's identity includes what another imagines him or her to be.

All the characters in *The Blacks* are types rather than personalities. Members of the White jury are designated only by role: missionary, judge, Queen, and so on. The Blacks have flamboyant, borrowed, suggestive names: Archibald Absalom Wellington, Stephanie Virtue Secret-rose Diop, and Felicity Trollop Pardon, to name a few. All the Blacks' names are hyperboles. The Missionary condescendingly says of them, "Their dusky bodies were allowed to bear the Christian names of the Gregorian calendar."[240]

Archibald quickly sets up the basic dramatic contradiction of the play. He makes participation in the audience equivalent to being an oppressor. "You are White," he accuses, "and spectators."[241] Throughout the play the implication is that White audience members (who are, of course, not actors—at least not in the theatrical sense) are role-playing as much as the Black actors are. And it is typical of them to sit back, at a distance, where they can judge things aesthetically and spectate without having to participate. Spectating is a White ceremony inasmuch as it is how we Whites define ourselves as a group, just as play-acting and dissimulating is how the Blacks define themselves in the play. Archibald, who announces that the Blacks' sole concern is to entertain us, says, "By stretching language we'll distort it sufficiently to wrap ourselves in it and hide, whereas the [White] masters contract it."[242] Each group needs the other for this reciprocal ceremony to continue.

Bobo describes the White court, a group that functions as a kind of chorus or onstage audience, as a "pale and odorless race, [a] race without animal odors, without the pestilence of our swamps. . . ."[243] Whiteness in this ceremony-drama symbolizes death and disease, not purity, and the Blacks seethe with a rage to slaughter Whites "down to your White powder, to your very soap suds. . . ."[244] The Missionary is sure God is White, but the Judge, just as he is being shot, makes a declaration to his executioners: "Act of July 18th. Article 1. God being dead, the color Black ceases to be a sin; it becomes a crime. . . ."[245] Blackness in the performance is not only an inherited skin tone but a quality that is earned.[246] One performs, not only inherits, blackness. Archibald orders his actors to *be* black, to negrify themselves, to persist in doing what they are condemned to do.

This persistence in doing what one is condemned to do is one of Genet's most recurrent themes, and it is at the root of his own life as a thief. Caught stealing as a child and then labelled a thief, Genet learned to perform and ironically sacralize those actions he was condemned to do. The Blacks, from whom Whites are advised to flee and who are supposed to have affinities with night and Black cats, ritualize the views held of them by their White others. By embodying and mirroring them before Whites, they begin to turn the tide of negatively functioning stereotype toward positively valued archetype:

> We were the shadow, or the dark interior, of luminous creatures. . . . I know not whether you are beautiful. I fear you may be. I fear our sparkling darkness. Oh darkness, stately mother of my race, shadow, sheath that swathes me from top to toe, loving sleep in which the frailest of your children would love to be shrouded, I know not whether you are beautiful, but you are Africa, oh monumental night, and I hate you. I hate you for filling my Black eyes with sweetness. I hate you for making me thrust you from me, for making me hate you. It would take so little for your face, your body, your movements your heart to thrill me. . . ."[247]

In the midst of the polarized otherness that characterizes the world of *The Blacks*, attempts at mediation are bound to arise. Ritual emerges in situations of insurmountable ambivalence and social contradiction. It hides as well as bridges the gaps, so its mediations can be false, masking contradictions rather than healing them. Diouf (Mr. Vicar-General, as he is sarcastically addressed) wants to straddle the fence. He embodies the liberal attempt to mediate social—in this case, racial—contradictions. The performance, he hopes, will reestablish a psychosocial equilibrium by presenting so harmonious an image that the Whites will see the beauty of Blacks. When the Missionary inquires if the Blacks would have them make the host black or, say, brown like gingerbread, Diouf suggests a compromise: Why not a grey host, or black on one side, white on the other?[248] Genet conducts a fierce slash and burn on quick resurrections and easy reconciliations.

The ending of *The Blacks* is not happy, and the alternatives are not encouraging. The only symbolic mediation between blackness and whiteness is the formality of the ceremony itself. The rite does not point to reconciliation, but by ceremonializing opposition and otherness, it has identified and commented on a fundamental social contradiction. A White man wrote the script for Black actors who would be performing in front of White people. It calls attention to the social status of the theatrical event itself and does so by performing, rather than avoiding, the usual stereotypes. Blacks and Whites are forced to play, rather than be, themselves. The very fictionality and reflexivity of the ceremony represent the only possibilities for insight. But, of course, neither playing nor self-awareness assures racial harmony, and we are left expecting the playing/ spectating cycle to continue.

We readers ought neither reduce *The Blacks* to the playwright's text nor isolate it from its cultural setting and time. We need to imagine it as performance, not just as text. The Grove edition of the play has notes about its first American performance in 1961 as well as photographs that remind us of the separability of text and performance, a basic fact that many who study ritual texts regularly overlook or minimize. The first French production (directed by Roger Blin) at Theatre de Lutece in Paris was surely different from the one at St. Mark's in New York (directed by Gene Frankel). And, no doubt, it makes a difference how the reader imagines or reconstructs the performance—if we know, for example, that Godfrey Cambridge played Diouf; James Earl Jones, Deodatus Village; and Cicely Tyson, Virtue; Roscoe Lee Brown, Archibald; and Maya Angelou, the Queen.

It is important, when studying a ritual or dramatic text, to be aware of what is missing from it. Readers who study the text would, of course, recognize that the bodies, voices, and stage are missing. But an audience is part of a performance, even if in some cultures a relatively passive part. The role of the audience is particularly accentuated in *The Blacks*, and what we do not know from the text is how audiences responded. Were they threatened? Defensive? Humor-filled? What were the differences between White and Black responses? What were the consequences after the play—fighting, friendliness, fear?

A performance-based approach (as opposed to a text-based one) would bump us into recognizing that we have a hard time guessing what the audience's response was, because we do not know the *tone* of the acting? Was it played ironically? Straight? Like a minstrel show? The entire dynamic *between* actors and audience is missing. And in this instance it is a more crucial factor because the actor/audience dynamic in the stage drama parallels (or *is* a condensation of) the larger social drama. The esthetic drama implicates the social drama. Consequently, White audience members cannot watch with immunity, cannot have the luxury of mere formalistic "appreciation."

An enacted fiction is potentially more dangerous than a read one, and this play, particularly when first performed in the U.S., must have had its threatening, perhaps even terrifying, moments when the decorous line between stage and street seemed shaky. Archibald shouts furiously, "This is the theater, not the street," and we feel safe. But his next phrase undoes the first and sends shivers through the audience, "The theater, and drama, and crime."[249] Archibald has to struggle with all the actors, including himself, to maintain the formal tone expected of ceremony. Periodically, we witness rage boiling up under it and wonder what it would take for us spectating Whites to become the next occupants of the bier. Felicity, a 68-year old earth mother, costumed as an African shaman, ends her invocation of Africa in a way that threatens to turn a play into a sacrificial rite:

> Dahomey! Dahomey! To my rescue, Negroes, all of you! Gentlemen of Timbuctoo, come in, under your white parasols! Stand over there. Tribes covered with gold and mud, rise up from my body, emerge! Tribes of the Rain and Wind, forward! Princes of the Upper Empires, Princes of the bare feet and wooden stirrups, on your caparisoned horses, enter! Enter on horseback. Gallop in! Hop it! Hop along! Negroes of the ponds, you who fish with your pointed beaks, enter! Negroes of the docks, of the factories, of the dives, Negroes of the Ford plant, Negroes of General Motors, and you, too. Negroes who braid rushes to encage crickets and roses, enter and remain standing! Conquered soldiers, enter. . . . Walk gently on your white feet. White? No, black. Black or White? Or blue? Red, green, blue,

> white, red, green, yellow, who knows, where am I? The colors
> exhaust me. . . . Are you there, Africa with the bulging chest
> and oblong thigh? Sulking Africa, wrought of iron, in the fire,
> Africa of the millions of royal slaves, deported Africa, drifting
> continent, are you there . . . ? I call you back this evening to at-
> tend a secret revel. (pondering) It's a block of darkness, com-
> pact and evil, that holds its breath, but not its odor. Are you
> there? Don't leave the stage unless I tell you to. Let the specta-
> tors behold you. A deep, almost invisible somnolence emanates
> from you, spreads all about, hypnotizes them. We shall pres-
> ently go down amongst them, but before we do. . . .[250]

If theater-goers are not ill at ease contemplating the possibility that the action might spill off the stage and into their laps,
then surely they must worry about the offstage actions or
wonder about the post-performance consequences of the play.
Is the hatred real? Is the restraint? And the role-playing—is it
not just as real in the society at large as on the stage? White
fantasy goes on a rampage: What is to keep this from being a
charade while our daughters or babysitters are being raped
and our banks robbed?

The performance event involves, to invoke Richard Schechner's terms, neither an "accidental" nor an "integral" relationship between actors and audience.[251] Perhaps some audience
members attend hoping they will be allowed the safety and
comfort of being accidental. Others may have come hoping for
some sort of participation, which would make them integral.
But the audience/actor relation is better understood as antithetical rather than either accidental or integral. A liberal inte-
grationist might want to insist that an antithetical relation is a
subcategory of Schechner's "integral" relation, but it is hard to
imagine Genet's accepting such a view. The performance shat-
ters all but the most dogged estheticism. Critics, interpreters,
and reports have noted again and again how taken or offended viewers were. There was no escaping the fact that they
were implicated—and not just during the time of the show but
afterward, in their very social being.

One indication of ritualizing in theater is an audience's
increased participation. There were other plays, *Hair*, to cite an
example from the same era, that allowed audience more actual, overt activity in the theater. But participants in *Hair*, by

dancing on the stage, became, in effect, extras. In *The Blacks* the audience is made to play a leading, villainous role. Though physically more passive in *The Blacks*, the audience role is more significant than in *Hair*. To return to Schechner's terminology, the audience role is more integral to *The Blacks* than to *Hair* precisely because it is antithetical. In *The Blacks* the social and theatrical roles of audience members are inseparable. And they are antithetically related to those of the actors. When actors play themselves, they move away from entertainment toward efficacy, which is how Schechner describes the movement from theatricalization toward ritualization.[252] Not only is Genet's play *about* the integral/accidental/antithetical relations between Blacks and Whites, it *enacts* these relations. The same is true of entertainment/efficacy. The play *uses* entertainment to cover up and then reveal efficacious events going on elsewhere.

Is it a measure of efficaciousness or of entertainment value that the play had a record run in New York—four years and over a thousand showings? From this sort of data alone we cannot decide. However, if one compares the French and American productions, it is clear that the historical and social situation in the United States was more ripe. The play "took" in the States in a way that it did not in France, although the French production was itself highly acclaimed (and widely condemned) and approved by Genet himself.

Ceremonial Irony

Though *The Blacks* is both theatrical and ritualistic, it is neither theater in the conventional sense nor ritual in any traditional sense. If we are to ponder its ritual dimension, then it is probably best understood as ceremonial irony. Ceremony is a ritual mode emphasizing group-to-group, rather than face-to-face, encounter.[253] In ceremoniously defined situations personal ritualizing presents severe difficulties; it seems self-indulgent and uncommitted. In ceremony, a group's solidarity is buttressed to set it off from outsiders, so there is little room for personal nonconformity or indecision. Diouf's fate illustrates well the conflict between the social solidarity of ceremony and the individualism of personal ritualizing. He remains, pitifully, with the Whites even after they have departed to die and removed their masks. In the end he has neither community nor self-identity, only a pretty dress. He thinks that the antagonism between races requires polite decorum. He imagines that attentiveness and courteous patience will convince Whites of the humanity of Blacks.

Archibald, the master of ceremonies, runs the show, introduces characters, explains things to the audience, reminds everyone that the event is a ceremony, and directs the action like an on-stage manager. He plays with polite decorum, but he periodically rips off its face full of pleasantries to reveal the seething chaos that is the generative center of ceremony:

> This evening we shall perform for you. But, in order that you may remain comfortably settled in your seats in the presence of the drama that is already unfolding here, in order that you be assured that there is no danger of such a drama's worming its way into your precious lives, we shall even have the decency—a decency learned from you—to make communication impossible. We shall increase the distance that separates us—a distance that is basic—by our pomp, our manners, our insolence—for we are also actors. When my speech is over, everything here—(he stamps his foot in a gesture of rage) here! will take place in the delicate world of reprobation.[254]

The Blacks follow Archibald, their master of ceremonies, rather than the old man Diouf, who wants peace at any price. Archibald does not submit to the demands of decorum; he uses them for ceremonial ends. He is ironically polite and subtly caustic to the audience. Theatrically, he conducts the show for the entertainment of Whites, but socially its effect is to negrify the attitudes of the actors and to judge the White audience. By donning the personae dictated by White fantasies, the Blacks are able to Blacken their blood and thicken their own ties.

Durkheim's theory of ritual is most applicable to the ritual sensibility that I am calling ceremony, because it interprets references to the divine as symbols of a group's own social structure and ideals. Durkheim defines religion not just as a web of beliefs and practices but as constituted by the sacralization of community.[255] Accordingly, he understands the dominant function of ritual to be that of legitimating and symbolizing the group that enacts it. In his view, ritual always functions ceremonially, because every enactment of sacred togetherness engenders a sacred group of others who are profane because they are beyond the boundaries staked out for insiders.

The difficulty with Durkheim's functionalist theory of ritual is that it cannot account for ritualized resistance. *The Blacks* is a ceremony of resistance in which Black types resist White types. Perhaps an apt term for this sort of ceremony would be Max Gluckman's phrase, "rite of rebellion."[256] One might compare it with Black worship services held under conditions of slavery: some were covertly revolutionary.

In ceremonies participants come to know who they are by declaring who they are not. This act of negation is not just a peculiarity of Black-White relations but an inevitable ritual dynamic, the "original sin," if you will, of ceremony. Although the oppressed are far more likely to have to employ ritual as a facade for defense or as symbolic guerilla warfare, all ritualists, including liturgists, are to some degree engaged in a contest. Even when the audience of the ceremonializing is the Wholly Other itself, rather than a group of self-satisfied Whites with a long history as oppressors, the enactment not only connects worshippers with the divine but also holds to object of worship at bay and erects protective barriers. All rites, sacred liturgies as well as politically or ethnically charged ceremonies, contain this cycle of defensiveness and attack.

The ceremonial frame that Genet creates in *The Blacks* has a number of functions: (1) to create the semblance of a reassuring setting ("it's only a play") and then to undermine its safety; (2) to emphasize the mutual otherness of antagonistic roles (Black-as-actor and White-as-audience); (3) to act out roles that usually operate as self-fulfilling prophecies which evoke repetitions of fixed, ritualized patterns; (4) to consolidate (and relativize?) "us" and "them" as groups; (5) to provoke power struggles without actually engaging in violence; and (6) to allow dramatic conflict of symbols without the necessity for forcing a narrative resolution.

The dominant ethos of ceremony in *The Blacks* is that of irony. Tom Driver, one of the few North American theologians to write in a sustained way on ritual and drama, says of irony:

Twentieth-century drama has been notable for the variety of its styles, motifs, and intentions. Yet its principle growth has been toward an ever more pervasive irony, by which is meant the maintenance of an attitude of affirmation and negation toward whatever is in the field of vision and the accompaniment of this attitude by acute self-awareness. The ironist is not always sure what he sees is real, but he is sure that he sees it. He knows that the reality he seeks lies neither in the subject nor in the object alone but in the interchange between them.[257]

Genet's way of plaguing the theater so fiercely that its ceremonial dynamics are exposed depends on irony rather than analogy, difference rather than presence or identity. It is crucial to understand how the ironic mode works as it passes over the boundary between theatre and ritual, since we normally associate belief, not irony, with participation in ritual. After all, the devil, according to tradition, is an ironist. Genet is playing devil's advocate by implying that social unity is not a prerequisite for ceremony. Most social anthropologists and liturgical theologians assume the necessity of social cohesion for the production of ritual. They take ritual to be essentially metaphoric, symbolic, or analogical but do not consider the possibility that it may be ironic. In this view, which is dominant, "ceremonial irony" would be a category mistake of the same order as "a thirty-pound nightmare" or "a green idea." And it is not just theorists alone who mistrust irony. Sophia Antonovna in Conrad's *Under Western Eyes* advises, "Remember . . . that women, children, and revolutionists hate irony, which is the negation of all saving instincts, of all faith, of all devotion, of all action."[258]

So we have to leave open the possibility that ceremonial irony is morally bankrupt, an expression of cultural decadence. If irony negates not only social unity but faith and action, how is ritual irony possible at all? Max Gluckman has said, "I consider that rituals of the kind investigated by van Gennep are 'incompatible' with the structure of modern urban life."[259] It is a widely held view that not only rites of passage but all kinds of ritual have difficulties surviving in industrialized cultures. Ritual survives, some scholars seem to suggest, but only in enclaves removed from the voluntarism, privatism, technology, and, we should add, irony of the contemporary urban world. Despite this view ritual irony is emerging from complex, large-scale cultures as surely as it has thrived in small-scale ones. We have to allow for the possibility that irony can be as fertile a soil for ritual as either tragedy or comedy has been. Some obvious, familiar examples are Bread and Puppet Theater's annual *Resurrection Circus* in Vermont and the work of England's Welfare State International.

Since ritual is sometimes understood as a performed metaphor, it may help us grasp ceremonial irony if we follow the lead of Wayne Booth on irony. He will not allow irony to be defined so broadly that it becomes a synonym for metaphor.[260] Interpreting a metaphor, he says, requires one to explore or extend, but not to reverse or repudiate, a first reading. In the case of irony we can be shocked by the absurdity of what is said into actively exercising negative judgments as we search for meaning other than the surface one. Both metaphor and irony make us look elsewhere, but the kind of movement required of irony is more disjunctive than that of metaphor, which, in the end, balances identity and difference.

Booth distinguishes two types of irony, stable and instable. Stable ironies are (1) intended, not unconscious or accidental; (2) covert, but with reconstructible meanings that the user would seriously hold; (3) finite, not mocking all effort to interpret them; and (4) fixed, not requiring further demolition once the covert meaning has been apprehended.

Ritual irony of the unstable variety is exemplified by Kierkegaard's "knight of infinite resignation," Samuel Beckett's *Waiting for Godot*, and by *The Blacks*. In all three cases we cannot be sure what the users would seriously hold. In addition, protagonists get closer and closer to their goals but never quite arrive. Their movement tends to become infinite, without limits in its application. The ironies of ritual clowns in tribal cultures or traditional rites of inversion are more local, less infinite, therefore more stable. Their duration is limited and their extent bounded by non-ironic constraints. In contrast *The Blacks* keeps an audience constantly in the process of inverting what is said and done, and it leads actors and audience into sharing a ceremony at the very moment they repudiate one another. Not just lines in the play, but the situation itself, is ironic and unstable—hardly the basis for community but certainly the basis for enduring social antagonism.

How might we recognize unstable ceremonial irony? Learning from Genet and others, these are some preliminary cues suggesting its presence: (1) ultimately valued actions that are held subjunctively, playfully, or negatively; (2) actions that function as inactions or cover-ups for other actions; (3) words that function as deeds, or deeds that do not "do" anything except "mean"; (4) "received" or "revealed" actions that are actually improvised; and (5) actions that require collective action while leaving participants alone in their solitude. On such a basis ritual is possible though unstable. But instability does not automatically ensure a short life. Instability can endure for very long periods. The ritualization inherent in gender- and race-subordination are the best examples.

An ironically enacted ceremony requires a double-take of an interpreter. Our usual assumption is that acceptance and participation in ritual appear in tandem, but it is quite possible to participate in ritual without the attendant beliefs that are conventionally assumed. Ironic participation in ritual calls into question this claim by Roy Rapport: "By performing a liturgical order the performer accepts, and indicates to himself and to others that he accepts, whatever is encoded in the canons of the liturgical order in which he is participating."[261]

When they began to emerge in the 1960s, theologies of play, death of God theologies, subjunctive renditions of ritual (such as that advocated by Victor Turner), and fictive interpretations of religion (such as that proposed by Lonnie Kliever) treated religion and its constituents (such as theology or ritual) as ludic modes of consciousness that are closer to make-believe that to belief. Suspension in play theologies, negation in death of God theologies, second naiveté in fictive religion, and bracketing in theories of subjunctivity seemed at first to lead to the end of religion as well as theology. But, in fact, the perceived incongruity of negation and ultimacy have heightened, rather than lessened, religious urgency. Playfulness has not prevented seriousness in ritual. If not ironic in themselves, these theologies and theories are tacit recognitions that ceremonial attitudes are not necessarily literal or naive. So we should not miss either the playfulness or the ironies of ritual. Missed ironies make fools of their interpreters.

Ritual irony has dangers even though Wayne Booth insists that the use and interpretation of irony can be an exceedingly social act. Irony may also create victims or outsiders who do not "get it." Irony can intensify we/they boundaries. Victimization, though not a necessary consequence of irony, is sometimes associated with irony, because there are always implied *unsound* readers, readers who "choose to dwell in happy ignorance."[262] They are the ones who have not climbed to the hidden, superior level of meaning. Even when one is being ironic about oneself, there is always the repudiated, old self to be better than.

Consider poor Diouf. Dressed in a wig, mask, and gloves, he is ready to begin his life in the White world. He is about to abandon his life in the Black world, give up his old self. He is listening to Virtue chant the "litany of the Livid" when he loses control of his bowels. Snow, seeing shit flowing down his stockings, muses, "So it was true, Lord Jesus, that behind the mask of a cornered White is a poor trembling Negro."[263]

On the one hand, Genet's irony seems to offer hope that Black/White dualism is not final, because inside every White is a Black. On the other hand, Diouf, though his skin is Black, is really White. Genet does not offer any hope that a White can ever learn to negrify. The only ceremonial option that onstage Blacks are offered is that of performing for Whites or killing them, and Diouf's attempt at whitewashing only brings about his death. So unstable irony embedded deeply in a social drama, can be deadly.

Ironic action, like ironic rhetoric, can become stable only if there is a common base of shared cultural experience between the user and interpreter. Ironic acts are most likely to be confused with straight ones when the user's and interpreter's beliefs or communities diverge. Stable, conscious irony must be witting and thus hold the possibility of being enlightening, but a great deal of the unwitting, unstable variety is endemic to the social situation ceremonialized by Genet. Consequently, it strikes terror; we Whites fear the actions will spill over their dramatic bounds and become ceremonial sacrifice with us as victims. Blacks, perhaps, fear that the action will never move beyond the stage. Between Blacks and Whites the threatening promise that ritual action may become real action has seldom been so acute and so chronic. Irony holds this social contradiction in momentary suspension, exposing this clown show ceremony for what it is but threatening at any moment to transform stage play into social drama. How can it be that such an unstable enactment is such an old, old story?

11

The Ritualizing of Passage: Elie Wiesel's
Gates of the Forest

GREGOR IS NOT THE BOY'S REAL NAME; THIS IS HIS "CHRISTIAN" name. But he is not a Christian. He is a Hungarian Jew hiding from Nazis in a forest cave. The clouds are Jews too, incinerated ones. Like the forest, the clouds seem to be everywhere.

Someone is coming. His father? A captor? No, it is a stranger with a peculiar laugh—a Jew who says he has lost his name. He queries Gregor: "It was by naming things that God made them. True?"

"True," murmured Gregor.

"You admit, then, that a name has a fate of its own, independent of the life and fate of its bearer. Sometimes a name ages, falls ill, and dies much before the man who bears it. Well, my name has deserted me. Now do you understand."[264]

We are no more sure of the identity of this stranger than Gregor is. The boy decides to give his own real name to the stranger: Gavriel, "man of God." Now, who is this "other" man? Gregor's alter ego? A heavenly messenger looking for a message? A madman? The man, if that is what he is, explains that dying men take their souls but leave their names to survivors.

This nameless man, whom we will now call Gabriel, insists that Gregor remember laughter, "God's mistake."[265] Gavriel vows to be the boy's shadow, to protect him.

195

Gavriel tells a story about Moshe, whose tongue had been cut out. This mute beadle, he surmised, was a procrastinating messiah who did not know how to disobey God so the people might be saved. After telling this story, the stranger laughs. He does so in such a way that Nazi dogs find him instead of Gregor. Now the boy must wonder, "Was Gavriel the messiah? If so, why am I still alone?"

Gregor makes his way to a Rumanian village and finds that Maria, dear Maria, lives there. Not a Jew, she was once his nanny. At the sight of Gregor, she cries out, "Dear Lord Jesus, dear Mother of God, have mercy on me!"[266] How can she hide this Jewish boy in her village? Christians and Jews, like Blacks and Whites, are each other's shadows. During a holocaust where do shadows hide? Before she convinces him to pretend he's mute, he reminds her that Jesus was a Jew and that Jesus too is a cloud—because he never learned to laugh. (But Gavriel knew how to laugh, and laughter did not save him.) Where is Gavriel now? He was supposed to shadow Gregor, to protect him. Gavriel had taught the boy what Gavriel had learned from Moshe: that God is silence. Now the boy must be silent or die.

Time passes. Gregor the mute is passing as the son of Maria's sister Ileana, a whore who has fled the village. The villagers are certain his muteness is a punishment for the mother's sin. Nevertheless, they put it to good use by treating him as a safe receptacle for their secret sins. Then, as if ritualizing had not already begun, the local school teacher, who mistrusts comedy and prefers tragedy, begins to organize the village children to present a play about Jews. Following Ministry of Education orders, the teacher chooses to perform one about Judas Iscariot and the betrayal. But no one volunteers to play Judas.

Of course. Why not the son of that Ileana, the love goddess whose body could have corrupted the savior himself (as it had Mihai, a local carpenter)? By now Gregor is "custodian of their liberties."[267] Even the local priest has confessed to him.

So a passion play of sorts ensues. The schoolmaster has convinced Maria that the role of Christ requires the mute. This role is the mute's call of duty—as surely as if he were being drafted into the army. Maria feels she has no choice. The village must have its Judas, its self projected as an other, an other playing itself. We know what has to happen.

The performance gets out of hand. In the third act Judas, having been judged in the first two acts by weeping disciples, is confronted with his Christ-killing deed. The audience begins to throw things; it wants confession, repentance, blood. This mute, boy-Judas is not who they think he is. Yet he is not who they imagine either. He is more Judas than they know, less Judas than they imagine.

The drama becomes a scapegoat rite, and the fiction onstage becomes more real than the "reality" of peasant village life. Mihai shouts at the mob. Momentarily, it stops short. Then it resumes furiously. Only Gregor's voice breaks their stride. Stunned, they are certain his gust of speech is a miracle: "St. Judas, only you can forgive us." Mihai convinces the mob that Judas, not Jesus, was (and is) the true victim, and the whole crowd repeats after him, "Judas is innocent and we humbly implore his forgiveness."[268]

Moved, Gregor confesses he is Gavriel, a Jew. He is not really the son of Ileana.

His tongue must be cut out at once, screams the audience.

Petruskany, who once knew Ileana, whisks him away from death's gate.

Again in the forest, Gregor joins a band of partisans. Leib the lion, their leader, had once saved him from an anti-semitic gang in the town where they were classmates. Along with Clara, his girlfriend, and other partisans, Leib is organizing Operation Gavriel to free the stranger whom Gregor had met earlier in the cave. Gregor and Clara are sent to be certain that Gavriel is, in fact, there in prison. They are to pretend they are lovers, and they are to con the information from a guard. In three days Gregor is no longer merely pretending to be her lover. Clara continues playing her part well, but not too well; she still loves the heroic Leib.

After a long wait, word comes. The only Jew in the prison is Leib, just captured today. Now Gregor's and Leib's battles must be fought "not alone, but separated."[269] Gregor and Clara return to the partisans. They force Gregor to tell and retell the story. The repetitions exhaust him: "Listening to his own voice, he found it false. This isn't the true story; you're holding that back. The repetition of the truth betrays it. The more I talk the more I empty myself of truth."[270]

Like the Judas pageant, this recital becomes ritualized. And with the increased ritualization, comes an intensification of fictionality. And with the emergence of fictionality, the truth of the story-become-rite grows more profound. The more Gregor tries to convince the partisans that he is one of them, an extension of the group, the more they stare at him. Their eyes demand a miracle. They want Leib, their Samson, alive. Five times Gregor is forced to retell the story, but "a thousand times one still makes one."[271] The repetition deepens the guilt—his, theirs, all of those who are not victims. And so in the face of their suspicions, he offers them the confession they wish to hear: "Yes, I betrayed Leib the Lion."[272] With these words Gregor hopes to push himself to the uttermost limits of evil. By expressing such a fiction, he hopes to be freed. Suddenly he understands why, on Yom Kippur, Jews beat their breasts and accuse themselves of crimes they have never committed. They hope to exorcise evil. Perhaps the scapegoat, driven into the wilderness, will come back with the face of a hero, the nimbus of the supernatural.

Gregor begins laughing. Only Clara's intervention keeps the partisans from killing him and enables them to see that his laughter is an expression of suffering. Suddenly, they recognize that he is not a traitor, or that if he is, they all are. Storytelling, confession, and laughter have thrown a shaky bridge over the abyss between Gregor and the group. Saved, Gregor prefers solitude. He would not yet have his love for Clara known, but the companions find out anyway. And they accept it. Yehuda says to him:

> It's inhuman to wall yourself up in pain and memories as if in a prison. Suffering must open us to others. It must not cause us to reject them. The Talmud tells us that God suffers with man. Why? In order to strengthen the bonds between creation and the creator; God chooses to suffer in order better to understand man and be better understood by him. But you, you insist upon suffering alone. Such suffering shrinks you, diminishes you. Friend, that is almost cruel.[273]

Soon afterward, Yehuda is killed.

Years pass. Gregor and Clara are married, childless, and living in Brooklyn. Gregor, who is never sure whether Clara is still embracing the dead Yehuda or if they are still pretending to be lovers in the midst of the forest, is about to leave her.

He happens by a Hasidic celebration. The dancers, singing repeated phrases from the Psalms, leap vertically as if reuniting God and humanity. The presence of both God and the Hasidic community is so stifling that Gregor, who has come to say goodbye to the city, his name, friends, and job, holds back. Eyes fixed on the Rebbe, he cannot sing, drink, or pray. The Rebbe—Gregor can see it in his demeanor—will have none of Gregor's solitary self, none of this God-the-stranger. Gregor asks what is being celebrated. He is told: The death of the Zaddik, a righteous man, dead for more than a hundred and fifty years.

Gregor and the Rebbe had once argued about the Holocaust and believing in God. Gregor could not believe. A friend had sent him to the Rebbe after telling him that no one can go it alone; only for two or more is victory possible. Gregor, closed within himself, had tried without success.

There is joy as well as fury in the Hasid's dancing. Dancing is his way of proclaiming, "You don't want me to dance; too bad, I'll dance anyhow. You've taken away every reason for singing, but I shall sing. I shall sing of the deceit that walks by day and the truth that walks by night, yes, and of the silence of dusk as well. You didn't expect my joy, but here it is; yes, my joy will rise up; it will submerge you."[274] Gregor's desire to cling to his solitude wilts. He wishes only to be able to cry, but the Rebbe will not put up with this childishness: "That's not enough. I shall teach you to sing."[275] Later, singing a Hungarian army song, as if the words were of no hindrance to the soul, Gregor joins the celebrants.

Suddenly he sees a man he imagines is Gavriel. The crowd becomes a single person; the song, a single laugh. Gregor, recognizing that he has been alone and leading a false life, asks for his name back. The stranger refuses to be questioned about his identity and wrestles him down as the angel did Jacob. Who is Gregor imitating? Why is he drunk without drinking? The stranger persists with questions until Gregor has re-told the whole story of what happened after the meeting in the cave.

Perhaps Gregor is mistaken. Maybe this is not Gavriel. He looks like Gregor's father. The stranger claims not to understand the stories, saying that he listens just because he likes stories. He refuses Gregor's request to provide a demonstration laugh. On and on Gregor talks—of Leib, the dead partisan companions, his troubles with Clara.

We never learn the identity of the stranger.

Gregor's last words to him before falling asleep are about the forest, where a man is "alone with God, against God." He says, "The man that chooses solitude and its riches is on the side of those who are against man, who pay with the blood and tears of others."[276]

The morning after, a Yeshiva student finds Gregor asleep. The stranger is gone. Asked who he is, Gregor answers as usual: "Gregor." Then he corrects himself. "Gavriel," he says.

He says the Kaddish for his father, then for Leib, and, finally, for God. Then he goes home to Clara.

The Ritualizing of Passage

Gates of the Forest has had considerable impact not just in literary and Jewish circles but on the study of religion. The book appears frequently on reading lists for religious studies courses, especially those on religion and literature. This little parable, which precedes the novel, is widely referred to and quoted as a justification for making narrative a central consideration in the study of religion:

> When the great Rabbi Israel Baal Shem-Tov saw misfortune threatening the Jews it was his custom to go into a certain part of the forest to meditate. There he would light a fire, say a special prayer, and the miracle would be accomplished and the misfortune averted. Later, when his disciple, the celebrated Magid of Mezritch, had occasion, for the same reason, to intercede with heaven, he would go to the same place in the forest and say: "Master of the Universe, listen! I do not know how to light the fire, but I am still able to say the prayer." And again the miracle would be accomplished. Still later, Rabbi Moshe-Leib of Sasov, in order to save his people once more, would go into the forest and say: "I do not know the prayer, but I know the place and this must be sufficient." It was sufficient and the miracle was accomplished. Then it fell to Rabbi Israel of Rizhyn to overcome misfortune. Sitting in his armchair, his head in his hands, he spoke to God: "I am unable to light the fire and I do

not know the prayer; I cannot even find the place in the forest. All I can do is to tell the story, and this must be sufficient." And it was sufficient. God made man because he loves stories."[277]

This parable depicts a ritual solitude which foreshadows that of Gregor. This brief tale is, of course, a clue to reading the novel, but the novel is also a clue to reading the parable, which is often misread. Since the story of Gregor ends with the reclaiming of his name, saying a prayer, and going home, I read the parable's statement about the sufficiency of story in a way that differs from the conventional theological reading of it. Usually, the statement is taken to mean that story as such is sufficient. This interpretation is then used to buttress an argument that religious studies should concern itself centrally or primarily with narrative. My counter-argument is that Gregor's story does not dispense with enactment in favor of narrative. Rather it narrates a ritual act. The parable is about the domestication of ritual (as it moves from forest to armchair) and about the primacy of ritual acts (telling) over ritual places (the forest) and ritual objects (the fire). After the ritual setting and paraphernalia are stripped away, there remains the ritual act: storytelling. In the end it is not story as such, not narrative alone, but story*telling* that remains and that God loves.

This interpretation is supported by the final scene in the novel itself, which ends with the recovery of prayer, clearly a ritualistic, specifically liturgical, act. The prayer is, after all, the Kaddish. So the parable's point is not that story displaces rite, serving as its adequate replacement, but that the telling *is* the rite. As such it *preserves* the ritualizing impulse, thereby allowing for the possibility that it may once again be re-elaborated into liturgical prayer or dance and reintegrated into community.

Gates of the Forest is not a rite of passage, nor is it about one. But the novel is fraught with ritualization, and it is about passage, both literal and symbolic. In a male rite of passage initiating elders typically take boys into seclusion and, in the context of trials and deprivations, saturate them in the lore of the culture. The boys return men, themselves now potential elders. In *Gates* Gregor is largely alone, even when he is with others; he is not part of an age cohort with whom he will be bonded for life. There is no group of elders. Gregor's instruction comes at the hands of miscellaneous individuals or the partisans, a group of peers. The most obvious elder is Gavriel, but Gavriel may be Gregor himself, in which case their relationship would imply a kind of self-initiation. Gregor's going "home," is not to Europe but to the United States. Although at the end of the story we know that he has in some sense returned to Judaism and that he is on his way back home to Clara, we are unable to say how fully he will be reincorporated into either his religion or his marriage. So if we want to think of *Gates* as a rite of passage, we have to put both "rite" and "passage" in quotation marks.

Ritualization processes, unlike liturgies, often imply isolation from the collective. The parable, like the novel, struggles with the problem of solitude. But they have differing views of it. The parable is not about the loss of collective ties nor about the degeneration of congregational praise into private ritualizing, but about changes in solitary meditation, which begins in the forest and ends in the armchair. Nowhere does the parable suggest that solitude is a problem, much less a sin. Perhaps it assumes that meditation in the forest is liturgical in quality, therefore an expression of collective identity. In contrast to the parable, the novel has Gregor uttering the words, "The man that chooses solitude and its riches is on the side of those who are against man, who pay with the blood and tears of others."[278] In the wake of these words he is able to embrace his identity as Gavriel. Embracing his old name, he becomes a Jew in community with other Jews.

Whether in the village with Maria, on stage in the Judas play, in the forest with the partisans, in his marriage to Clara, or attending a Hasidic celebration, Gregor is simultaneously with others and by himself. He is alone within community. The one state does not cancel the other. Gregor's relation to his people and tradition is like his relation to God—"with" and "against" at the same time. Divine and social others are both his antagonists and the repositories of his identity. We do not have to be Durkheimians or Jungians to see the stranger Gavriel as a collective figure. Not only is he Gregor's self-as-other, he is Every Jew, particularly every nameless Jew who keeps in trust Gregor's true name until he is ready to assume it.

Name-changing or name-taking is often central to ritual passages. Gregor's two names, along with Gavriel's treatment of names as separable and as having wills and fates of their own, are two primary examples of the importance of the theme to the cosmology of *Gates of the Forest*. Gregor's two names suggest a polarity between a self that is his own and a self that is not. But which is which? The two are separate and in contest; yet they are identical. In one sense the answer to the which-is-which question is obvious. Gavriel is the real, which is to say, Jewish name, and Gregor is the imposed, therefore inauthentic, Christian name. When Gregor reclaims the name Gavriel at the end, we are hopeful: he is embracing who he is.

In another sense the answer is not so obvious. Wiesel forces us to puzzle: which is self and which, other? Can we be sure whether the stranger is Gregor's ideal self rather than, say, God or an angel? Is the stranger inside or outside of Gregor? Or, is he both? I assume that the name "Gregor" (whose name is reminiscent of that Christianizer of the calendar, Gregory the Great) is a function of non-Jews' images of Jews. Even so, is our protagonist any closer to being Gavriel than to being Gregor? Isn't Gavriel (as aspired-to self) as distant as Gregor (as socially imposed persona)?

Being between names is both an expression and a function of being homeless, between two worlds. This sort of liminality is far more dangerous than the liminality that marks the middle phase of a rite of passage, because it has no boundaries and no "safe" zones. Gregor is unable to dwell in a single, coherent social or religious system. He is a wayfarer, less by choice than by necessity. His religious nomadism makes him a stranger, a living invitation to the ritualized social drama we call scapegoating. Showing up as a stranger on some dramatic occasion such as war, systematic acts of genocide, or an Easter play becomes the occasion of a "scene," a momentous occasion fraught with danger and possibility. Like Genet's white dummy, Wiesel's mute Judas, played by Gregor, is ushered to a privileged seat only to find it earning him special hatred and envy. Strangers are potential objects of ritual activity, as easily subject to scapegoating as to veneration. Scapegoating is ritualization run wild, a ceremonious means of shipping off a cargo of profane otherness in hopes that "we" may be purified by this act of ritual exclusion. The usual way is to unload what is defined as other or profane onto a transient outsider. This possibility is what makes the solitary ritual stranger's quest so dangerous: the world of "insiders" can cast themselves as heroes and heroines in a self-righteous morality play at his expense.

This ritual stranger's most positive roles are hearing confessions and interpreting rites. By having heard confessions, he becomes dangerous, particularly insofar as he has been privy to the inner workings of sacred liturgies set in the midst of pious social dramas. He is in danger, not just as recipient of damaging gossip, but as bearer of potentially de-mystifying knowledge that could shatter the bubble of liturgical insularity, that could break the bounds erected to protect "us" from "them."

Ritual insiders, who play roles opposite those of ritual strangers, are often called by kinship terms: brother, father, mother, sister. Outsiders are those others without kin or name. Within every camp there are those who cross, legitimately or illegitimately, the boundaries. Every polarized or distanced interaction between groups generates third-parties, anomalous insider-outsiders. These become interpreters and culture-brokers; they also become traitors, Uncle Toms. The proverb, "Translation is betrayal," is felt not just in the translation of language but the translation of culture as well. Not every interpreter is a traitor, because not all forms of boundary-hopping are the same. But the interpreter or hermeneut (from *herm*, "boundary marker"), who maintains simultaneous insider and outsider status, is an ambivalent, therefore ritually evocative, personage.

Becoming a foreigner by entering another cultural domain and thus bracketing one's own values and practices (that is, by losing one's name) precipitates a high degree of self-consciousness. Self-consciousness escalates as other-consciousness does; the two states co-vary directly, not inversely. Self-consciousness and other-consciousness become acute, if not chronic. In a state of acute self-consciousness, one cannot dance, but only watch. Only watching makes one a voyeur. Gregor's watching from the sidelines leads to his being gouged by elbows that resent his spectating. It is one thing to sit reading the Torah, another to sit surrounded by dancing Hasidim. When Gregor goes to the Hasidic celebration, we do not know why. Though he has argued with the Rebbe and has practicing friends, he seems to be a non-practicing Jew. However, to recall the opening parable of the book, he manages to reach "the place" where the fire is lit in this urban forest. He tells his story, but probably would have been unable to had not the Rebbe *become* the fire with his song and dance. Gregor is not quite a stranger here, but neither is he a member of the congregation. His hanging on the periphery is emblematic of the ritual stranger's dilemma. Not interested in inventing rites or searching for them, he is nevertheless drawn. Gregor asks questions, but they make him distant. He uses reflection as protection. A Hasid tells him he should have something to drink, "Sometimes drink is better than prayer."[279] What the Hasid perceives, I suspect, is that drink, for a man like Gregor, might lead to prayer. A while later, the stranger whom he thinks is Gavriel asks him if he is drunk.

Gregor's moment arrives when the group of celebrants appears to be a single person. His acceptance of the inescapable sociality of life hinges on this ritual celebration. It does not jolt him out of aloneness into polite socializing but provides him with a visionary image of all people as one person. Participation in celebration does not necessarily demand socializing or obviate solitude so much as it requires the performance, the dance, of community. There are many ways to enact community: by drinking to it, dancing with it, sleeping in it. Enacting community may be a prelude to its actual formation, or it may be simply what is necessary for an individual to continue on his way. At the end of the story Gregor may be on his way into communal practice; he may not.

Gates of the Forest is a story containing a celebration that evokes a story that leads to the liturgical rite of the Kaddish. The narrative-enactment-narrative chain is long; the layers are many. The narrative is ritualized not only by being linked to ritual performance but by being repeated. If Gregor had been believed when he first told the story of Clara's and his search for Gavriel in prison, the outcome would have been a report. But he had to ritualize the telling. He repeated the account five times. At first the account sounded false even though it was true. Later, it became confession, ritualized truth-telling. Even though what Gregor said was really a lie, what he enacted was true. In the ritualized re-telling, Gregor recognized that he was no longer a child. Repetition of the story does what a rite of passage in tribal cultures does: it marks his entrance into manhood.

12

Reading, Writing, and Ritual: Jean-Paul Sartre's *The Words*

THE WORDS IS MORE PORTRAIT THAN STORY. BITS OF PLOT ARE EM-
bedded in it, but the book does not develop chronologically.
Most of the action in it consists of "Reading" and "Writing,"
the titles of its only two chapters. The ritual qualities of the
narrative and the metaphors used to describe the actions are
perceived by an elderly narrator who eventually finds in reading and writing, not just an alternative to, but an extension of,
the priestly domain.

> I had found my religion: nothing seemed to me more important
> than a book. I regarded the library as a temple. Grandson of a
> priest, I lived on the roof of the world, on the sixth floor,
> perched on the highest branch of the Central Tree: the trunk
> was the elevator shaft. . . . I would lend my rags to the low-
> lands, but my glorious body did not leave its perch; I think it's
> still there. Every man has his natural place; its altitude is deter-
> mined by neither pride nor value: childhood decides. Mine is a
> sixth floor in Paris with a view overlooking the roofs. . . .

> The Universe would rise in tiers at my feet and all things
> would humbly beg for a name; to name the thing was both to
> create and take it. Without this fundamental illusion I would
> never have written.[280]

Sartre's sixth floor is sixth even when he lives at the top of a ten-storey building. Like ritual space, his place is irreducible to literal geography. While correcting the manuscript for *The Words* and looking out a window at a cemetery, he is aware that, obstinately, he has not escaped the beginning of his life. Writing, he returns. And return, Eliade assures us, is the essence of ritual.

Little Jean-Paul is in church kneeling in prayer, his mother and grandmother at his side; his father is dead and his grandfather, at home. The boy pretends to be a statue, not wiggling despite a cramp. What if he were to pee in the baptismal font or yell, "Boom!" He is tempted to "act out," as the child psychologists say, to "show out," as the mothers put it. If he were to do so, this worship service would be transformed into a social drama, a scene requiring ritual redress to repair the breach of sanctified decorum. One way to discover the meaning of a rite is to violate it. But Jean-Paul does not yell or urinate, so surely he must have character. He can resist temptation: "I am bad soil for evil," he boasts quietly to himself.[281]

Jean-Paul Sartre's *The Words* is autobiography. It is at once the best illustration and most strident critique of a claim I hope to make. I want to show how inextricably related reading, writing, and ritual can be, and this boy-sized book treats them as virtually identical activities. But Old Man Sartre slaps his reader with a tough choice. Take your pick, he orders: living or telling stories. Trying to have it both ways, that is, wanting to live your life in the light of storytelling, amounts to ritualization. And ritualization, Sartre is sure, is a bourgeois neurosis, one that he himself barely escaped: "A man is always a teller of tales, he lives surrounded by his stories and the stories of others, he sees everything that happens to him through them; and he tries to live his life as if he were recounting it. But you have to choose: to live or to recount."[282]

The young Jean-Paul, who has the cramps at mass, is five. The elderly Sartre, who begins writing an account of his childhood in 1954, will die in a few years. Such retrospective distance makes the book, in the author's view, fictive. At five, the boy is busy "making himself up."[283] The old man, as author, continues to create himself by writing. Fictionalizing is the glue that cements the world of the old man to that of the boy.

The young Jean-Paul's grandfather is lordly. His child, Jean-Paul's mother, has returned home a widow. Grandfather Charles likes to pronounce oracles; he finds prophecies in children's words. He has read Victor Hugo's classic *The Art of Being a Grandfather*, and his yellowish-white beard entitles him to strike portrait-like poses in the attitude of God the father. So the grandson, instead of sneaking away to play games, plays at being good. The boy is a precious little angel; he does not leave this role to girls. His early years (1905-1914) leave a "funereal" taste in his mouth:[284] he is the child of a dead father and the grandchild of Charles Schweitzer, who is already, as they say, making his way back to nature.

Reading as Ritual

Of medieval monks who spent hours illuminating the first letter in a manuscript of the Gospel of Luke we would have little doubt that their act of writing was ritualized. And when societies of Moroccan Jews in modern Israel recite the *Zohar* aloud without knowing its meaning, we do not need convincing that their reading is a ritualistic action. There is little question that in some contexts reading and writing are, in fact, rites. Like speaking, eating, and other more universal human activities, reading and writing can be embedded in activities that most people would regard as ritualistic. But can autobiography writing ever be ritual?

The Words is rife with the rhetoric of ritual, applying it repeatedly to the acts of reading and writing. In ordinary usage we associate rhetoric with inflated, or empty, language. As with "ritual," so "rhetoric" can be heard as suggesting whatever is mindless or rote—the mere shell of something else. In scholarly usage, however, the terms are more descriptive, sometimes even positive; they are more suggestive of cultural richness. "Rhetoric" refers to the dynamics of performer/audience or author/reader interaction, and "ritual" connotes valued, stylized interaction.

After reading Sartre, one is forced to ask whether his rhetoric of ritual is of the empty sort. The answer is, not quite—at least, not in the ordinary sense of the term. For him the rhetoric of ritual that so pervades *The Words* is useful precisely because of its suggestion of emptiness.[285] Sartre's rhetoric, though it at first seems to empty "ritual" and associated terms of meaning, does so in order to turn his story into a gesture. Just as Sartre's antitheism depends on the gods, and is, strictly speaking, not atheism, so his antiritualism leads him to depend on the very emptiness that ritual provides. He employs the rhetoric of ritual to evoke simultaneously the sacred and the banal.

Jean-Paul's early life is a ceremony—he says so—and books are his most sacred objects. When his grandfather handles them, he is an "officiant."[286] When his grandmother reads, he is filled with a "holy stillness"; he thinks of the Mass, death, and sleep. He describes a scene with his mother:

> While she spoke, we were alone and clandestine, far from men, gods, and priests, two does in a wood, with those other does, the Fairies. I simply could not believe that someone had composed a whole book to tell about that episode of our profane life, which smelled of soap and eau de Cologne.

> Anne Marie [his mother] sat me down opposite her, on my little chair. She bent forward, lowered her eyelids, fell asleep. From that statue-like face came a plaster voice. I was bewildered: who was telling what and to whom? My mother had gone off: not a smile, not a sign of complicity, I was in exile. And besides, I didn't recognize her speech. Where had she got that assurance? A moment later, I realized: it was the book that was speaking. Frightening sentences emerged from it: they were real centipedes, they swarmed with syllables and letters, stretched their diphthongs, made the double consonants vibrate. . . . As for the story, it had got dressed up: the woodcutter, his wife and their daughters, the fairies, all these little people, our fellow creatures had taken on majesty. Their rags were spoken of with magnificence; the words colored the things, transforming actions into rites and events into ceremonies.[287]

Jean-Paul does not like improvised stories, the told kind. He would be unhappy with my retelling of what he so carefully etched in a book. He prefers the eternally recurrent, read stories—the ones in which every word, every name, returns in the same impeccable, liturgical order. He illustrates Roy Rappaport's attempt to make invariance definitive of ritual.[288]

From now on discourse will be ceremonious for Jean-Paul.

He will find Reality in books, and for the next thirty years reality outside them will be only a dim reflection of what can be found "on the right page." Life outside books is banal; wildness and adventure dwell inside them. They are sacred objects, and more: they construct sacred space and time; they generate a cosmos.

David Winnicott would likely refer to Jean-Paul's books as "transition objects." Such objects, which are neither identical with ourselves nor fully detached from us, are essential for ritualized regression to an undivided state. Jean-Paul's books are not so obviously linked to mothers as Linus blankets or pacifiers are, but they do transport him to a liminal zone "betwixt and between" self and other. Interaction with transition objects happens this way:

(1) An infant assumes rights over an object, and its parents agree to this assumption, even though they abrogate the child's omnipotence regarding it.

(2) The object is affectionately cuddled, excitedly loved, and regularly mutilated.

(3) The object must never change, unless changed by the infant.

(4) The object must survive instinctual loving, hating, and aggression.[289]

Is Jean-Paul's fetishization of the book neurotic? Winnicott thinks one can decide by weighing the results of being attached to a transition object. Sartre will remain attached for some time, and as an adult he will express contempt for this neurosis. Eventually, he will believe he has outgrown the need for the ritualization of reading and storytelling. He will become, by Winnicott's standards, healthy:

> Its [the transition object's] fate is to be gradually allowed to be decathected, so that in the course of years it becomes not so much forgotten as relegated to limbo. . . . In health the transitional object does not "go inside" nor does the feeling about it necessarily undergo repression. It loses meaning, and this is because transitional phenomena have become diffused, have become spread out over the whole intermediate territory between "inner psychic reality" and "the external world as perceived by two persons in common," that is to say over the whole cultural field.[290]

Jean-Paul is always ascending. Ascension is a habit that he tries to cure by weighting himself so he will sink. He draws books to himself; maybe they will ground him. No such luck: good boys live above the rooftops of the world. Realistic hope of keeping their feet on the ground is scant. Ritual directions, upward, for instance, are our cardinal directions. They draw us. We do not make them up on the spot or deliberate over and choose them. Rather, we find them choosing us. Sartre chooses to descend, but ascent chooses him. The regions below will remain mythic for the rest of his life. So he will make friends of criminals and write a mythic biography, a hagiography, of a French thief.

As with space, so with age and time. Jean-Paul is not what he aspires to be. He is always old, making grown-up remarks, reading the end of *Madame Bovary* twenty times, and already, at a very young age, finding the human heart shallow when compared with what he reads in books. At nine years old the boy is planning to live his life on the basis of this novel. Souls, he imagines, are pressed between pages, looking out at the reader.[291]

This is the stuff of grandfather religion, not the girlfriend religion of Dom Casmurro or the fiance spirituality of Kierkegaard, on whose lives and ritualizing we will soon ruminate. The grandfather is lord, and the child becomes for the grandfather a living book of magic. The elder prefers reading young boys because printed books are dead for him. So the child must perform. His character is formed by his becoming a character. He lives as if in a book; morality and fiction are wed in him. "Even in solitude I was putting on an act," he recollects.[292]

Among mystics "recollection" is not merely a synonym for "remembering." To recollect is to re-call oneself—ascetically and stringently to gather oneself together. Sartre is no mystic; he has too much fear of being swallowed up by otherness for that. Yet his act of recollecting in this little autobiography has something monkish about it. He is not simply replicating his life as a child, he is purging it, judging it, trying to burn it off. As I read *The Words*, I cannot help imagining an immolation or sacrifice: Old Man Sartre grabs Young Boy Sartre by the nape of the neck and drags him to Abraham's altar.

Anna Marie buys books for her son, hoping they will give him back his childhood, which he is giving up before he has lived it. When Jean-Paul's mother is discovered giving cheap adventure stories to her son, Grandfather Charles, an educator, at first loses his temper, then regretfully tolerates the stories, but finally counters by enrolling the boy in the lyceé. For our boy-priest-hero, school is supposed to function as a rite of seclusion to cure him of base appetites.

Children hide from their elders to avoid having to dramatize their goodness. The hide so they can repeat what counts rather than what is expected. Public performance demands the semblance of bread, but the sequestered ritual allows for the substitution of chocolate. Drama demands ritual. Ritual demands drama. Jean-Paul finds the one when he finds the other. He observes his elders' ceremonious use of the book and their perpetual role-playing. In this way he not only learns to read but he discovers drama. He wants to become a hero for the same reason most of us do; he has no scene of his own.[293] Family ceremoniousness has taught him that everything has a place and reason, but he has not yet found his reason or his place. He is abstract, without soul; he is superfluous. He resorts to ritual because it proceeds by necessity.

Jonathan Z. Smith defines ritual in a way that makes clear this necessity and its accompanying "perfection":

> I would suggest that among other things, ritual represents the creation of a controlled environment where the variables (that is, the accidents) of ordinary life have been displaced precisely because they are felt to be so overwhelmingly present and powerful. Ritual is a means of performing the way things ought to be in conscious tension to the way things are in such a way that this ritualized perfection is recollected in the ordinary, uncontrolled, course of things.[294]

Jean-Paul has no such necessity; his rite is far from perfect. He is a bourgeois child in a state of inaction, a dog gracing the family hearth. He could die and no one would sense his absence. No place, once filled by him, would seem empty if he were dead. "I had an appointment with death every night in bed. This was a rite," he confesses.[295]

The fictionality of "interaction ritual" is learned early and applied to liturgy.[296] Jean-Paul is raised a Catholic by women who attend Mass to hear good music, who believe only as a matter of discretion. Jean-Paul is a Catholic in order to be normal, like his mother and grandmother. Like his nominally Lutheran grandfather, who fled to become a circus rider rather than become the minister his father intended, the child becomes both "priest" and "performer"—in quotation marks. The performance is inside his own head, where he is a hero. Outside is the ceremony.

Sartre recalls:

> I had been playing with matches and burned a small rug. I was in the process of covering up my crime when suddenly God saw me. I felt His gaze inside my head and on my hands. I whirled about in the bathroom, horribly visible, a live target. Indignation saved me. I flew into a rage against so crude an indiscretion, I blasphemed, I muttered like my grandfather: "God damn it, God damn it, God damn it." He never looked at me again.

> I have just related the story of a missed vocation: I needed God, he was given to me, I received him without realizing that I was seeking Him. Failing to take root in my heart, He vegetated in me for a while, then he died. Whenever anyone speaks to me about Him today, I say with the easy amusement of an old beau who meets a former belle: "Fifty years ago, had it not been for that misunderstanding, that mistake, the accident that separated us, there might have been something between us."[297]

The loss of faith, whether of the living or of the merely convenient sort, does not bring with it the loss of ritual. It may, in fact, intensify one's need of it. Now Jean-Paul has to play at ritual and overplay the family drama. He withdraws into himself as he continues to play hero: "Someone's missing here. It's Sartre."[298] A champion, he arrives atop a flaming roof, carrying an unconscious woman. And as always, the drama will be finished in the next installment. The child is a future hero, lest a climax precipitate melancholic depression. God for him is all but dead, but magic is still alive—in the cinema. In the movie theater is a ceremony more compatible with the ritualized internalization of drama:

> The social hierarchy of the theatre had given my grandfather and late father, who were accustomed to second balconies, a taste for ceremonial. When many people are together, they

must be separated by rites; otherwise, they slaughter each other. The movies provided the opposite. This mingled audience seemed united by a catastrophe rather than a festivity. Etiquette, now dead, revealed the true bond among men: adhesion. I developed a dislike for ceremonies, I loved crowds. I have seen crowds of all kinds, but the only other time I have witnessed that nakedness, that sense of everyone's direct relationship to everyone else, that waking dream, that dim consciousness of the danger of being a man, was in 1940, in Stalag XII D.[299]

In the movies Jean-Paul finds an absolute world, one in which the last musical chord and the climactic gesture can be made to coincide. The Catholic liturgy is not so well timed; in it one still senses the superfluous despite the order. In the cinema, on the other hand, ritual and drama remain synchronous, complementary. But the ending—how does one stand the world after such transport and possession? In the movies one knows for sure; there is destiny, necessity. Heroes are made. But outside, on the sidewalk, we know we have made it all up from a string of disconnected events.

Readers less enamored of ritual than Jean-Paul will insist that cinema is cinema and ritual, ritual. Perhaps film is film and acting art, but going to the movies, always on Saturday, always sitting on the right side just below the half way mark, is ritualized behavior. Who can say that the heroes of Saturday and the saints of Sunday do not share some secret berth?[300]

In adolescence the Sartre boy can neither convincingly invent himself nor locate the mission for which he is specially chosen. He is just a short kid, not quite at home in his body, ill at ease among children. The drama in his head both condemns and saves him. It condemns him always "to be continued." It saves him from urinating in the baptistry. The result is social pantomime—actions that do not speak and stories that are not incipient acts but only substitutes for actions.

Writing and Ritual

Between the ages of eight and ten Jean-Paul begins to write novels to replace the movies. Now he can be both author and hero. Even though he leaves them unfinished, as he does his fantasies, he begins to find himself. The self who is beginning to separate from adults is the self who can write. Writing becomes for him a clandestine ritualizing. A male child cannot initiate himself; he needs elders, and the elders need him to need them. So they become supportive and declare to the boy, "He will be a writer." But can one live by the pen? No, he says to himself, he should be a teacher-writer like his grandfather. Then Jean-Paul can write without having to live the life of a writer.

Abruptly, initiation leads to disenchantment. One minute writing is sacred; the next it is not. The moment Jean-Paul discovers his gift, his grandfather's clerklike view of writing begins to corrode the discovery. Is this all there is, asks Jean-Paul of himself—a few essays, an exactly described armchair? His confirmation becomes a form of containment, and the grandfather's supervision threatens to make the writer more clerk than creator. Already the newly initiated self is beginning to be lost. The child who charged into his calling a hero is in a few weeks merely resigned. This is his calling: to write labored, rather than gifted, works. He loses innocence in the very moment of the revelation of his calling. When he discovers himself, in the same instant he bumps against its limits and others' investments in him. He falls into writing; it is just another way to be a good boy.

The socialization of Jean-Paul's pen is an initiation, though no one calls it that or designs it deliberately. Van Gennep's three stages—separation, transition, incorporation—are collapsed into a single, triple-layered event. And there is no brotherhood of initiates to share the hazing that foreshadows the more serious fall. Punishment can break the skin, but disenchantment breaks more. At fifty Sartre will still be trying to satisfy a long dead grandfather by writing books the old man would have repudiated. One can acquire a shade or tutelary spirit whether or not formal rites of passage are undergone.

What saves Jean-Paul is a meta-fiction, a fiction about fiction. He dreams:

> I was in Luxembourg, near the pond, facing the Senate Building. I had to protect a blonde little girl from an unknown danger; she resembled Veve, who had died a year earlier. The girl looked up at me calmly and confidently with her serious eyes.

Often she was holding a hoop. It was I who was frightened: I was afraid of abandoning her to invisible forces. But how I loved her, with how mournful a love! I still love her. I have looked for her, lost her, found her again, held her in my arms, lost her again: she is the Epic.[301]

The boy makes a subtle shift and thereby stages his resistance, weak though it may be. He makes the author, not the main character, the hero. He will grow up to be a writer-as-knight, not a literary clerk or heroic character. The fall becomes a fortunate fall, a predestined event. He has created a fictive (not fictional) character, the writer-knight, who will resist the fate of becoming a writer-clerk. He has turned a foreshortened rite of passage into a lifelong quest: "I confused literature with prayer, I made a human sacrifice of it. . . . The soldier quietly gave way to the priest. . . . I decided to write for God with the purpose of saving my neighbors. I wanted gratitude and not readers."[302]

The ritualization turns in on itself, as private rites sometimes do. The neighbors, for whom one might write, are easily reduced to oneself. Jean-Paul writes in order to write. This formalism is a meta-rite. He does not write about, to, or for anything beyond the act itself. Jean-Paul writes because he is chosen—by what he later calls a "holy ghost," which is to say, for no particular reason. If one writes for a reason, he will be no better than a clerk. Sartre "martyrs" words—he says so. He stretches and squeezes them, but does not do so for anyone in particular. This is what it means to write at the call of the holy ghost, this compelling vacuum.

When Jean-Paul discovers playmates who need him to receive their tossed ball, he, for a time, gives up play-acting. Likewise, he is able to forget about literature for a while when the war conflates his sense of fiction and reality and heroism becomes commonplace. What is a child to do when adults claim heroism as their own possession? He and his mother, whom he now experiences as his own age, become confidants and maintain a "sweet friendship."[303] Chatter, like playing ball and war, momentarily replaces writing. This is an interlude. No longer trying either to create characters or be an author-as-knight, his own character development becomes his mandate. For an moment he lives in his bones, not his stories; in a

group, not on the sixth floor. He is a boy, not a little man skip-
ping over decades and bent on immortalizing himself in
words. No longer seeing himself, he simply carries through
and is happy.

But soon he is back at it again. In writing, Sartre becomes
other. But in becoming wholly other, he is among the dead.
He becomes an object both to himself and others. He tries to
beat death by evacuating himself into volumes of print. So
when "that day" arrives, "Death would be taking only a
dead man."[304]

Sartre's life, as he authors it, takes religion as a model but
carries atheism to its conclusion. At twelve, in 1917, the Almighty "tumbled into the blue and disappeared without explanation."[305] Nevertheless, the holy ghost continues to hand
him anonymous literary mandates. Sartre is a "believer" but
only in the sense that he believes names are the things they
name. He believes in the magic of language, though his belief
in it is ironic, subjunctive, fictive. He is among the elect, in the
company of masters of the word who doubt the very words
they create.

Sartre says he throws himself without reservation into writing,[306] but eventually he evacuates every structure he builds.
Even writing, though he never gives it up, is emptied. So in
retrospect he sees everything, including his autobiography, as
waiting on a final validation that never comes. With hindsight
his every action, at least until he is beyond thirty, is considered fake "to the marrow of [his] bones."[307] This is the case not
because he is insincere but because what he creates in one moment he destroys in the next. When he publishes his autobiography in French in 1963, he claims to have cast out even the
holy ghost. Once again he feels like a boy without a ticket on a
train. But the habit is the habit; the rite of writing goes on, authorized or not. No longer does worship consist of going to
church or being a man of letters. Nevertheless, Sartre writes
on, uncured of himself.

Reading and Writing as Funerary Gestures

The Words can be read as story or as philosophy. It must also
be understood as a gesture, one of the fundamental units of

analysis in ritual studies. At ten Jean-Paul, virtually alone among adults, lets his actions become gestures;[308] for Sartre "gesture" always means "gestural lie." The boy is just barely aware that acting is a possibility. Until now he has done it without awareness. Now actions begin to degenerate into gestures in anticipation of their reception by judging audiences.

If Sartre's writing is not, strictly speaking, a rite, it is ritualized. More specifically, it is funerary. Sartre's life, at least as he tells it in *The Words*, reeks with a mortuary odor, especially when he tells how he becomes a mere symbol for his own work. Around 1955 he finds himself on a shelf of the National Library:

> I, twenty-five volumes, eighteen thousand pages of text, three hundred engravings, including a portrait of the author. My bones are made of leather and cardboard, my parchment-skinned flesh smells of glue and mushrooms, I sit in state through a hundred thirty pounds of paper, thoroughly at ease. I am reborn, I at last become a whole man, thinking, talking, singing, thundering, a man who asserts himself with the peremptory inertia of matter. Hands take me down, open me, spread me flat on the table, smooth me and sometimes make me creak. I let them, and then suddenly I flash, I dazzle, I command attention from a distance, my powers shoot through time and space, they blast the wicked, protect the good. No one can forget or ignore me: I am a great fetish, tractable and terrible. My mind is in bits and pieces. All the better. Other minds take me over. People read me, I leap to the eye; they talk to me. I'm in everyone's mouth, a universal and individual language; I become a prospective curiosity in millions of gazes; to him who can love me, I step aside and disappear: I exist nowhere, at last I am, I'm everywhere. I'm a parasite on mankind, my blessings eat into it and force it to keep reviving my absence.[309]

Writing is a rite of making oneself into a medicine bundle that speaks. No one is there inside a book; nevertheless, pages speak. Some would experience this fetishization as a virtue; they might hope to write oracular books that speak with authority and not as the scribes. . . . But for Sartre this process is a reduction of action to gesture. Sartre does not like gestures: "Acts themselves," he tells us, "cannot serve as a measuring-rod unless one has proved they are not gestures, which is not always easy."[310] For him an action is guilty of being a gesture until proven otherwise. For him "gesture" connotes "only" an "empty" action. Such a gesture is decadent, done emptily because some social scenario demands it.

"Rhetoric," "storytelling," and "fiction" can be empty in the same way. They can easily be made to suggest "lie" or "inauthenticity." But a gesture can have full, as well as empty, versions. A gesture can be a reservoir, always in the process of filling up or being emptied, but Sartre, it seems, notices only the emptying. A gesture can function as a way of waiting, a way of preparing for the eruption of renewing energy that fills. A gesture is not by definition an empty action, one devoid of commitment and motivated only by compliance. The view that the older Sartre perpetuates is not the only possible one. For instance, Antonin Artaud, his fellow countryman, exclaims:

> I am adding another language to the spoken language, and I am trying to restore to the language of speech its old magic, its essential spellbinding power, for its mysterious possibilities have been forgotten. When I say I will perform no written play, I mean that I will perform no play based on writing and speech, that in the spectacles I produce there will be a preponderant physical share which could not be captured and written down in the customary language of words, and that even the spoken and written portions will be spoken and written in a new sense.[311]

> The grammar of this new language is still to be found. Gesture is its material and its wits; and, if you will, its alpha and omega. It springs from the NECESSITY of speech more than from speech already formed. But finding an impasse in speech, it returns spontaneously to gesture.[312]

> It is certain that this aspect of pure theater, this physics of absolute gesture which is the idea itself and which transforms the mind's conceptions into events perceptible through the labyrinths and fibrous interlacings of matter, gives us a new idea of what belongs by nature to the domain of forms and manifested matter.[313]

Now we have two choices: gesture as decadent compliance or as ecstatic embodiment. Jean-Paul is cursed with the former and cannot attain the latter. His alternative is to privatize many of his actions and later to "crucify" [my term] or "martyr" [his term] them. Thereby he can dramatize his rituals (thereby making them interesting) and ritualize his dramas (thereby making them important).

The choice between the two views of gesture precipitates some hard questions: Is letting action lapse into empty gesture the occasion on which we devise dramas to cover our rituals? Without an audience, are our actions more likely to return to the source of their nourishment? Do not all rituals become dramatized and emptied as soon as they become collective and overseen by elders? Is authentic ritualizing only possible in solitude, in seclusion from the mothers and grandfathers? If an author is not a knight-on-quest or priest of literature, how does he or she prove an action is not a gesture?

Sartre repudiates early versions of himself as he flees forward. He admires those who are tenacious of their memories and mementos, particularly women, but he himself is lucid, reflexive, forward-looking. He slays the dragon of his past. In this way he can always be newborn. He is unfaithful to his own emotions.[314] He knows he repeats himself but ignores the fact. The result is that he experiences himself as a fictional character,[315] constantly being made up as he goes along. In not being faithful to either the past or his emotions, he regresses; he claims he lacks substance.

I do not believe Sartre is quite the faker he claims. He does not convince me that his every act is a vacuous gesture. It is his returning, his repetitions, his ruts and rites, that convince me. He returns. So if he is a faker, he is a consistent one. And a consistent faker is better understood as a highly reflexive actor than as a liar. What does Sartre mean by claiming that he gestures or that he is unfaithful to his emotions? Why does he think he must deny them validity shortly after feeling them? In order to go forward?

I suspect that Sartre's gestures, the primary one being his writing, are permeated by the intentions and dynamics of a ritual sacrifice. He sacrifices himself to his reader. He exposes the child Jean-Paul. The act is a gesture in the empty sense because it is a smokescreen, a mask. It attracts our attention and keeps us from seeing that the mature Sartre has not transcended little Jean-Paul. But if we see this repeated, as we do in the story, we begin to see through it. And then we discover that, for Sartre, seeing through is a gesture—now, not in the sense of an empty deed, but in the sense of an ultimate deed. Sartre says he will continue writing without feeling the need to justify it. A gesture becomes a ritual practice if it so compels ritualists that they have no choice but to repeat it, even when they would like to flee it. Such are the actions liturgies are made of.

Sartre's view of his childhood commits an error he criticizes in others, "the error of perspective" or "retrospective illusion." The elder Sartre makes young Jean-Paul a grave-digger. I wonder, if, by loathing his childhood, the senior Sartre is not burying Jean-Paul, the boy. Is he not conducting a funeral in the telling of this story? The child sees with future eyes; the fifty-year old, with retrospective ones.

Sartre the autobiographer is a man engaged in carving his own monument.[316] And monuments are ritual objects. Author Sartre asks, "Does anyone think that children don't choose their poisons themselves? I swallowed mine with the anxious austerity of a drug-addict."[317] He reads his own early life through his late life. The poison is the poison of storytelling and ritualizing. But the author cannot help inventing when he writes about himself as a child-writer. He cannot avoid the error he has identified—that of starting at the end and writing everything else so it arrives at the very point where he presently stands. This is how God is supposed to see things.

Sartre the autobiographer wears a divine mask—he can gaze across the whole landscape of his life. As we once imagined God watching our every action, Jean-Paul the young author, envisions future generations reading him in the way he watches movies. He will have weight, necessity, destiny, because someone will have need of him. However, the fifty-year old will judge the young man a fake. Sartre knows that Jean-Paul writes, hoping always to find himself on the other side of a page. On this side is fiction. But the other side. . . . Ah, to reach it. Things will be factual over there, won't they?

The Words is an example of counter-ritualization in which the rhetoric of ritual, instead of leading to its enactment, leads to its repeated deferral, or more accurately, to its cancellation as an overt, embodied act and its reinstatement as a decaying, verbal one. As a gesture it is a funeral oration by an old man for a young boy. As a religious artifact it is a small gravestone. The book haunts my sense of ritual in a way that neither liturgies nor theories of ritual do. After dwelling within and walking around Sartre's slim little life of himself, I cannot walk past either baptisteries in churches or large leather bound volumes in libraries without feeling that I ought to tiptoe, without being tempted to snicker as I once did on the back pews.

13

Sweet Masses and Ceremonial Promises: Machado de Assis' *Dom Casmurro*

THE NARRATOR OF MACHADO DE ASSIS' *DOM CASMURRO* HAS SEV-eral names. Though born and baptized Bento Santiago, he is nicknamed Dom Casmurro in Portuguese. In English we would call him Lord Curmudgeon—but only behind his back. Our narrator received his pejorative title from a neighborhood acquaintance, a young man who insisted on reading him poetry as they rode the Brazil Central to the suburbs. Sr. Santiago became drowsy and let his eyes flutter shut two or three times. The next day the offended young poet began berating him with the nickname which is the title of Machado de Assis's novel. Helen Caldwell, translator of the story, tells us that "Dom" suggests aristocracy and divinity.[318] In Brazil a member of the higher nobility or higher clergy could have borne such a title. A casmurro, the narrator tells us, is "a morose, tight-lipped man withdrawn into himself." Now at fifty, he recollects the days when his mother insisted on addressing him by the diminutive, Bentinho.

The Sweet Mass

Furtively, Bentinho and his fourteen-year old sweetheart are having fun. His mother would not approve of playing at such things. José Dias, the family servant, has already intimated to Dona Gloria that her son and Capitú are snuggling in the corners.

Shouldn't Bentinho be sent off to seminary? He's fifteen already; the clergy is still important in Brazil. And a promise is a promise, the servant reminds her.

Dona Gloria had begun her "ecclesiastic projects" in 1842 when Bentinho was conceived. Her first child having been stillborn, she had made a pact to give God a priest if she were allowed to bear a living male. Now she has one, but he is hiding and playing, though not quite what the servant suspects he is playing. Rather, Casmurro tells us,

> I was being accustomed to the idea of the Church: children's toys, devout books, images of saints, conversations at home, everything converged on the altar. When we went to Mass, she [his mother] would always tell me it was to learn to be a priest and that I should watch the padre, that I should not take my eyes off the padre. At home, I played Mass—somewhat on the sly, because my mother said that Mass was not a matter for play. We would arrange an altar, Capitú and I. She acted as sacristan and we altered the ritual in the sense that we divided the host between us; the host was always a sweet. During the time that we used to play this game, it was quite common to hear my little neighbor ask: "Mass today?" I recognized what that meant, answered in the affirmative, and went to ask for the host under another name. I would come back with it, we would arrange the altar, mumble the Latin and rush through the ceremonies. Dominus non sum. . . . I was supposed to say that three times but I believe that I actually said it but once, such was the gluttony of the padre and his sacristan. We drank neither wine nor water: we did not have the first and the second would have taken away the savor of the sacrifice.[319]

I read this and I remember playing preacher. And Tarzan. And cowboy. My female friends tell me they played nun and Jane. And cowboy. I catch myself longing to celebrate a sweet Mass as if I had grown up Catholic rather than Methodist. But this is Bentinho's story; I must not read myself into it. Do I have a choice? I picked up Machado de Assis's book to be a reader, not a character. But the narrator is as subtle as a serpent, and I am gullible. The narrator tempts his readers to play fiction with him. I like to play, but sometimes I like to step out of bounds to ask my own questions: If Mass is not a matter for play what is it for? Why do we have to make up ceremonies on the sly? Why do practitioners and theorists insist that we cannot invent them? Is the played mass of Bentinho and Capitú any less serious than *the* Mass in all its solemnity? How does their playful rite differ from the "real" ones priests perform? What constitutes the reality of ritualizing and of liturgy?

The narrator lures me to ask my questions in, rather than of, his story. Whereas Sartre wanted to convince readers of the emptiness of rites, gestures, and stories, Casmurro assures us, "This book is the absolute truth."[320] No priest has promised more. And I have the author's word—in writing. I agree to play fiction with the narrator, but I do not promise to refrain from arguing about the rules.

"Fictive"—the word is from the past participle of the Latin *fingere*, "to touch," "to mold," "to make." Sometimes I imagine that child's play is to adult life what a novel is to everyday life. Both are fictions of sorts. In childhood, play is just play, but childhood recollected during adulthood is fictive. Something is fictive if it is made-up in such a way that it re-makes us.

In childhood there are two hosts—the disappointing Sunday one that tastes like fish food, and the sweet Saturday one that we share in secret with real or imagined sweethearts. It is not true that we pass from innocence to experience. We pass from innocence-in-experience to innocence vs. experience. We are lucky if we have a third alternative.

Bentinho is a teen-ager; he knows the sweet Mass is not real. He also knows that the not-real is quite real. What neither Bentinho nor his mother knows is how thoroughly her projects and his play are entwined. Is he just playing? Or is he, as the psychologists say, "acting out?" If he is acting out, his fictive activities are not unreal; they are meta-real, reality-forming. They are commentaries on a reality that surrounds him.

Bentinho is acting out the fears and promises of his mother. By doing so ritually, however, he is unwittingly subverting them and unconsciously foreshadowing what is to come. The present sweetness of play will lead to future bitterness.

Casmurro does not say they used chocolate, but I insist on it. I have an imagination too. What other sweet has comparable sacramental qualities for teenagers? My substitution is little enough interpretive license even if Brazilian kids in 1900 had in fact other cravings. Not only does Bentinho use chocolate instead of bread, he makes other substitutions that church folk would excuse with great difficulty, and then only for pre-adolescents:

> I, future padre, thus stood before her as before an altar, and one side of her face was the Epistle and the other the Gospel. Her mouth the chalice, her lips the paten. It only remained to say the new Mass, in a Latin that no one learns, and that is the catholic language of men. Do not hold me sacrilegious, my devout reader; purity of intention washes away whatever may be slightly uncurial in my style. We stood there with heaven in us. Our hands united our nerves, and made of two creatures one—and that one a seraph. Our eyes continued to say infinite things, only the words in our mouths did not attempt to pass our lips; they returned to the heart, silently as they had come. . . .[321]

Freud considers religion a collective version of the personal neurosis he labels "obsessive compulsion."[322] After him there has been a tendency among therapists and theologians alike to condemn personal rites as neurotic and private ones as magical. This view misses a crucial point best made by Daniel O'Keefe. "Magic," he says, "helped develop the institution of the individual."[323] We do well to consider the possibility that private and personal rites have the capacity to soften or dissolve collective obsessions and compulsions.

A Protestant-minded reader might call Bentinho's actions idolatrous, because Capitú has been elevated from celebrant's accomplice to object of veneration. A more Catholic reader might graciously allow that these are children, Brazilians, and characters in fiction. Besides, Casmurro insists on the purity of his intentions: they were only speaking "the catholic language of men," the language in which gesture exceeds word. However, if all we can do is excuse or condemn this behavior, we misunderstand it. This daring superimposition of adolescent mooning on liturgical imagery makes the Mass momentarily new and sacralizes the romance. Bentinho's perception seams together what is rent apart in his experience, religion and romance. All rituals, I believe, are fictive attempts to act out the dualisms in our psyches and cultures. In rites we have our sweets and eat them too.

Bentinho and Capitú are not doing in the corners what Dona Gloria and José Dias think—at least not until Bentinho overhears the servant speculate and recommend seminary as the cure. Then, of course, they do. They plot and plan and vow to keep Bentinho from becoming a priest. In the midst of the scheming, Bentinho embarks on manhood; he undergoes the rite of the first kiss. The boy's oscular reminiscences exceed his liturgical ones:

> Of all my memories of the time, I believe that this one is the sweetest, the most fresh, the most all-embracing—the one that entirely revealed me to myself. I have others, vast and numerous, sweet also, of various sorts, some intellectual, likewise intense, when I had become a grown man too, but the mark they left was less.[324]

"I am a man!" he declares, and his initiation is begun. Playing Mass and the first kiss are cornerstones, secret ritualizings, that will be more foundational than the authorized liturgies. Only Jung's childhood ritualizing compares with them.[325] Whatever José Dias says is only the bones of truth. Truth itself now resides in flesh and blood. Capitú's eyes, which are like the tide, have begun to drag Bentinho into himself. Although his "ideas are without legs,"[326] he assures us he is no longer imitating anyone.

The predictability of adolescent love is probably no greater than that of mature love. Perhaps it seems so ritualized because we recall it with longing and assure our children, "It's only a phase; you'll outgrow it." Bentinho's first love is different. Everybody's is. The rite of first kissing is unrepeatable, and every person suffers it as if it were unique. The event is absolutely unique, also absolutely common. The burden of the Mass is that it must be done over and over. The pain of the first kiss is that it can never be done again. The Mass is a rite of sustenance; the kiss, of initiation. Even if adolescents can conflate sustenance and initiation, adult males rarely do. Except fictively.

We aspire to perform our rites of sustenance as if for the first time, but to our chagrin, we cannot forget the previous times. So we are bored or loathe the repetition. We aspire to make our rites of initiation durative—as if first kisses, or first anything, could really last so long. The loss of ritual innocence (or is it "the ritual losing of innocence"?) begins the moment we perform an action, remember it, and then enact another for the sake of avoiding or repeating the original one.

Bentinho tries to kiss Capitú a second time and quickly discovers that "gesture requires an accord of wills."[327] She resists. Locked in struggle, their mouths jerk. And he misses. The search for primal deeds, as well as the effort to sustain them, will, in the end, cost us our naivete and instruct us in the laws of religious and interpersonal entropy.

The Opera and the Lottery

Dom Casmurro, unlike Sartre's *The Words*, is not shot through with rites and ritual motifs. Casmurro's is not a ceremonially constructed cosmos, nor is his life in the town of Matacavallos a never-ending Lent as it is in, say, Juan Rulfo's *Pedro Paramo*, nor is it a conflation of magic and celebration as in Jorge Amado's *Tent of Miracles*. Bentinho's cosmology is split between two dominant metaphors, neither of them ecclesiastical: the opera and the lottery.

Marcolini, an old Italian tenor full of chianti, tells Bentinho before he goes to seminary: "Life is an opera and a grand opera. The tenor and the baritone fight for the soprano in the presence of the basso. . . . God is the poet. The music is by Satan, a young maestro with a great future. . . . The whole thing would have ended," he says "if God had not written a libretto for an opera, and thrown it aside, because he considered that type of amusement unsuited to eternity. Satan carried off the manuscript to hell."[328]

If God is too grown up for operatic amusements (though he is a poet) and Satan carries off to the corners of hell what the Father throws away, who is running the show in which our Bentinho is the main character? Is his fate going to be the result of God's plot or the devil's ambitious editing? Not only is there dramatic tension in the opera of this life, there is dramatic uncertainty in the very question of author- and directorship.

Bentinho often resorts to the lottery as a second metaphor for the world. He compares the conjugal felicity of his mother and now dead father with winning the grand prize in a lottery.[329] Since Bentinho suspects life is a lottery or, more hopefully, a barter, rather than a drama with music, he promises to pay God a thousand paternosters and a thousand *Ave Marias* if Dias can get him out of seminary. But he has bargained like this before and failed to make payment. So he feels he has to offer a substantial sum to cover arrears. Like his mother, he hopes to find a way of "extending the note"[330] held by the Great Creditor.

Capitú's father, Sr. Padua, asks for a memento from Bentinho before his departure to seminary. Bentinho gives him a lock of hair. Padua is effusively grateful, but his face betrays a look of disenchantment "like a man who has spent his whole hoard of hopes on a single lottery ticket and sees the cursed number come out a blank—such a sweet number!"[331] A mere scrap of hair when he had hoped for a son-in-law!

Later, when Bentinho gets to seminary, he will dream that some young buck hands Capitú's father a lottery ticket with a beautiful, mysterious "4004" on it, but he loses anyway, because the roulette wheel breaks down. Meanwhile, Capitú is giving Bentinho "all prizes, great and small." When he awakens, he tries unsuccessfully to force his way back into the dream. He concludes that "one of the offices of man is to close his eyes and hold them tight shut to see if the dream that was interrupted when the night was young will continue through the dead hours."[332]

Life-as-lottery is a world where wins and loses are not proportionate to investments and in which neither effort nor pious complaint to heaven determines who is to be the recipient of a windfall. You are not "chosen" either for victory or suffering. Even surmising that the game might be fixed is an oblique way of hoping someone cares.

Life-as-opera is a different matter. Someone directs the show. But who? Machado de Assis's actors do not know for sure; they play out someone else's scenario onstage. The difference between "All the world's a stage" and life-as-opera is the high stylization of the latter. In opera conflict is not simply undergone, it is gesticulated, elevated. In life-as-opera the audience does not have to infer emotion, because the performers project it as music and posturing. Nor is an audience in suspense about the outcome. Even if the libretto is not printed, it is nevertheless known.

Neither lottery nor opera is ritual, even though lotteries probably developed from divination rites, and operas (at least those under the influence of Wagner) became cultural celebration rites. Except for divination, rites leave little to chance. They generate a controlled theater of action. If one thinks of the sweet Mass as ritually controlled play, then it makes sense to consider the lottery metaphor as a symbol of the uncontrolled and uncontrollable and the opera metaphor as a symbol for the predictable, fated outcome.

Bentinho is only in his teens and already life for him is an opera and a lottery. As if the contradiction within each model were not enough, there are severe clashes between models. So what can he and Capitú do? They do what we always do in the face of deep contradictions. They resort to ritualization. At first it was ritual play; now it is ritual combat. In sum, the scene goes like this:

She: Between your mother and me who would you choose?
He: You.
She: Liar. I'll not marry you.
He: So? The life of a padre is not so bad.
She: I promise not to miss your first Mass.
He: Promise that I alone will hear your confessions and that I will be the priest who marries you.
She: I promise that you may baptize my first child.

The last remark leaves him unable to reply. He is without a gesture. Shortly afterwards, they displace combat with ceremonial promises. They swear by almighty God to marry each other, come what may. Now they feel clear of danger; they are religious, relieved of dread, sanctified. Each Saturday they will light a candle to Our Lady of the Conception to commemorate the vow. They do not recognize how prophetic is their choice of this particular representation of Mary. Their promise to maintain the devotional act will, they hope, snare the favor of heaven and compensate God for his loss of a clergyman.

Now the future is doubly mortgaged—by Dona Gloria's vow and by the counter-vow of the adolescents. Just as the mother, faced with the death of a child, binds her future, Bentinho and Capitú pledge their love in the face of separation. But the formal promising does not obviate the combative prelude to it which gives the readers an edge over the characters, because the characters cannot imagine what it foreshadows. The vowing and combating seem contradictory but only because a reader with retrospective distance can view them side by side. Both the threats and promises will in some sense prove to be true. All the ritualizing will be prophetic—the sweet Mass, first kiss, ritual combat, vows, and commemorative devotion. The celebrative play and ceremonial promises foretell the couple's fate in the Grand Lottery, but who in the story can yet divine the secret of these rites? Only we readers can, because we have the benefit of the narrator's hindsight; he is more indulgent that Old Sartre. To read is to divine. Life is like that. We repeat the rites bequeathed us, and our variations and secret versions hold the keys to the world we will create. In our own ritualized lives we are, unfortunately, only characters, not readers. Life is like that; it is not a novel we can read. It is a fiction we are in.

The Seminary of the World

In honor of his new status I will now drop the diminutive and call him Bento. At seminary they will make him a man (by, of course, denying his "manhood"). He has kissed Capitú and entered the Seminary of St. Joseph, named, you will remember, after that saint who had such a terrible time believing his betrothed's pregnancy story. Bento has been sent here to keep him out of corners with his sweetheart and to fulfill his mother's vow.

With sufficient prompting, I might argue with both the Italian tenor and Bento. Having been there, I would declare, "The world's a seminary, not a randomly stopping roulette wheel. The world is neither dramatically conclusive nor musically inspiring. We are not tenors or gamblers but priests and acolytes. So our mothers and fathers all send us to their equivalent of seminary hoping "the call comes with habit."[333] I would drone on: Since life is not an opera (God threw away the libretto) nor a lottery (no one ever really wins), it must be a seminary, a liminal zone in which we try to snare the dove of divinity with the nets of curriculum.

But I have no one to prompt me, so I will not pursue this line of thought. I will follow the narrator's instead.

No one volunteers to go to seminary, as Dias says, "to be anointed with the holy oils of theology."[334] We are called, sent, or dragged. We go objecting. Why bother with rites and doctrines when there is business? Or industry? Or science? Or love? Dietrich Bonhoeffer is said to have advised his seminarians not to pray while making love; it would not add a whit to their piety. Those who send us to seminaries hope to divert our attention from the romantic and dramatic to the habitually important. But as every wise seminarian soon learns, ritualizing is a kind of acting out, therefore it is potentially subversive. In ritualizing we do those things which, said aloud or done straightforwardly, would erupt into the deepest quarrelling. The vocation of ritual custodian seldom saves us from the opera.

Bento goes to seminary having secretly sworn to marry Capitú. By weathering it for a year, he can avoid swearing in vain and can honor his mother's oath as well. He will "seek, in appearance, the sacerdotal investiture; and before it, the call. But the call was you, [Dear Capitú], the investiture, you."[335] This is the call that will become his habit of being (as one of his professor-theologians might have said). There were other agendas for seminary as well: "Come back a Pope!" his Uncle Cosme says with a laugh as Bento kisses him good-bye.[336]

Religious institutions are often dialectically or ironically related to ritual intentions. Institutions are tough "sacred canopies" constructed to protect tender processes. The aim of a liturgy is communion with the sacred, but institutions sometimes prophylactically interpose structures that prevent the very conceptions religious people espouse.

Much to our regret, Bento does not tell us much about his courses in moral theology, worship, and homiletics, because, as he says, one chapter would not be enough. Instead, he takes six chapters to tell us about a twenty-nine page paper called "Panegyric of Saint Monica" written by a classmate whose name he can not recall. We are made privy to little of the content of the panegyric. The narrator has forgotten most of it.

But he tells us, "The fact is, everything is to be found outside a book that has gaps, gentle reader. This is the way I fill in other men's lacunae; in the same way you may fill in mine."[337] Dear reader, here is your invitation as well as mine.

The time spent at seminary is, as theologians are wont to say in sonorous German, *zwischen den Zeiten* ("between the times"). The Seminary of St. Joseph and the "seminary of the world"[338] overlap, creating a liminal zone, a swamp breeding ritualized action. It is a time-out-of-time and, accordingly, Bento has to improvise or invent what he "forgets." He not only gives us associations rather than interpretations of the panegyric, he reads the rest of the novel into this paltry paper. In addition he forgets what he had vowed to remember. I read him to remember what I have worked to forget.

During a moment of tenderness the adolescent lovers had once heard the song of a peddlar selling sweets: "Cry little girl, cry/Cry 'cause you haven't any penny."[339] They had vowed to remember this lyric always. Now, in seminary Bento begins to forget the words and tune, so he resorts to having them written down. Later, he will forget them altogether and have to rummage for the scrap of paper to avoid violating his oath.

Forgetting is like having no penny; he will be unable to pay the price for sweets.

As old Casmurro is trying to recollect in the gaps, he tells us that in seminary he writes a poem, a kind of panegyric of his own, to Capitú. He invents the first and last lines for a sonnet that he is unable to complete because he cannot figure out the middle. As with his life, he is unable to tie the two ends together, so he offers the lines to you and me—or to "the first soul who wants them"—to finish as we will.

The first line is, "O flower of heaven! O flower bright and pure!" He suggests that we may substitute Capitú or virtue or poetry or religion or liberty or charity for "flower." Worn out with waiting for the remaining verses "to spring forth in a bath of inspiration," our seminarian suddenly reverses the last one, "the golden key," so that it reads ironically: "Life is won, the battle still is lost" instead of, "Life is lost, the battle still is won."[340]

The panegyrics to Monica and Capitú, I am tempted to suggest, are metaphors for the book *Dom Casmurro*. If we were to follow the lead of the main character, we would treat the novel as commentary on the gaps in the "Panegyric" or the gaps between the first and last lines of the sonnet. The "Panegyric" was finished but Casmurro cannot now remember what it said. The sonnet is unforgettable (you must agree) but unfinished. Fortunately, Machado de Assis is a better novelist than Bento is a poet, and his work is more memorable than that of Bento's old classmate.

Inspired for a moment to write fictive theology, I could tell you what a seminary really is. Seminary is any place in which one discovers that the metaphysical order is unfinished like the sonnet or forgettable like the panegyric. It is where we receive ultimate fictions to fill the gaps. A panegyric (Greek: *panegyrikos*) was originally either a festival oration or a funeral eulogy. We usually forget orations and cannot tie up the loose ends of eulogies. The purpose of "seminary" education is to train "priests" for a world that cannot remember orations or finish sonnets. These priests perform the liturgy of remembering what they never knew and invent stories that enable them to forget. The people at St. Joseph's engage in what Richard Schechner calls the "restoration of behavior," of which he says, "Restored behavior offers to both individuals and groups the chance to become someone else 'for the time being,' or the chance to become what they once were. Or even, the most often, to rebecome what they never were."[341] The restoration of behavior, one of the major functions of ritual, allows people to behave as if they were "transition phenomena."

Bento's classmate dedicated his term paper to St. Monica, Augustine's devout Christian mother, who eventually prayed his soul away from paganism and his mistress and into the arms of Mother Church. Dona Gloria is not so fortunate. Her son goes from the arms of the church to those of Capitú, then to writing books. Need I say it? For Bento the book will become the place where one does what one used to do in seminary. In the book we who follow Bento's example will get our training in formalization, metaphysics, and love. Formalization and narration will be our way of biding time in the gaps between God and ourselves, between our lovers and ourselves.

Seminarian Bento squeezes almost as much from the "Panegyric" twenty-six years later as I do from his own story. As he says, "All this the devil of a little book kept telling me. . . ."[342] After reminding Bento of that unfinished sonnet from long ago, the little book evokes one other presence, that of Ezekiel de Souza Escobar, his best friend, a man able to seduce Bento with words. Escobar pushes his way into the story. Bento tries unsuccessfully to cut off his recollections only to find the memory evoked by the yellowed pages of the "Panegyric" reasserting itself and carrying him all the way to the end of the book *Dom Casmurro*, in which it is embedded. If sweetening the Mass sacralized Bento's romance, seminary has provided a sacred place that hatches a fated friendship.

"Real" Life in the Suburbs

The habits inculcated by mothers and mother churches do not automatically became callings, any more than meditation rites produce mystical experiences or weddings produce marriages. After a year, Dona Gloria is regretting her vow. She wishes her son would marry and have children. With Bento away at school she and Capitú have become friends, almost mother and daughter. But unlike her son, whose God is a Rothschild capable of foregoing collection on promises, Gloria feels morally bound.

Leave it to Escobar. His calling is to commerce as Bento's is to Capitú. This best friend divines a way to reformulate the mode of re-payment: Dona Gloria needs only to underwrite the theological education of some poor student who would be otherwise unable to fulfill his calling. She can purchase a substitute, he suggests. The substitutionary logic makes perfect seminary sense. The exchange is made, and God has his priest; a mother, her son; a lover, her beloved.

Bargaining and vowing require one another. Symbolic substitution is the currency that mediates exchange between heaven and earth. All might have gone well were it not for the cascading of exchange rates. Liturgical economics carries the story along for three-quarters of the book. But as soon as Bento Santiago, his seminary days long behind him, has his law degree and wife in hand, the operatics once again intrude upon the ritualization.

The honeymoon almost disproves the Italian tenor's theory. It is a veritable Song of Songs chanted in such harmony that one would never suspect that lotteries or operatic counterpoint could disturb it. But the seeds of drama have been sown already. (Which is it—ritual or drama—if the tale is an old, old story, and we can guess its ending?) On the one hand, the predictable ritual economy. On the other, the dramatic irruption of chance and fate. In seminary they try to teach us how to mediate between the two.

Just before he is to marry Capitú, Senhor Santiago (he has degrees now, thus my formality in referring to him) hears an invisible fairy assuring him that he will be happy. His old servant warns that the voice is Bento's own. The prospective groom muses, "It is probable that the fairies, driven out of tales and verses, have taken up their abode in people's hearts and speak out from there inside."[343]

The wedding and honeymoon ratify the fairy's assurance. Soon afterwards two couples, Mr. and Mrs. Santiago and Mr. and Mrs. Escobar, are friends. These perfect, turn-of-the-century suburban couples share one another's company. They have dinners and children together. They fancy that their children will marry. The Escobars name their daughter Capituzinha in honor of Mrs. Santiago, and the Santiagos name their son Ezekiel in honor of Mr. Escobar. Naming is a creative act, not a mere strumming of vocal cords with breath. To name is to forge a relation, to empower with character.

As he grows up, Ezekiel develops the features and mannerisms of Escobar, rather than Santiago, his Father. But. Well. . . . He imitates other people too. Maybe that explains it. Probably just a fortuitous resemblance. Or are our lawyer's eyes getting clouded by middle-aged jealousy? Now the opera begins. Or is it the lottery? Is the resemblance chance, or is it hidden narrative design?

The vows are questioned. The old ritual combat is reenacted. Mom and Dad are watching one day when little Ezekiel spies a cat with a mouse:

> Capitú also wanted to see what the boy was doing. I went along. As a matter of fact, it was a cat and a mouse, commonplace event. Without interest or charm. The only peculiar circumstance was that the mouse was alive, kicking, and my little

son entranced. But the instant was short. As soon as the cat saw more people, it prepared to run. The child, keeping his eyes on it, again motioned us for silence, and the silence could not have been greater. I was going to say religious; I scratched out the word, but I put it in here once more, not only to signify the totality of the silence but also because there was in the action of the cat and the mouse something akin to ritual.[344]

The cat and mouse game, which our storyteller sees as a kind of liturgy (and which readers trained in seminaries would prefer to keep at a safe distance with the label "ritualization"), symbolizes what is going on in Gloria, which is the name the Santiagos give their home in order to honor Bento's now deceased (and therefore mythic) mother. Metaphor is not allegory, so we poor readers cannot be sure who is cat and who is mouse. We know there is a mystery here, but we do not know what it refers to. We sense, though, that we are approaching an abyss.

Old Casmurro tells us he should now be at the middle of his book; he is starting to run out of paper.[345] He begins to cut short his reflections. Social drama, the uncontrollable, unrepeatable side of performance, creeps upon us, driving us to the edge of a precipice. Much happens in a few pages; things fall like overripe fruit.

One night Santiago feels attracted to Escobar's wife, but he resists. Shortly thereafter, Escobar drowns. Bento delivers the funeral oration, resists poisoning his own son, almost commits suicide, and finally exiles Capitú and Ezekiel to Switzerland. The wife dies there. The son returns much later, looking even more like his father's best friend. Eventually, Ezekiel dies in Jerusalem.

Vowing and Wedding

The story is over. Just like that. We never know for sure whether our narrator is right about the paternity of his son. Does the tragedy consist of his wife's infidelity or of his jealousy? Is his story a gloss on *Othello*? The abrupt climax of the plot does to me what the end of his marriage does to Casmurro. Madly, I plow back through the story searching for clues to what really happened. I am compelled to figure out what I missed. If I cannot find out, like old Casmurro I will have to make up something to tie the two ends together.

It seems to me that a great deal hinges on the tension between vowing and fate or, to put it another way, liturgical fidelity and cosmic pattern. A vow is a hinge joining the moral and ritualistic, as well as the ritualistic and the cosmic. Avowal is more than frank admission. It is confession in the religious sense, a declaration of faith and aspiration, coupled with promises that bind the future. It is a trusting, yet audacious, action. About to marry, we know conditions will change, both inside and outside us. Yet we have the presumption and courage to declare what we will do. Who knows what we will in fact do, unless we also know who we will in fact be? And who can know that, except imaginatively?

A man and woman exchange vows in a ceremony. A little satin, a few tears, a word or two, a bit of pulpy cake, and it is done. Where else could such fictions be made except in heaven?

The convention is that marriage begins with a rite, the wedding. Only a curmudgenous theologian would suggest treating marriage itself as ritualized—which is almost to say, patterned, stylized, emploted, fated. Not only can relationships routinize, but wedding rites can inject themselves into a marriage far beyond the few hours of their duration. Ceremonies continue to wed, or to inhibit wedding. And marriages seem in retrospect to have been rites unwittingly planned and executed. Couples are held together by a multitude of things other than love—economics, inertia, children, a house, a trajectory initiated in a childhood game. They are driven by unwitting acts of ritualization such as the choice of a best friend and by experiments with ritualizing such as sweet masses. The rite makes us; maritally, the wedding is our first step of formal entry into marriage, but what if ritualization also constitutes the long middle phase, the marriage itself? You think I am being curmudgenous?

Not every rite does its appointed work. Not every wedding produces a marriage. Some are, as Bentinho would have said, "ideas without legs."[346] Only a paltry theology would treat wedding ceremonies as mere reflections of social and spiritual realities. Strong rites make up realities; they do not merely imitate them. Most of our rites for bonding and binding are fictions in the weak sense; they are "false." They would be "fictive" if they made us up in a way that convinced us to suspend disbelief.

One day, while home from school, Bentinho spied a dandy riding by. Capitú and the horseman eyed one another. And the trumpet of jealousy was blown. Bentinho, after hiding out for a day of anguish, tells Capitú of his suspicion. She wept that, after their oath, he could think her so faithless. She does not know the dandy, she claims. She will not look out the window any more, lest her eye fall on another man. Besides, that other man is getting married, to another girl. Bentinho misses the contradiction between her claim not to know him and her declaration that the dandy is marrying another.

No, no, Bentinho insists, feeling guilty, You don't have to promise me that!

Fine, she replies, as she withdraws the promise.

Now she substitutes a threat instead. She will dissolve the romance at the next sign of suspicion from Bentinho, "It was my first suspicion and my last," he concludes.[347] Without a doubt, he believes her; he will not question her fidelity again. Aloud.

Jealousy in the wake of a vow is evidence that our rites do not bind us with the same force that nature drives us. A vow binds from on top: one wills it and declares it, formally. But nature, the cosmos, the lottery is that which we cannot bind; it binds us. From below. Jealousy is to love what doubt is to faith. Faith must include doubt, says the theologian.[348] Jealousy reminds us of the limits of ceremonial promises. It is necessary but can as surely wreck an avowed relationship as doubt can faith. Jealousy as recognition that no ritual of commitment can fully bind either the world or two people is one thing. Jealousy as an attempt to control a person's soul is another.

An action dictated by a ceremonial promise made in the past is peculiar. Since it does not quite "do" what it "says," it is not a performative utterance.[349] Such an action enacts the promise in a manner resembling scripted action on a stage. It is molded from a template. It is formative, not formalized. This is what lends it a ritual-like quality without making it a rite proper. Actions such as remaining faithful to marriage vows or carrying out the conditions of an oath to avenge a death are not of the same order as actions done in the shadow of a memory. The disciples meet the risen Jesus in the act of breaking bread. Who has not stumbled into a web of evocations at the discovery of a forgotten lock of hair in the corner of some old box?

Jesus' "Do this in remembrance of me" binds Christians in memory (like the lock of hair), but it goes further. It binds them morally as well: you ought to do it; you vow to do it. Liturgical ritual often has both a mnemonic and a moral function. The two functions are similar but not identical. The violation of a memory is not the same as the violation of a vow. The difference between the violations lies in their direction: I violate a memory and I walk on the dead; I break a vow and I damage the future.

Ritual vows mortgage the future on the grounds of the credit rating of the past. But the rating is no guarantee of future payment. Bentinho anticipates this discrepancy even in adolescence: "It was we who were the same: we sat there reckoning the sum of our illusions, our fears, and already commencing to count our memories."[350]

It is a false procedure based on deluded premises to regard the making of covenants solely as a form of moral obligation, words offered as guarantees of future actions. Covenanting is also a recognition (and in this respect not a "making" of anything) of a shared repository of memories that will be honored in the relationship. Ritual vows, of which a wedding is but one sustained example, is a cultural device for joining the commemorative and the promissory in a single action.

A sworn oath has been the epitomizing gesture of romance from its medieval to its modern forms. In oath-making the knight attaches himself to a lady or a brotherhood and thereby establishes a center to which he returns from wandering. Nothing is so poignant as the situation of two lovers bound by an oath but separated by obstacles. And nothing is so peculiar as the lovers' contrivance to create those obstacles. Both parties unconsciously enter into collusion to maintain the distance in order to fuel the passion.[351]

When are the seeds of ceremonial cynicism sown? Does Capitú make her vows already knowing she will violate them?

Does Bentinho vow without really trusting Capitú? He fears she will not keep the vow, though he tells us otherwise. She fears he will question her fidelity. The fears that lead them to make the pledge are the ones that undermine it after it is formalized in marriage. We would not vow if we had no fear. Yet, if we have nothing to fear, we have no need to resist making promises.

Bentinho's and Capitú's vows are secret. Ordinarily, avowal is a public action. Besides giving my word personally, I do so publicly as a way of insuring that violation will result in shame. I invoke witnesses to hold me in contempt if I do not live up to my side of the contract. Even God's covenant with Abraham is with a people, not just an individual; this is one of the major points of the Isaac story. The secret, romantic vow was uncharacteristic the ancient Near Eastern world. Secret vows assume that individuals really have the power to do what they intend. You begin to be a theologian by remembering how seldom people have such power. Ancient vows had gods and communities as guarantors. Secret romantic vows have the unconscious. But we postmoderns have few guarantors. The law can govern only the economic and political aspects of marriage. Who guarantees the religious and emotional ones? Casmurro seems to think only his storytelling can now serve as guarantor.

Ritualizing and Feminizing

Dom Casmurro is ritualized in several respects: (1) Ritual play (the sweet Mass) and private rites (the vows and commemorative candle lighting) are part of its content. (2) The role of husband displaces, and therefore carries some of the valence of, the ceremonial role of priest. (3) Though the writing is superb, the plot is stock, so we read the story as if re-reading it. (4) The narrator's act of writing enshrines and lays to rest the object of his devotion, whose simultaneous presence and absence inspire the story.

Had it not been for the female sex, Casmurro philosophizes, this book "would perhaps be a simple parish sermon if I had become a bishop, or an encyclical if Pope, as Uncle Cosme had charged. . . ."[352] When the story ends, two questions still cling like burrs to the brain: Who is this female? And what sort of book is this? There are two obvious, direct answers: (1) Capitú, (2) a romantic novel. However, having devoured the sacramental sweets, weathered the seminary of the world, and killed three times over the baritone who fought me for the soprano, I have developed a taste for more devious answers.

Is not this an old, peculiarly masculine tale: mama's good boy, on the way to higher or holy things, is bemused by girl with eyes like the tide. She becomes the new object of veneration, only to be trapped, killed, or sent away. Then, he turns to storytelling and enshrines her. Finally, the reader, or other sympathetic ear, is seduced by the story.

The simple answer will not do. Casmurro says, "The female sex," not "Capitú." He is not talking about the bare fact that he married a woman instead of becoming a priest, nor even about the loss of his wife. He is alluding to the muse. So let us speak of femininity.

For men femininity is a myth; feminization, its corresponding ritual. To be feminized is not the same as being female, feminist, or effeminate. Feminization is the elevation of the symbolically female in order to contain its mystery and have access to its succor. It is the ambivalence-fraught process whereby men hope to make the transition from authority to inspiration. The transition, though necessary, is exceedingly dangerous, because men are likely to confuse women with muses. If women are confused with muses and "man" is vaunted into a generic term, he becomes entranced. Actual women are rendered "dead" to the extent that they are volatilized into muses, and men are driven to the madness of bemused writing. Just as Casmurro speaks of casmurricity,[353] momentarily transforming himself from a character into a principle, so Capitú becomes abstracted into "the female sex" (or what I am calling "femininity"). Properly, muses are other; they are spirits. They belong in fiction or religion.

Casmurro becomes old by exiling his wife and son to Switzerland. With her across an ocean, he begins to write inspired books. Whereas bureaucrats are kicked upstairs, muses are booted out the door or across the ocean. No woman ought to put up with this. But every muse must insist on it. A woman is a female. A muse is feminine. Men and women have equal competence in conducting rites and writing theology. But Man is lord of theology and Woman, queen of ritual. Panegyric, in which theology is at one with ritual, requires androgynous thinking.

Seminary fosters the collusion of Bentino's mother and his girl friend, both of whom are repeatedly praised as angels. Women do not attend the seminary, so Woman runs the show. And Man fancies that he is really doing something by planning, plotting, and fraternizing. In "seminary," the enclave of men aspiring to authority, we are instructed in dogma and morals. Meanwhile, ritualization of our relationships sets in. Things begin to go in circles and triangles until everyone has lost perspective. In the end, Capitú, like the old ones, has "gone to study the geology of holy ground"[354] and Casmurro is trying to write a "history of the suburbs," a story solid enough to be a monument over his tragedy. His act of narration is a simultaneous containing and conjuring up of shades—a counter-funerary rite, an interesting counterpart to Sartre's "funeral" for his childhood.

Having lost his first love, Casmurro turns to two tasks both of which are ritualized attempts to contain his losses. In the suburb named Engenho Novo he builds a new house that is a replica of his adolescent home in Matacavallos. There he writes the story in which we are presently entangled. He both writes and builds while looking backwards. The house contains busts of emperors from Roman history, and the book is the beginning of a "history" of the suburbs. I would call it a mythology. In any case, it is there that Lord Curmudgeon is biding time and keeping to himself. No longer stranded in a premarital frenzy at the seminary, he is now going to the theater to see *Othello* in a state of post-marital withdrawal.

Old Casmurro is telling us his story. He wants desperately for us to believe him. He addresses us directly and intimately but never presumptuously. After all, he is a Brazilian gentleman. As he tries to "tie the two ends of his life together,"[355] he is polite. He calls us "dear lady" and "senhor." He goes to great pains to provide us with short chapters ("just another five minutes," I say to myself), summaries, and asides that both keep us oriented and distract us from the pain. I become so attentive, so taken by his attentions, that I do what Machado de Assis the author never did. I become identified with Bento, with Casmurro. When he finds that his child Ezekiel looks like his old seminary friend, I want to do exactly what Casmurro does. No, I want to do more. I become Casmurro's defender. How could his best friend? How could he? Dom Casmurro is telling the absolute truth. Isn't he?

Machado de Assis, the author, did not confuse himself with Bento, his character. The novel is not an autobiography. As far as we know, the author had no lovely Capitú in his life. Ms. Caldwell, the translator, assures us that he was married for thirty-five years to the same woman—"a legend of conjugal devotion that bedims the Brownings."[356] Neither the author, his friends, nor the critic José Verissimo regarded Bentinho as a mere mask for Machado de Assis himself. (Ms. Caldwell cites two letters, however, in which Dom Casmurro is treated as real—as real for him as he is for us.)[357]

I see no reason why we should exclude fictive ex-seminarians from our authorities. Casmurro exercises priestly powers over his readers. Perhaps he learned something in seminary after all. Why should we listen to real people when fictive ones are wiser? He seduces us with his story as surely as Capitú seduces him with her eyes, and Escobar with his words. Casmurro, though he was never ordained, and is "only," as they say, a fictional character in a turn-of-the-century Brazilian novel, can instruct us well in some of the elementary lessons of fictive ritual and ceremonial promising.

I have gone too far? I should not claim so much for Casmurro? I hear you reminding me that he was, after all, only a student of theology—one who never finished his degree or completed his ordination. Yes, I know that his "Dom" is partly earned, partly ironic—like most of our degrees in divinity. (In what sort of a world is it possible to master divinity?) But still, what can you expect from an ex-seminarian, especially one who finished, if not a little creative exegesis in the gaps?

14

The Denial of Ritual: Søren Kierkegaard's *Repetition*

A BOOK'S TITLE PAGE AND COVER ARE ITS PERSONA, AND OUR PE-
rusal of them is analogous to an introduction between two
people. In his wry, perceptive treatments of "interaction rituals," that is, occasions on which we present ourselves in everyday life, Erving Goffman labels as "front" that part of an "individual's performance which regularly functions in a general
and fixed fashion to define the situation for those who observe
the performance."[358] The front matter of a book is supposed to
provide readers with clues for reading the whole thing—with
summaries, outlines, key words, epigraphs. We expect it to
give us general information, not randomly selected items. We
take a title page as a fixed reference point for construing the
ethos of the entire book. In the beginning we readers may allow a title page to tease us, but in the end we do not want it to
deceive us.

I have only to open the latest translation of Kierkegaard's
Repetition to discover that I am in trouble.[359] Ignoring the obvious problems implicit in its being a translation, I am immediately foiled in my formalist ploy of "just" reading the book by
two elementary facts. First, *Repetition* is preceded by the trans-

lators' (Howard and Edna Hong) introduction as well as another book by Kierkegaard, *Fear and Trembling*. Second, the title page at the front, dated 1983, lists Søren Kierkegaard as author, whereas the reproduction of the original title page, dated 1843, lists Constantin Constantius as author.

I could plunge onward and treat Constantin as author by assuming either that this is what Kierkegaard must have wanted or what Danish readers in 1843 were forced to assume even if they had doubts. Alternatively, I might follow the contemporary practice of assigning authorship to Kierkegaard as if we scholars had uncovered the secret of his pseudonym and can now justly saddle him with a responsibility he tried to escape. The first way fails because it leaves a huge remainder unexplained and the second, because it leaves none, having reduced all the characters to the author's neuroses and passions. Instead, I will follow a third strategy, that of regarding Kierkegaard as author and Constantin as narrator. One reason for trying this is that Kierkegaard never disclaimed authorship even though he did not want the fact publicized—at least not initially. Later, he not only claimed authorship but purported to explain it in *Concerning My Work as an Author* published in 1851 and *The Point of View for My Work as an Author: A Direct Communication, Report to History* published in 1859. His use of pseudonyms, he claimed, was an exercise in indirect communication, which he hoped would free readers from the tyranny of authorial authority. Unfortunately, Kierkegaard's pseudonymous authorship has often had the opposite effect, that of teasing readers into a hunt for the real author.

Henning Fenger[360] doubts that Kierkegaard himself knew how much of his self was contained in his pseudonyms. Kierkegaard, he thinks, was constructing personae. That he was not hiding behind a *nom de plume* is probable since, as Mackey points out, there was little doubt in Copenhagen who had written *Repetition* and the other pseudonymous works that we now attribute to Kierkegaard.[361] Therefore, I take pseudonymous authorship to mean that *Repetition* is best read as a fiction of sorts, as "imaginative construction."[362] It would violate the author's explicitly, albeit retroactively declared, intention if we were to read *Repetition* autobiographically rather than fictively.

Kierkegaard's intentions were split. He had more than one audience. Both Regine, his ex-fiancé, and the public were intended readers. So the way we define the genre of *Repetition* depends on whom we construe as audience. If the public, then the book is fictional; if Regine, then it is epistolary. How far to carry this epistolary reading is hard to determine. In 1840 Kierkegaard had written directly to Regine in the so-called "Wednesday" correspondence, about which Henning Fenger makes an important but undeveloped observation.[363] The letters, he notes, were part of a courtship ritual. During the first part of the engagement their "day of love," Wednesday, was celebrated to commemorate a Wednesday in July of 1839. This was the time of their second meeting and the beginning of their love affair, and it was commemorated by a weekly letter. The couple lived only a few minutes away from each other, and the letters were delivered by Kierkegaard's servant.

Upon analysis, these earlier, "direct" letters turn out to be somewhat indirect. Their rhetoric is formal, due in part to the ceremonial occasion. Conversely, the later, indirect communication published under the title *Repetition* can be read as direct communication with Regine, though the public had to read it indirectly, that is, as fiction.

So from the very beginning—I am not yet past the title page—a fundamental intertextuality is forced upon the reader. I am compelled, despite my purist intentions of reading this document on its own, to read it in terms of other documents. Even if I can resist playing if off Kierkegaard's journals or letters, I have been led by a subtitle and "author's" name to posit a mixed or undefinable genre. Before reading a word of the book proper, I have had to take a quick trip to the end, not to mention to the critics, in order to make the provisional judgment that *Repetition*'s is overtly fiction, but covertly correspondence. Nevertheless, for the moment, hoping to carry out my aim of just reading the text, I will bracket out the correspondence hermeneutic, since it was intended "for her."

I am left with my fictive, public reading. What is implied by reading it as fiction? Does this way preclude reading it as autobiography, philosophy, or theology? Does it lead to construing the book as entertainment or not taking it seriously? For now it can mean only that I should enter the work in a subjunctive mode. This tactic amounts to exercising an active suspension over my desire to read it in a way that immediately refers it to a pre-selected context—Kierkegaard's world, my own interests, or the history of its interpretation. To regard it as fiction means that although the author, like any artist, inescapably wrote it out of his own life, I cannot read it back into that life. This interdiction is true for the reading of any work of fiction, but especially of one by a pseudonymous author. Non-fictional works are those we can read directly back into authors' mouths, heads, lives. Here, interposed between us and the author like "two soldiers with crossed bayonets," is a hiatus created by the invention of a fictive author, whom I am going to call the narrator so as not to identify him with Kierkegaard.

The alert reader already suspects I have smuggled in a modern way of talking about authors and narrators. My reading will have to show this ploy is fair. By treating *Repetition* as a work of fiction, I implicitly invite comparison with other fiction writers. But Updike, for instance, signs his works "Updike," so I have had to say *Repetition* is a fiction "of sorts" because its "author," not its main character, is the first invention a reader encounters.

The alert reader also suspects my discussion of genre cannot depend only on the title page, but also on a retrospective view possible only after reading the text and interpretations of it; otherwise, I would never have known that a work subtitled "experimenting psychology" (or worse, "experimental psychology" in Lowrie's 1946 translation) was not a lab report by a pre-Skinnerian behaviorist.

The Narrator's Recollections

I hurry past the epigraph, knowing one does not understand such things until later; (on retrospect they are supposed to make sense). And soon I reject the editors' running head, "Report by Constantin Constantius," because reading a few pages convinces me that what I am reading is closer to reminiscence, reflection, or story than to report. In addition, the story is not only by him, it is about him. The editors give away the narrator's identity too soon, so now my readers will have to pretend they do not know his name until they reach the end of the book with me.

The storyline begins to emerge like threads from a tangled skein of philosophical windings: "When I was occupied for some time. . . ." "At home I had been practically immobilized. . . ."[364] A first-person, narrative voice is reflecting on the topic of movement and repetition. The narrator, whose name and identity we are not yet supposed to know, tells us that recollection "faces backward," while repetition "faces forward." As soon as he elaborates the distinction with a series of comparisons, thus completing a kind of prefatory statement that links repetition to happy love and recollection to unhappy love, he himself begins to recollect: "About a year ago, I became very much aware of a young man. . . ."[365]

The young man appears on the scene repeating a verse by Poul Moller, "Then, to my easy chair,/Comes a dream from my youth. To my easy chair./A heartfelt longing comes over me for you,/Thou sun of women."[366] By his refrain he seems to be acting out the narrator's own reflections on the notion of recollection. Not only is the young man unhappy, the poem he is quoting seems more appropriate to a reminiscing older man than to a passionate, aspiring poet. The following passage illustrates most of the interactions and themes that will follow:

> About a year ago, I became very much aware of a young man (with whom I had already often been in contact), because his handsome appearance, the soulful expression of his eyes, had an almost alluring effect upon me. A certain toss of his head and flippant air convinced me that he had a deeper and more complex nature, while a certain hesitation in inflection suggested that he was at the captivating age in which spiritual maturity, just like physical maturity at a far earlier age, announces itself by a frequent breaking of the voice. Through casual coffee-shop associations, I had already attracted him to me and taught him to regard me as a confidant whose conversation in many ways lured forth his melancholy in refracted form, since I, like a Farinelli, enticed the deranged king out of his dark hiding place, something that could be done without using tongs, inasmuch as my friend was still young and pliant. Such was our relationship when, about a year ago, as I said, he came to me quite beside himself. He appeared more vigorous and handsome than usual; his large glowing eyes were dilated—in short,

he seemed to be transfigured. When he told me that he had fallen in love, I involuntarily thought that the girl who was loved in this way was indeed fortunate. He had been in love for sometime now, concealing it ever from me, but now the object of his desire was within reach; he had confessed his love and found love in return. Although as a rule I tend to relate to men as an observer, it was impossible to do that with him. Say what you will, a young man deeply in love is something so beautiful that one forgets observation out of joy at the sight. Usually all deeply human emotions disarm the observer in a person. One is inclined to observe only when they are lacking and there is an emptiness or when they are coquettishly concealed. Who could be so inhuman as to play the observer if he saw a person praying with his whole soul?[367]

The plot of *Repetition* is thin but essential. It turns on two sets of interactions, that between the narrator-confidant and the young man and that between the young man and his lover, who never enters the story as a character. The action is not shown to us through the eyes of an omniscient narrator but recollected in the mind and memory of a narrator who, because he is also a character, we already suspect of bias; he is "interested."

Even though he is reflective, capable of observing and even criticizing the fact that he is an inveterate observer, he is not neutrally omniscient in the modern literary sense of the word. He lures the young man and leads on his readers. Far from being detached, he actively attracts and teaches the young man, whose passion he needs as much as the young man needs the elder's reflective abilities. The young man's being emotionally beside himself is both countered and complemented by the narrator's being "above" himself reflectively. The older man admits to being enamored with the younger.[368] Specifically, his attraction is to the transparency and spontaneity of the young man's gestures. This is what he tells us. As reader, I decide to wait and watch. The young man's act of confiding is compromised by his selectivity and concealment. The confidant's compromise consists of his having designs for the relationship, even though they may include such honorable intentions as enticing the young man away from his romantic melancholy.

The narrator thinks the young man's soulful expression reflects a life lived in "more than one register."[369] The boy is at that age when a person's spiritual voice begins to change. The confidant, normally a reserved man, is drawn into the wake of this spiritual adolescent who seems to be "praying with his whole soul."

Our aspiring poet needs a presence in which he can talk aloud to himself. The older man needs vicarious participation in an energy more impassioned than his own. As he says of his young friend, "How consistent even an abnormal state is if it is normally present."[370]

By this point in the reading we have crossed the threshold. Major characterizations are now evident: the spiritual adolescence of a young male, the female love object almost within reach, and a recollective character embodied in an aging, male spirituality. The basic parameters are established. With a minimum of cheating by looking ahead or at other sources, we have tentatively posited the genre, pegged the relationship between author and narrator, learned that the narrator's intellectual preoccupation is with the idea of repetition, characterized his tone and attitude as recollective, been introduced to what will turn out to be the other main character (a nameless young man), and tentatively posited plot and theme problems: how to resolve the two relationships and how to integrate the idea of repetition with the events in the story. In five short pages we are boiling in a stew of unanswered questions: Is the confidant's interest sexual? Why is the young man's name withheld? Does the narrator know it, or is he concealing it? Can we trust the narrator? What image of his reader does the narrator hold? To what degree are these passions of nineteenth century romanticism literary conventions and to what extent, emotions?

The two men go for a carriage ride together. Soon the youth becomes deeply melancholic. Before he has taken the first real step toward marriage, he has, by anticipating the outcome of the relationship, already become an old man with respect to marriage. His mistake, the confidant observes, is that the young man stands at the end instead of the beginning, and he is too soft to counter this erotic anticipation with an ironic resilience that might save him.

The elder invites the younger to his home, and the conversations deepen. One difficulty is that his lover has awakened the young man into thinking he is a poet. (I am skeptical; so far I have only heard him quote poetry.) By becoming his muse, the girl has signed her own death warrant. (But then who made her his muse?) Now the young man longs for her but cannot marry her. In the end he is certain he will make her unhappy, but

> to explain this confusing error to her, that she was merely the visible form, while his thoughts, his soul, sought something else that he attributed to her—this would hurt her so deeply that his pride rose up in mutiny against it. It was a method he despised more intensely than anything else. And he was right in that. It is contemptible to delude and seduce a girl, but it is even more contemptible to forsake her in such a way that one does not even become a scoundrel but makes a brilliant retreat by palming her off with the explanation that she was not the ideal and by comforting her with the idea that she was one's muse.[371]

The would-be poet, horrified at the discovery that he regards his fiancé as a mere rung on a ladder beyond which he has already climbed, wants to find a way to extricate himself that will not lead to his being guilty of mistreating her or to her being further enamored by his poetic melancholy. He anticipates that, despite his moods, she would cling to him to prove her love. Even the narrator, whose constancy is suggested by both his first and last names, is put off by this brand of fidelity. He wishes his young friend had sufficient humor to convince the girl that he has deceived her (though, in fact, he has not). So the confidant advises ending the relationship in the following manner:

> Transform yourself into a contemptible person whose only delight is to trick and deceive. If you can do that, a balance will be established, and there can no longer be a question of esthetic differences that gave you a higher right in comparison with her, something people are much too often inclined to grant to a so-called unusual individuality.[372] She is the victor, she is absolutely right; you are absolutely wrong. But do not go about it all too suddenly, for that would only inflame her love. First of all, try, if possible, to be somewhat unpleasing to her. Do not

tease her—that stimulates her. No! Be inconstant, nonsensical; do one thing one day and another the next, but without passion, in an utterly careless way that does not, however, degenerate into inattention, because, on the contrary, the external attentiveness must be just as great as ever but altered to a formal function lacking all inwardness.[373]

In addition, the confidant recommends starting a rumor that the young man is having an affair, a rather unpoetic one, with a seamstress. The youth agrees to try the strategy. Then he abruptly disappears.

By now the reader has been lured by the narrator into being far more interested in the young man's fate and in the confidant's response to his friend's absence than in any theories of repetition. But the narrator, feeling that he has gone on too long recounting what he now wants to reduce to an illustration, reminds the reader that his aim all along has been to demonstrate that love based on recollection makes one unhappy.[374] I imagine female readers, frustrated, complaining about male characters who ransack relationships to make them illustrate of principles. And what about male authors who read other men's works as illustrations of categories like ritual? This is going to be a less than happy reading.

One begins to wonder whether *Repetition* is going to turn into philosophy illustrated by characters—whether the fiction will be weighed down by reflection. If so, let us pause so our narrator can catch his breath. Meanwhile, I will make one short observation. Notice how the weaning strategy is supposed to work: formalizing will be used as a facade that simultaneously hides and displays the young man's lack of heart, his inability to continue in the relationship. If there is a definition of ritual anywhere in the book, it is this "formal function lacking all inwardness."[375] This is a widespread view, particularly in Protestant-dominated cultures such as Kierkegaard's and ours.

The narrator is more convinced than I am that the young man really loved the girl but was in a poetic confusion which, presumably, he would have been free of had he believed in repetition. "Repetition" begins to sound like "salvation," but can one be sure? Would "repetition" lead to the young man's abandoning the young woman in order to clear up his confusion? Would such an act eventuate in his returning to her? Is repetition the courage to will a renewed relationship? Whatever it is, whatever it implies, the narrator thinks "great inwardness" would be the result. (I recall from the introduction that the editors think "faith" and "spontaneity after reflection" are synonyms for "repetition," but I prefer to wait and see.)[376]

During the young man's absence the confidant recollects the time the youth recited the poem, because it was such a concentrated, "feminine" moment of presentiment. In the narrator's recollections the young man's "investigative rapport with reality"[377] was "pregnant—every subsequent moment seemed to be prefigured in it." This rumination leads him, by association, I suppose, to recall an incident six years ago in which he gave a young girl a ride in his carriage without, he insists, feeling tempted. She was so modest that she did not evoke "the interesting" (that is, his interest?), which he considers a better defense than "feminine cleverness and cunning."[378] So moved by her trust was he that he walked the last two miles to Copenhagen so she would not feel uncomfortable in his presence.

I cannot help suspecting that there may have been motives. This gentleman seems in awe and fear of a female when he is least able to reduce her to an interesting temptation. In other words, if she is not an erotic object, the she becomes a sacred subject upon whom one must not intrude: "If a man has gone astray in the interesting, who is to save him if not a girl?"[379] The double bind seems to be that a girl is blamed if she evokes interest, but if she does not, she is obliged to save a man from going astray. This young woman has done neither, consequently she escapes from the bind only to be made a pleasant recollection in the narrator's memory. Quickly, her image becomes fuel burned to crank the engine of intellectual reflection toward the idea of repetition (not to be confused, he insists, with Hegel's notion of mediation). Why would the narrator even bother to mention Hegel? Is the narrator a philosopher? At this point in our reading we are tempted to give up our assumption of the fictionality of the work. Mention of Hegel by itself, however, is insufficient warrant. After all, Hegel can be made a character like anyone else.

The Narrator's Investigative Journey

Since our confused boy poet has disappeared from the city, our narrator decides to tell us about his own experiment in re-peating a trip to Berlin to attend the Königstadter Theater. The account is replete with humorous details about his travel con-ditions and room, the gestures of the actors, and the comport-ment of the audience. This sort of logic ("now that he's gone I have time to talk") and style (travelogue) arouses in a reader the suspicion that the genre has degenerated from fiction to journal.

The Talisman, a farce, is the play our narrator sees more than once, each time hoping to re-experience the pristine state of joy in which he originally saw it, but, he is forced to conclude, not even theater performances of the same play are really re-peatable. All he is able to repeat is the experience of the im-possibility of repetition.

The bodily imagery in the narrator's account of his experi-ment is striking. On one segment of his trip to Berlin he finds himself so cramped in a carriage with other people that he can no longer distinguish which legs are his. Later, he describes the posture of Mercury as posed by an actor in the farce. After the play, back in the privacy of his room, the confidant, like Mer-cury, stands there on one leg, flooded with humorous relief.

What seems to the narrator distinctive about farce is that in it neither characterization, language, nor reflection is as im-portant as action. He is impressed by an actor named Beck-mann, who illustrates this fact:

> In an art theater proper, one rarely sees an actor who can real-ly walk and stand. As a matter of fact, I have seen only one, but what B. is able to do, I have not seen before. He is not only able to walk, but he is able to come walking. To come walking is something very distinctive, and by means of this genius he also improvises the whole scenic setting. He is able not only to portray an itinerant craftsman; he is also able to come walking like one and in such a way that one experiences everything, surveys the smiling hamlet from the dusty highway, hears its quiet noise, sees the footpath that goes down by the village pond when one turns off there by the blacksmith's—where one sees B. walking along with his little bundle on his back, his stick in his hand, untroubled and undaunted. He can come

walking onto the stage followed by street urchins whom one does not see.[380]

The narrator argues that farce, because of its stronger emphasis on action than characterization or thought, is least susceptible to repetition. Not only does he fail to find Beckmann funny the second time around, but different social classes at the performance respond in radically different ways; their reactions do not reflect one another. In a brilliant treatment of the sociology of theater, the narrator shows how much one's social role and physical location in the theater affect the way a performance is seen. The cultivated have a difficult time with farce. Unless viewers can achieve naivete, it is lost on them. Newspapers, which ritualize theater by prescribing in advance how a performance is to be responded to, can least determine a person's response to farce. Skilled farcical actors seem able to achieve the sort of repetition which is a recovery of pristine spontaneity free of ceremonialized order and the solemn pretentiousness of art-as-salvation:

> They are not so much reflective artists who have studied laughter as they are lyricists who themselves plunged into the abyss of laughter and now let its volcanic power hurl them out on the stage. Thus they have not deliberated very much on what they will do but leave everything to the moment and the natural power of laughter. They have the courage to venture what the individual makes bold to do only when alone, what the mentally deranged do in the presence of everybody, what the genius knows how to do with the authority of genius, certain of laughter. They know that their hilarity has no limits, that their comic resources are inexhaustible, and they themselves are amazed at it practically every moment. They know that they are able to sustain laughter the whole evening without its costing them any more effort than it takes me to scribble this down on paper.[381]

This section of the narrator's story, though delightful and perceptive, is at first elusive. What is a piece of theater criticism combined with a treatise on the sociology of theater doing in a book on repetition? Is this just some arbitrarily chosen way to mark time during the young man's absence? The point, we surmise, is that actors are professional repeaters; they do the same play over and over. Farcical actors, unlike ritualists, do so with spontaneity. Even so, a viewer cannot see the same

play twice any more than Heraclitus could step twice in the
same river. The narrator can no more repeat something religious than he can repeat laughter; a deliberate, self-conscious
effort destroys both. As he understands it, farce is the opposite
of ritual, which, in his view, is an arbitrarily or deliberately
imposed solemn order. Farce lacks heavy rubrics; it does not
have posted over it a sign, "Not for Pleasure Only," as did the
Royal Theater of Copenhagen.

To anticipate, Kierkegaard is using farce as a parody, and
therefore, a foreshadowing, of true, religious repetition. "Making the religious movement," as he will call it, is not possible
by ritual means. Rather ritual is the farce that results from trying to make such a movement by deliberate, self-consciously
willed acts. The lowest type of theater dialectically presses toward its opposite, the transcendent action of faith that Kierkegaard calls "making a religious movement." The narrator
seems to imply a set of distinctions among (1) spontaneous action, (2) dramatic action (that is, scripted spontaneity), (3) behavior (that is, ceremonialized interaction), and (4) religious
movement. The last is not a synonym for "liturgy" or "ritual."

The author has his narrator arrive in Berlin on the first day
of Lent and speak of other days as having the air of Ash
Wednesday about them (a sarcastic criticism of the climate).
Going to the theater is treated ironically, as quasi-liturgical activity. Any author who would declare, "People nowadays go
to church to be entertained and to the theater to be edified,"[382]
would not be above having one of his characters sit watching
a farce while imagining that he is in the belly of the sea mon-
ster that swallowed Jonah.[383]

What attracts the narrator to the farcical actors is their lack of
self-consciousness and ability to yield to spontaneous impulses. They do not have to reflect or calculate as he himself does.
Like his nursemaid, whom he remembers fondly, they do not
compel themselves. Instead they yield to laughter in a theatrical miracle that once succeeded in engulfing him in its wake:

> My unforgettable nursemaid, you fleeting nymph who lived in
> the brook that ran past my father's farm and always helpfully
> shared our childish games, even if you just took care of your-
> self! You, my faithful comforter, you who preserved your inno-
> cent purity over the years, you who did not age as I grew old-

er, you quiet nymph to whom I turned once again, weary of people, weary of myself, so weary that I needed an eternity to forget. You did not deny me what men want to deny me by making eternity just as busy and even more appalling than time. Then I lay at your side and vanished from myself in the immensity of the sky above and forgot myself in your soothing murmur! You, my happier self, you fleeting life that lives in the brook running past my father's farm, where I lie stretched out as if my body were an abandoned hiking stick, but I am rescued and released in the plaintive purling!—Thus did I lie in my theater box, discarded like a swimmer's clothing, stretched out by the stream of laughter and unrestraint and applause that ceaselessly foamed by me. I could see nothing but the expanse of theater, hear nothing but the noise in which I resided. Only at intervals did I rise up, look at Beckmann, and laugh so hard that I sank back again in exhaustion alongside the foaming stream.[384]

This passage is the most joyful one in the book. Insofar as his trip to Berlin was not a detached experiment, but rather a nostalgic attempt to recover lost times, this is its apex. It evokes memories of two other "girls" (making four that the narrator has recollected so far). One he observes in the theater; her presence helps him yield to pathos in the farce. The other is a milkmaid, whose memory helps him find repose.

The great pool of laughter into which the narrator fell when he first saw the play is one way of accomplishing what the girls symbolize—lost innocence, repose, lack of self-consciousness. Laughter momentarily relieves him of his role as audience member, but when he recovers, it leads to voyeurism, albeit of a chaste, timid sort. If such a girl became aware of his gaze she would have been spoiled—herself the victim of self-consciousness. Love, it seems can no more recover the light of a primordial erotic gaze than a theater-goer can repeat the experience of a delightful first performance.

The narrator's point in including the vignette seems to be to connect the story of the confidant's experiment with the tale of the young man's dilemma. The young girls are the connective tissue. But the confidant's girls cannot be recovered, whereas the would-be poet's girlfriend cannot be properly disposed of. We can always object to the narrator that he should not be so romantically foolish as to hope a primal gesture can be sustained. He and the young man should let their relationships mature, one might advise. But the "should" does not alleviate the expectation. Does some force in us mere mortal males always long to return, even when we command ourselves to forge ahead? Is not ritualizing an impossible effort to recover the sources from which we have already emerged?

At the end of part one the older man is desperate. Death is becoming terribly persuasive, because life, like a river, is hurriedly losing itself in the sea. Like a coach horn, life never sounds the same note twice. All is loss; nothing is recoverable. If life were a drama, no one could name its genre, because the whole shows is not over yet. For this aging male there is only wearying, rigid repetition, which leaves the doer feeling guilty. He can find no happy repetition steeped in repose or spontaneity. What was a pool of laughter the first time becomes stagnant with reflection and recollection the second. A man "quivering in fateful rapport"[385] one moment, can sink into the "abyss of despair" the next. Recollection is just a treacherous retake.[386] Repetition, authentic repetition, would have to transcend this mere recycling of things with its accompanying nostalgia, voyeursism, and despair.

Reader-oriented criticism occurs in the "blanks" between "theme" and "horizon" (Iser's terms). Theme is the viewpoint of the moment; horizon, the cumulative viewpoints from other moments of reading. Kierkegaard put it more simply when he observed that he reflected in other writers' gaps. In any case, I pause at this break in the text before the mail carrier delivers the prodigal young man's letters. What is probably obvious by now is how much my "horizon," fight it though I may, influences my reading. Whether I want to or not, I am looking for something. In this instance it is for fulfillment of my expectation that a book on repetition by a philosopher of religion should help me understand the idea, if not the practice, of ritual. What I have found instead is a high degree of reflexivity and histrionics, a great deal of posturing and gesturing, and a nostalgia for spontaneity—in short, a male post-protestant spirituality with a penchant for romanticist melodrama but with a strong dose of irony that forces consciousness to one-up itself continually. Surely, we must be desperate to know:

Where will all this lead—to what Freud will call "repetition compulsion?" To private piety? To unwittingly entered, vicious circles with God and girlfriend?

The Young Man's Letters

Kierkegaard's only formal division of his work occurs here, and he marks it with a repeat of the original title, *Repetition*. The effect is not just to remind a reader of the topic but to precipitate a question: Is the second half an image of the first, or is it a completion, a repetition that transcends the first? I will return to the question later. *Repetition*, part two, consist largely of eight letters preceded by the narrator's introduction. The part is interrupted once by his observations, and followed by a letter from him to the reader. The tone of this letter is quite unlike that of the narrator's earlier recollections. It reads as if it were written by a third party capable of understanding and including both him and the young man. I hear it as the voice of the ideal reader. You perhaps? This reader feels forced either to take it as the voice of Kierkegaard himself or to assume that the narrator has been playing a role, which he now reveals by putting aside.

The narrator's introduction to the young man's letters is actually the conclusion of the story of his own investigative journey. Having failed to achieve authentic repetition (which we mere readers are still standing on tiptoe to comprehend), recovering neither his original theatrical laughter nor his domestic bliss, he allows his servant, "a housewifely Eve," to ritualize his daily existence by establishing a "monotonous and unvarying order."[387] Even the flies in the room, he quips, are carefully restricted to three, and they must fly at specified times. Not only is this inflexible routine dull, hardly a substitute for original spontaneity, it absolutely inhibits responsive behavior. Far from giving up his attempt to repeat, the narrator has now raised it to the second power, thereby transforming an experiment into compulsive ritualization. His attempt to repeat a dramatic experience transformed it into a rote pilgrimage. With its failure he pursues a second ritual aspiration: to go home again. The impossibility of this second experiment forecloses the possibility of real action and leads him to live in a state of world-forgetfulness. Almost.

Always there is an almost, a remainder, an unordered event. A letter arrives. The young man wants to pour himself out like a river over this "petrific" (William Blake's term) confidant, but he includes no return address. The young man not only demands absolute confidentiality, he wants one-way communication. He is even so bold as to suggest that, because of the confidant's theoretical detachment from the people he listens to, he is a little mad. While the narrator is entombed in his repetitions that do not regenerate, the young man is swamped with the self-contradictions of romantic melancholy.

Meanwhile, the narrator has figured out who the young man's girlfriend is and has made her the object of yet another scrutiny-at-a-distance, which we now recognize as his characteristic stance. That he really meets her, knows her pain, and has access to her "solemn declarations,"[388] seems a boast to me, because all he shows us is his spectating on her. In any case, the narrator is jolted into reminiscing about the young man, and we see that this recollecting holds more promise for him than his ritualizing did; the former I take to be a disembodied version of the latter.

When the narrator speculates that the young man has nothing left to do except make a religious movement, a reader can be sure this is not the same as going to church every Sunday. In the confidant's view making a truly religious movement could lead the young man to transcend his need for feminine love, using the love affair only as "the occasion that sets him in motion."[389] Here we go again. This is another example of the "classical" muse complex, but the narrator has stated it ritually rather than mythically. By this I mean that the muse inspires action rather than poetry, imagination, or belief. The action it motivates is "by virtue of the absurd,"[390] which is to say, a leap across an abyss.

A religious person whose theology was grounded in the narrator's presuppositions would view the girl as bait used by God to capture the young man. This would make her a means to an end. But she is not only a means. She is the matrix of action, not merely a character or actor. With her as impetus, the young man could rise above himself, that is, achieve repetition—something the narrator confesses he himself cannot do.

Religious repetition in this view is not a sinking within or a centering upon but a rising above oneself.

At last, the author presents the letters for the scrutiny of us readers. By now we are eager to get directly to the young man without the overbearing mediations of the narrator. The young man, loathing the fact that he confided in the narrator, expresses disgust for his confidant's insights, advice, and silence. One can consider their relationship this way: as the poet is to his fiancé, so the confidant is to the young man. Each loves the idea, but not the concrete reality, of the other. Just as the young man should, in the narrator's view, put the relationship to death, so the confidant expects he will be put to death figuratively in the young man's act of confiding in him.

With indignation the young man anticipates the silent observer's calm reduction of his unhappy love affair to a set of symptoms. We readers, of course, know that the narrator struggles with similar symptoms, only on another level. The young man wishes he could observe the confidant day and night but finds he cannot act in the older man's presence. Being watched confounds the aspiring poet. By now the theme of being watched has constellated into a central one. The confidant watches others and himself; the poet cannot bear being watched; yet he watches his girlfriend, sometimes from a great distance.

In his letters our would-be poet confesses that he was unable to follow through with his advisor's plan. The aspiration to be a hero in his own eyes rather than those of Danish society is too high. He cannot make the "movement which would surpass knighthood." He is not artist enough to sustain the role. What kind of man can this confidant be? he wonders. This old man seems so thoroughly correct, so consistent. How can he think of following through such an awful plan to the very end? Only a deranged man could suggest appearing within sight of his fiancé with some seamstress hired to play the other woman.

What the young man has done instead is escape the situation by fleeing to Stockholm; he is hiding and refraining from using his fiancé's name. Unlike the confidant who cannot repeat, the young man goes in circles like a spinning wheel, beginning over and over again, but doing everything in reverse. He sleeps by day and lies awake at night. Wallowing in ambivalence, he shrieks contradictions into the silence. Certain that his love cannot express itself in marriage, he is just as convinced that he cannot accomplish the heroic theatrics of his counselor's plan. He talks to nobody; reflection becomes his scanty, bread-and-water diet. Initially, he signs his letters, "Your nameless friend." Eventually, he does not sign them at all.

One night the young poet conducts a melodramatic liturgy. He lights the candles in his room and begins to shout passages from the book of Job. Sometimes he hollers them out his window at the world. The scene is among the most pathetic in romantic literature. Though he repeats the passages, the words always seem new to him, which is more than the confidant was able to accomplish by his ritualizing. Sometimes the boy sits, shrunken into a corner, weeping with a nameless dread. Slowly, he begins to perceive his own contradictions and histrionics, and then he smiles at himself, as one does at children caught putting on their parents' clothes.

The confidant, he rails, is a friend of Job, a professional comforter, a mere master of ceremonies.[391] At least Job's friends gave him something to fly in the face of. But against the confidant the young man can only purify his conviction that, when it comes to making sense of suffering, all understanding is really misunderstanding. The young man concludes that his suffering, like Job's, is an "ordeal." Therefore, it has a transcendent character, not an esthetic, ethical, or dogmatic one. Job is not a hero of faith but a man thrown into a "purely personal relationship of opposition to God."[392] Job is not tranquil like a hero but filled with wildness and insurrection. The young man is enthusiastic about his new interpretation of the story of Job and regards his appropriation of it as a religious "baptism"[393] of the story and his letter to the confidant as an "initiation"[394] of the elder by the younger man.

At last, the rhetoric of ritual has risen to the surface of the story. Unlike Sartre who pummelled us with it, Kierkegaard has kept it hidden. The reader no longer has to read it between the lines, though it will soon submerge as abruptly as it has now surfaced. At least it allows us a momentary glimpse of the peculiar concatenation of acting out and private ritualization that lies at the base of the young man's personality, and perhaps Kierkegaard's nineteenth century, romantic, post-protestant spirituality.

In the two letters dated January 13 and February 17 the storm seems to be over or about to come. The poet, like Job after God's hierophany, is quiet. Thought, speech, and explanation have ceased. Job lost his case literally but won it eternally, before God. Our aspiring boy-poet remains *"suspenso gradu* without moving a foot or making a single movement."[395] He hopes for a thunderstorm, one that will make him capable of being a husband; he imagines it will crush his personality, making him unrecognizable in his own eyes. If this does not happen, he will pretend that his expectation—and himself—are dead.

The melodrama is unbearable, almost farcical. Notice the alternatives: theatricalized irruption or routinized pretence. The young man seems unable to imagine a third way, that of pregnant repetition or, to use a Buddhist phrase, "full emptiness."

Following the seventh letter the narrator intervenes. He is convinced the young man's strategy will not work. This poet is "born to be the dupe of girls."[396] Poets, with their fanatical faith in Woman, had better watch out for young women whose lives they construe as categories.

I breathe a sigh of relief. The narrator has finally said what I have been waiting to say. He almost redeems the book from its sexist romanticism. I say "almost," because I have not forgotten that he watches girls. What thread restrains his interest?

The suffering poet's final letter announces that his girlfriend has married someone else. He claims that as a consequence he is unified, doubly restored like Job. Are we readers supposed to believe he has achieved repetition? Once again, the poet is free to belong to his "idea"; he no longer has to grieve or account to anyone. When he comes home, no woman will be obligated to decipher the look on his face. He will not have to account for his moods—as if he could. And so he raises a chalice and pours a ritual libation to the girl who saved his soul by leaving him: "Praised be feminine generosity."[397]

Is he being ironic?

The content of the final letter consists of the narrator's reflections on the poet as "exception." People who are exceptions to universal patterns, he argues, are on their way to becoming religious personalities. Religious is what one becomes, not by following the herd, but by embodying the particular. If ritual is involved in religion at all, it must be a "ritual of rebellion"[398] against universals and perceived patterns. We might also call this counter-ritualization.

The narrator interprets the "dythyrambic joy" of the last letter as a latent religious sentiment, and by this he means a secret, inward, exceptional experience. In the confidant's judgment the young man does not make the transition completely and so remains a poet rather than a religious man. A religious man would have known how to find firmness in ambiguity—something the poet can only handle by constant movement and the confidant, by becoming an observer or imposing arbitrary order. Now Kierkegaard, through his old and young men, has described two sets of false substitutes for authentic religious action (which is what we like to imagine liturgy is): (1) theatricalized irruption and routinized pretence (the quasi-dramatic set); and (2) constant movement and arbitrary order (the quasi-religious pair).

The final letter is preceded by a drawing of an envelope marked, "Mr. X., Esq., the real reader of this book."[399] It is signed, "Constantin Constantius." Acknowledged at last, I the reader, Mr. X., Esq., breathe a momentary sigh. But the contentment is short-lived, because, with a sudden jolt he addresses me (his dear, clearly male reader): "You are indeed fictional."[400]

Kierkegaard has created a fictitious confidant who suddenly claims he has created the young man. Then he turns on us, claiming we too are his fictions. The confidant had earlier confessed his infatuation with the aspiring poet. He had admitted that he felt like he *was* the young man. And now he tells us he is merely a midwife, a ministering spirit, an elder spokesman and that "every word of [his] is either ventriloquism or is said in connection with him."[401] Finally, just before committing the act of signing his name, he declares himself a "vanishing person."[402] The signature is of the one named on the title page, but here, at the end, it stands like a name on a tombstone over an empty grave with the bones of neither character, narrator, nor author in sight. And the readers? Where have they disappeared to in this magic?

Re-reading as Ritual

Exiting, like entering, is a human activity that typically evokes symbolic behavior. For a reader entering and exiting from *Repetition* is a fictive rite of passage. The narrator speaks of his being "initiated"[403] into the young man's story; the young man later uses the same terminology.[404] When the act of reading becomes ritualized, one form it takes is that of re-reading.

There can be many reasons for re-reading. The usual one we offer is that doing so enhances understanding, especially when a book is a classic or is dense and we suspect that has an underlying clarity or important message. By itself the difficulty of reading *Repetition* is no justification. A better one is that a primary intention of the author seems to be that of provoking repetitive behavior in a reader. Some works leave the reader a choice; others do not. In *Alice in Wonderland* a book demands of Alice, "Read me!" *Repetition* is even more imperious: "Re-read me!" Not only does it force the attentive reader to look back upon reaching the middle, it provokes a double take at the end by pulling the rug out from under us. Even if we are not surprised that the narrator has invented the young man, we are not prepared for him to invent us and then disappear himself.

A potent sense of absence is a widespread motive for ritualization. At the minimum, termination forces a re-casting of the frame that has previously defined a relationship. In this case we are concerned about the relation between the two men, between the men and their various women, as well as that between reader and author. To re-cast we have to recollect. As soon as we do, we have been tricked into imitating the narrator's main activity. We have gone from reading, as an activity of following a narrative, to reflecting on the meaning of that activity. *Repetition* is not only about repetition, it tries to induce repetition into the act of reading.

Having read the end, a reader has a better view of what happened in the transition from the first half to the second half of the book. Stylistically, part two is no simple mirror image of part one, since the latter consists largely of eight letters, while the former is continuous prose. The two parts are less mirrors of each other than they are two sides of the same coin.

However, even this analogy flounders because both the coin (the whole) and one of its sides (the part) would have the same name, "Repetition." Therefore, the second part has to be read in several, partially successful ways: (1) as mirror image of part one. This is clearest when, for example, the young man describes his waiting for the moment of repetition as "standing on one foot."[405] This action is a metaphoric replication of the older man's having stood on one foot in imitation of an actor; (2) as antithesis of part one. The antithetical relations between the parts are fairly obvious. To cite the narrator's judgment,[406] the first part is the work of a prose writer, the last, that of a poet; (3) as completion of part one. The plot problems are concluded (not resolved) by the girl's marrying someone else and the narrator's dissolving the young man and reader into himself; (4) as microcosm of the whole book. The microcosmic effect, besides being conveyed by repeating the title as a subtitle, is reinforced when we learn that the narrator has invented the young man. The narrator is not just a character (a part) but also the inventor (therefore, the whole) of the other character. Incidentally, this interpretation also implies that he "contains" the girl as well; she is his projection.

To return to the pseudonym with which we began: The use of a pseudonym evokes a mood comparable to that of the use of masks in ritual. Our pseudonymous author-narrator disappears, leaving the reader to decide what to do next. This combination of leaving readers free and initiating them at the same time can either facilitate communication between reader and writer or prevent it altogether.

Reading and writing are not always complementary activities. Sometimes they are conflictual. We can think of reading as the completion of a communicative process initiated by writing. But we can also imagine it as an unravelling or inversion of what has been made by writing. Both the complementing-completing and conflicting-inverting models are probably operative in any act of reading, but the latter is highlighted by Kierkegaard.

What did Kierkegaard hope to achieve by writing? What were his explicit intentions in doing it? What intentions can a reader infer from the book? How can a reader get from the young man and confidant to Kierkegaard? How can we refrain from wanting to glimpse the author if the narrator evaporates on us? Who is left but Kierkegaard? Or maybe the important question is more fundamental: Why bother with Kierkegaard at all? Why not remain in the void created by the narrator's absence?

An absence can set readers in motion. They bemoan or chuckle at the word-magic of a narrator who disappears, or they set out to find a narrator behind the narrator, that is, the one I am calling the author. How can they sniff him out? If an author invents pseudonyms several times, he begins to leave tracks, and by leaving tracks he develops, like it or not, authority. Even if he tries to erase those tracks, as Kierkegaard sometimes did, the act of erasing leaves clues and traces of a pattern readers can eventually recognize as style. And style is the beginning of ritualization on the individual level. The search for the author is an attempt to recognize distinctive style. And even what we usually call "content," if it recurs, indicates style. Even though I can read *Repetition*, I can only get at Kierkegaard by re-reading. I have to peer back over first one work then the whole of his works and, by inference and comparison, imagine an author capable of animating these characters and those of other pseudonymous works. In short, I have to invent what reader-response theorists call "the implied author." This is necessary even when Kierkegaard writes directly, without the use of pseudonyms, because of his posturing and continual role playing.

When Kierkegaard is at his most perceptive, he anticipates his readers' worst habits and fends them off. One way of accomplishing this is by putting remarks in the mouths of characters. For example, the young man is caustic toward one who would read his letters as if they were a case history.[407] The narrator chides female readers who peek at the last page and judge everything on the basis of outcome—who want to know, Do the lovers get each other? Using a pseudonym anticipates the reader's bad habit of relying on authors to make their decisions.[408]

When Kierkegaard is at his worst, when he is just being defensive, he uses pseudonyms to take flight even from the rare, good reader. He hides himself in a series of Chinese boxes, allowing one-way communication to parade as indirect communication. The hiding game either turns readers off or teases them out, both of which responses the young man has toward the confidant. The implied analogy is that the reader is to the narrator as the narrator is to the young man as the young man is to the girl. The movement from girl to reader is toward the largest of the Chinese boxes, toward ever higher degrees of abstraction, perspective, and analytical power. The problem is that this movement erodes the possibility of spontaneous action and moves toward sedentary reflection; hence, the necessity for a discontinuous movement, a leap or thunderstorm, to reintroduce flow and decisiveness into action.

Some Biographical Perspective

If we remove *Repetition* from the brackets that I temporarily forged to safeguard its fictionality and then compare it with the "plot" of Kierkegaard's biography as reconstructed from his other works, journals, and papers, it is obvious that our text is neither pure fiction nor mere philosophy.[409] In 1837 Kierkegaard met Regine Olsen for the first time. Two years later he encountered her again at the Ibsen parsonage. By September of 1840, when she was seventeen and he twenty-seven (having just completed his theological examination), they became engaged, although it was generally supposed that she was informally engaged to Johan Frederik Schelegel. The engagement had lasted about a year when Kierkegaard returned Regine's ring. Shortly thereafter he went to Berlin where he wrote *Either/Or*, which he intended to serve as a communication to her regarding his reasons for ending the engagement. He hoped to do so in a way that would not encourage her to wait for him or continue wanting him. Kirkegaard felt that the marriage vows implied a requirement to "tell all."

> But if I were to have explained myself, I would have had to initiate her into terrible things, my relationship to my father, his melancholy, the eternal night brooding within me, my going astray, my lusts and debauchery, which, however, in the eyes of God perhaps were not so glaring; for it was, after all, anxiety which brought me to go astray, and where was I to seek a safe stronghold where I knew or suspected the only man [like his father] I had admired for his strength was tottering?[410]

During his stay in Berlin, Kierkegaard corresponded with his friend, Emil Boesen. In these letters we see Kierkegaard at his most manipulative. Not only does he counsel Boesen, who is also having problems with his girlfriend, to control every expression, be master of every situation, and make up stories on the spot,[411] he confesses his own "practiced dissembling,"[412] and views it as an act of chivalry that he is leading Regine to view him as a deceiver.[413] He confesses to Boesen, the only person he claims to trust, that he has not told him the whole story. Two considerations seem to emerge: (1) that Kierkegaard was unable to reconcile married life and a life of the spirit and (2) that he considered Regine unable to handle the knowledge of his true reasons for ending the engagement. Fearing that "she would vanish because of my singularity,"[414] Kierkegaard says he broke the engagement for her sake. Nevertheless, he is not as decisive as he sounds, because he regards the engagement as broken "only in a certain sense." Although he boasts that he is accustomed to mastering his feelings,[415] he is far from being in control of them. Kierkegaard condescends to Boesen, insisting that he has only "feelings" while Kierkegaard has "passion," and passion is a state of war: "That a girl should be unconquerable, that thought has never yet been entertained in my recalcitrant, if you will, proud head."[416]

Kierkegaard is unable to conquer Regine with the eight hundred pages of *Either/Or*. After a glimpse of her during Easter Vespers of 1843, he takes flight a second time to Berlin. During this second visit he writes *Repetition* and *Fear and Trembling*—again, both "for her." It would be hard to deny the truth of his earlier confession to Boesen, "If she had broken our engagement, my soul would soon have driven the plow of forgetfulness over her, and she would have served me as so many others have done before her—but now, now I serve her."[417] He at once serves her and uses her as muse. Not only do we see this side of Kierkegaard in the young man of *Repetition*, but we can also see in him the narrator's penchant for "benign" deception. Regine is sacrificed on a social level and raised up a muse on a poetic one. Making a "religious movement" would have meant leaving the muse complex behind, something Kierkegaard was never able to do.

Fear and Trembling, the companion volume to *Repetition* begins with several retellings of the story of Abraham, Isaac, and Sarah. Are we to see through Abraham to Kierkegaard and through Isaac to Regine? Probably. But later in his journals Kierkegaard imagines himself as Isaac and his father as Abraham. Unlike Abraham, Kierkegaard has to confess in his journal that he lacked faith in God; otherwise, he admits, he would have married Regine. Having been sacrificed, it seems, he has to sacrifice. The idea that his "sacrifice" of the relationship with Regine is a repetition (in the sense of re-enactment) of his father's relationship with him is not one he would have readily entertained. The young man's old-mannish tendencies probably stem from Kierkegaard's belief that his father's melancholy and debauchery, along with his once having cursed God—and confided all this to the young Søren—was a "sacrifice" that changed him into an old man.

Both *Repetition* and *Fear and Trembling* imply that Kierkegaard hoped to get Regine back again. But as we know now, repetition for Kierkegaard is not "back again" but "forward." And the only way he can get her back is by "willing repetition" (he might have said, by "being reborn"). But like the confidant, he was unable to do so. When he arrived in Copenhagen after his second journey, Regine was engaged to her old boyfriend Schlegel. Hastily, Kierkegaard re-wrote the end of *Repetition* so the young man, who in the original version commits suicide, now claims, ironically one hopes, to have achieved his aim.

In 1846 Kierkegaard went to Berlin a third time. In 1847 Regine married Schelegel. And in 1855 Kierkegaard died at forty-four, having willed his estate to Regine Schelegel, because for him "engagement was and is just as binding as marriage . . . therefore my estate is her due, exactly as if I had been married to her."[418] I would put it another way: he was married to the idea of her, consequently he could achieve only the idea, not the reality, of repetition. Whereas the idea continues to develop after the publication of *Repetition*, the relationship itself fixates and Kierkegaard has to "return" to it in a sense considerably less exalted than his definition of authentic repetition.

Repetition and Ritual as Subtext

The hinge of my interpretation of *Repetition* is the discovery that ritual is its subtext. By this I do not mean that the book is about ritual. Rather, it *is* a ritualization process. Ritualization processes arise when rites themselves, especially liturgical celebrations, are in a state of decadence or denial. There are better and worse reasons for denying ritual. Kierkegaard's motives may have been heroic or neurotic, but the result is similar in both cases: ritualization becomes rife in his life. Repressed, it returns. The forms that it takes are many, among them: (1) the glaring absence of any mention of ritual in a book on religious repetition; (2) the occasional emergence of ritual in the rhetoric of the characters; (3) the stylizing, formalizing, and elevating of their actions; (4) the twofold structure of the book and the ritualizing evoked by the act of re-reading it; (5) the analogical relations between characters and between narrator and reader; (6) the authorial *deus absconditus* created by his use of pseudonyms; (7) the epistolary courtship rite in which the book is entangled; and (8) muse-driven action and inaction.

It may make some difference whether we regard Kierkegaard as aware of the dynamic I am calling ritualization. Is he simply rejecting ritual? Or has he repressed it in the psychological sense? In my estimation, he is repressing it. Later, say, in *Attack upon Christendom* published in 1854-1855, I believe we find him rejecting it. As author of *Repetition*, however, he is still in the process of becoming conscious of his repression, but he is not yet there. Once fully conscious, he is free to accept or reject it. As we know, he will reject it. Upon his deathbed he refuses Lutheran communion from the hand of his own brother: Kierkegaard will not receive the elements at the hands of a servant of the state. With neither bread, wine, nor wife, his ritual sensibility entered a state of repression fixated almost entirely on the written word, and it led to isolation rather than communion.

One could argue that the actions of the plot of *Repetition* are incidental. The volume, some would claim, is not a novel but philosophical psychology on its way to becoming theology. If this were all there were to say, my taking the events as significant for understanding ritualization would misconstrue the genre, which, it is supposed, is a treatment of ideas rather than actions. The "rather than" is what I disagree with. Kierkegaard certainly was interested in the idea of repetition, but characters and narrative were not mere allegorical fronts for those ideas. Even if *Repetition* were essentially a book of reflections, it would be one in which we are shown the ritual and drama of reflecting. The ideas develop out of fictional-autobiographical events; consequently, they include a large amount of narration. And the events narrated are substantive rather than illustrative—the source of, not a front for, ideas.

The themes of *Repetition* are rendered as traits of three characters. Kierkegaard's poet is not one who writes poetry but one who, though embroiled in unhappy love makes his way to the edge of the religious. The prose-writing confidant, a perpetual observer, gets almost as close. The girl is at once the closest and farthest away—closest by virtue of her spontaneity, farthest by virtue of her pre-reflective innocence and exteriority. She does not even "exist" as a character but is off in the wings. She does not act. Despite, or because of, this she is the motive for all the activity in the story.[419] In the final scene, however, she alone can be said to engage in action, by which I mean an act taken to its completion. The narrator is stuck in his domestic ritualization and theatrical voyeurism; the young man, in his liturgized histrionics. The girl cuts through the Gordian knot by deciding to marry someone else. She functions, then, as both the origin and end of action, while the two males, the one collapsing into the other, barely bide their time in the middle of things by engaging in ritualized activities.

Seeing the characters as sources for understanding various aspects of repetition is easier upon re-reading the text. Upon first reading, we are pulled forward by the narrative; upon a second, a "vertical loop" enters an otherwise linear process. A more conventional way to put this is to say that I followed *Repetition*'s *mythos* (plotline), which began to circle, then I turned to its *dianoia* (theme) and *ritus* (style). Cross-cutting the path laid out by the author, I maintain, is precisely what he intended.

The crucial theme is, of course, repetition. Insofar as it is a positive quality, some associated images and synonyms are:

the thunderstorm, religious movement, the exception, ordeals, inwardness, and happy love—all, we must add, by virtue of the absurd. Preliminary, or even in opposition, to repetition in this Kierkegaardian sense are: recollection, unhappy love, poetic melancholy, vapid analysis, observation, reflection, mediation, commotion, doubling, and the merely decorous or formalistic.

Kierkegaard's concept of repetition inverts the ordinary usage of the term in favor of a more eschatological one. Ordinarily, we think of repeating as doing again something we have already done. We employ a spatial metaphor, "going back," to convey the temporal experience implied in "already." Kierkegaard parodies this view by having the confidant act out the metaphor in his attempt to return to Berlin. Seen as one might see a theater performance, his solemn experiment is as farcical as the play he attends. Kierkegaard is certainly not without humor as he portrays the enactment of this scene. The narrator's journey illustrates what I call the "repetition of nostalgia," because it depends on the abortive desire to recover in action what can only be recollected in memory. Though Kierkegaard does not raise the issue in *Repetition*, it is worth asking ourselves whether even memory can repeat the past, if by this we mean reduplicate it.

The young man's problem is the inverse of his confidant's. The confidant desires selected moments from the past; he is nostalgic for a nursemaid and a pool of laughter he once experienced. The aspiring poet, on the other hand, wants to escape his past, but mere escape from his relationship would create guilt. So would staying in it. And guilt will only perpetuate the very mistakes he wants to stop repeating. So what he needs is to find a way to transform the past, to tease a vicious circle out into a spiral, to "repeat forward." I call this the "repetition of hope." Kierkegaard sometimes speaks of it as the "expectation of faith."

Two more views of repetition emerged after the publication of Johan Heiberg's *Urania* in 1844. It contains a review of *Repetition* in which Heiberg distinguishes between natural and spiritual repetition. His model for the former is astronomy and the rhythms of seasonality. The model for the latter is human development and cultural progress. He says, "True, authentic change is a development—that is, in its repetitions it is new; every time it reproduces its contents, it carries along with it something that was merely a bud in the previous existence. . . ."[420] Nature, he claims, changes, but its changes do not progress. They exhibit being rather than becoming and are, therefore, a "resting eternity." This is repetition in the strict sense of his usage, but since the human spirit is characterized by becoming, it in effect annuls natural repetition. Natural repetition is "merely a setting for the precious stone" of human progress.

In *Open Letter to Professor Heiberg . . . from Constantin Constantius* and *A Little Contribution by Constantin Constantius . . .*[421] Kierkegaard exposes Heiberg's misreading of *Repetition* and takes issue with his ideas. Heiberg, missing entirely the irony, thinks the narrator (whom he too easily equates with Kierkegaard) should not have tried to return to Berlin. Furthermore, he thinks Kierkegaard does not distinguish natural from human-spiritual repetition and accuses him of trying to stretch the natural model to cover human activity. Kierkegaard flatly denies that *Repetition* shows any interest in natural cycles and rhythms and accuses Heiberg of sentimentality toward them.[422] Kierkegaard accounts for Heiberg's misreading by insinuating that he had read only the first half of the book and thus missed what becomes obvious only in retrospect after the second half, namely, that the trip was a parody of the sort of repetition he wanted to reject.

In his rebuttal Kierkegaard implies further refinements in his understanding of religious repetition. To summarize them, authentic repetition is (1) discontinuous, not continuous, with what precedes it; (2) individual, not collective ("world historical"); (3) freely willed and passionate, not caused, passive, or "contemplative"; (4) interior ("consciousness raised to the second power"), not bodily or exterior; (5) post-sinful, not innocent ("immediate").

Understood in this way, repetition can hardly be a fact, either bodily or social. In this view repetition, by definition, has nothing whatever to do with ritual. Ritual would be antithetical to it. So Kierkegaardian repetition is an aspiration, an object of faith and hope. This is why Kierkegaard insists that the question in *Repetition* is whether it is even possible. After all, neither the younger nor older man claims to have experienced it. This sort of repetition is not immanent in either natural cycles or cultural development. So its most distinctive quality is its discontinuity, which, if we value it, we might call "religious," or, if we examine it historically, "protestant."[423] Emphasis on continuity in repetition is more characteristically "catholic" and, Kierkegaard would have insisted, Hegelian. Religious repetition, in Kierkegaard's view, is emphatically not a synthesis or continuous development even though he implies an outline its three stages of emergence:[424] (1) Filled with a desire to exercise my freedom, I fear repetitive structures and flee them as traps (the esthetic stage). (2) Desiring to be wise enough to make the most of my experience, I recollect repetitive patterns in order to predict the outcome of various courses of action so I can choose the correct one (the ethical stage). (3) Religious repetition has no precedent, is transcendent, and is no mere recovery of the lost things of the past. The stages are discontinuous. Earlier ones do not contain the potential or "seeds" of later ones. Rather, later ones transcend earlier ones.

With religious repetition severed completely from whatever natural cycles and rhythms Protestant liturgy may have been in touch in nineteenth-century Denmark, ritualization is Kierkegaard's destiny. He is forced into it while he aspires to the impossible "repetition" of Christian faith. The neurosis of being unable ritually to embrace ordinariness persists today, and Kierkegaard remains one of our most instructive teachers.

Postscript

I AM DRAWN TO KIERKEGAARD, THOUGH I DO NOT MUCH LIKE him. He, like Sartre, Casmurro, and Henderson, leaves me depressed about the possibilities for a just, healthy, or nonsexist ritualizing of manhood. Sometimes I am tempted to deal with the problem by cheating, by invoking a short-cut: I write them all off as fiction. But *Repetition* and *The Words* are not merely fiction, and, as should now be evident, framing novels and plays as fictive would not protect me anyway. The frame does not make us safe, because fictions form us. I have lingered long in *Repetition*, because it is such a telling example of the male Protestant West's handling of ritual by repressing it, taming it into mere words, and unconsciously enacting it. We are just now catching up with Kierkegaard's insight into himself, but we should remember that his insights did not cure him. Collectively, we now face some of the same choices that he did regarding the repetitions, females, and older (or younger) men in our lives. It is pressing for us to envision conditions under which ritual might be able to provide us with "pregnant"[425] repetition instead of the abortive sort in which, "as we train our virtues, we cultivate our errors."[426]

Many of the works I have considered are narcissistic or reflexive. We use the former term when we sense their destructive possibilities; the latter, as we become aware of their promising ones. The sort of "narcissistic narrative"[427] that depends

279

on the projection of muses, who then become confused with actual women (as is the case in *Repetition*), is hardly the sort of reflexivity that ritual should be used to deepen. However much the conjunction of reading, writing, and ritual may enhance self-discovery, connectedness, and social change for contemporary Euroamerican women, African Americans, or others not among the class of Euroamerican males who have time to write books, the danger that this conjunction will become a means of self-enclosure, disconnectedness, and fictive self-authorization for Euroamerican men is considerable.

Lonnie Kliever, the most astute theorist of the fictive dimensions of religion, says, "Fictive rituals and symbols of transcendence can triumph over reality by dignifying our deeds and distracting our anxieties—but only for a time!"[428] By "fictive rituals" he does not mean only ritual as it appears in or around works of fiction (my usage in part three), but all ritual insofar as it traffics in symbols of transcendence. For him religion itself is fictive, though necessary. By "fictive" he means that is no longer rooted in primary psychological and social processes, and that it is increasingly the product of self-conscious assemblage. In other words, contemporary religiosity is largely a product of secondary processes, the outcome of deliberate, self-conscious reflection.[429] Therefore, in his view our fictive rites can dignify us only for a time, because we inevitably become aware that we have made them up. Thus, he says, "The burden of fictive religiosity is its inherent irony," and "The odd blessing of fictive religiosity is its inherent iconoclasm."[430]

I agree with Kliever, but with a caveat. Fictive consciousness is not a universal, and the statement, "Religion is fictive," cannot be "true." If all statements about the ultimate nature of things are fictive, so is this one. Consequently, we should only play it (or play with it), not state it as if it were a fact. And who is this "we?" The recognition (or claim) that ritual and religion are fictive arises only at certain times, in specific places. It does so more obviously among members of certain classes and professions. Perhaps it is more pronounced among members of one gender than another. So we should ask: Whose religiosity, whose ritualizing, is it that has become detached from primary processes? And whose ritualizing most requires the acid of irony (according to Sophia, the enemy of women and children) and iconoclasm?

If I were to make a list of candidates for inclusion, it would include all the male authors considered here. It would include many who hold positions of liturgical authority. It would certainly include professors like Kliever and me. But would it include the Blacks who endure our clown show, the Africans whose frogs we dynamite, the six million Jews who have now become clouds? Would it include Regine Olsen, "Renata," or Capitú Padua?

If not, the question is how "we" find our way from a fictive ritual that is tied tightly in knots of self-consciousness to some other kind of ritual that has serious and sustained connections with primary processes, because at the level of primary process there is neither "us" nor "them."

Notes

Part I
1. See, for example, Thomas, *Critical Ethnography*.

Chapter 1
2. Part of this chapter was delivered in 1990 as a lecture, "Ritual, Memory, and Meaning" at the Graduate Theological Union in Berkeley, California. In 1992 another portion of it was delivered under the title, "Reinventing Ritual," at the Centre for Religious Studies, University of Toronto. Original publication was in *Soundings* (75.1 [1992]: 21-41), a publication of the Society for Values in Higher Education. It is reprinted here with the permission of *Soundings*.

3. Hine, "Self-Generated." See also her "Self-Created."

4. See my *Beginnings*, 53 ff.

5. See, for example, Walker, *Women's Rituals*; Beck and Metrick, *Art of Ritual*; Budapest, *Holy Book*; Ruether, *Women-Church*; Procter-Smith *Rite*; and Iglehart, *Womanspirit*.

6. See Imber-Black, *Families*; Foster and Little, "Vision Quest."

7. See, for instance, Fernandez, *Bwiti*; Thompson, *Flash of the Spirit*; and Badone, *Appointed Hour*.

8. See, for example, Turner, "Dramatic Ritual."

9. Ritual, he says, is "prescribed formal behavior for occasions not given over to technological routine, having reference to beliefs in mystical beings or powers" (Turner, *Forest of Symbols*, 19). For a critique of this definition see Grimes, "Victor Turner's Definition."

10. Tambiah, "A Performative Approach to Ritual," 119.

11. Exemplary historical accounts of rites include Carnes, *Secret Ritual* and Watson, "Chinese Funerary Rites."

12. Hobsbawm and Ranger, *Invention*, 4.

13. Hobsbawm and Ranger, *Invention*, 1.

14. David Cannadine, one of the authors in *The Invention of Tradition*, calls these weddings "essays in television ritual" ("The British Monarchy, c. 1820-1977," in Hobsbawm and Ranger, *Invention*, 159).

15. See also Terrance Ranger, "The Invention of Tradition in Colonial Africa," in Hobsbawm and Ranger, *Invention*, 247.

16. Hobsbawm and Ranger, *Invention*, 2.

17. Hobsbawm and Ranger, *Invention*, 12.

18. Hobsbawm and Ranger, *Invention*, 8.

19. Bellah, *Habits*. See also Vitz (*Psychology as Religion*), who castigates it as both bad science and bad faith. Lasch's *The Culture of Narcissism* is the best seller that popularized the now widespread view of North Americans as narcissists.

20. Wagner, *Invention*, 122.

21. See, for example, Hultkrantz, *Native Religions*, 14; and Cooper, "Individualism."

22. Goody, "Religion and Ritual."

23. Wagner, *Invention*, 44.

24. Wagner, *Invention*, 55.

25. Wagner, *Invention*, 56-7. I have no doubt that this is sometimes—perhaps often—the case. The first few years of the life of the Ritual Studies Lab, about which I have written elsewhere, (*Ritual Criticism*, chapter 5.) were plagued by the problem of self-consciousness and a persistent sense of the artificiality of trying to learn and teach skills essential to the construction of rites.

26. Wagner, *Invention*, 29. Wagner wryly defines an anthropologist as someone who uses the word "culture" with hope, or even with faith. Anthropological understanding, he says, is "the metaphorization of life into culture" (28). Anthropology, he muses, is a Western "culture cult," parallel to cargo cults (31). The mysterious, magical, invisible, all-determinative cargo called culture only becomes visible when there is culture shock. Wagner argues that, subjected to experiences beyond one's own interpersonal competence, anthropologists objectify the discrepancy as an entity called culture (9). Culture is invented as a construct to account for the shock of difference. This construct accounts both for "their" otherness and "our" self-consciousness. Our self-consciousness leads to cultural relativism, the view that our values, rites, and symbols are not given but invented.

27. Connerton, *Remember*, 72-3.

28. Connerton (4) bemoans the fact that this type of memory has been given preferential treatment for two millennia of hermeneutic

inquiry, hence texts rather than the human body remain the determinative example in many views of social memory.

29. Connerton *Remember*, 94, 96, 100. Connerton seems unwittingly to compromise his critique of linguistic imperialism when he asks what it is that is remembered in commemorative ceremonies, and answers: "A community is reminded of its identity as represented by and told in a master narrative" (70). In effect, this statement implies that a ritual performance is dependent on a primary narrative, a linguistic text, specifically a "collective autobiography" [his term].

30. Connerton, *Remember*, 70. However, he appropriates the definition of ritual used by Lukes: Ritual is "rule-governed activity of a symbolic character which draws the attention of its participants to objects of thought and feeling which they hold to be of special significance" (44).

31. See Connerton, *Remember*, 40, 22, 35.

32. For more on the container/contained metaphor see Lakoff and Johnson, *Metaphors We Live By*, 29 ff.

33. Connerton, *Remember*, 64.

34. Connerton, *Remember*, 102.

35. On the cognitive dimensions of ritual see Jennings, "Ritual Knowledge."

36. Connerton's view of memory parallels his view of the body. Memory for him is a like funnel or filter. The filter metaphor is useful; it reminds us of memory's selectivity. But like all metaphors it obscures other important truths. Memory is also like a muscle: it grows stronger as exercised; it moves the body into action; it is a source of action, not merely the recipient of it.

37. Gill, *Native American Religious Action*, 58 ff. See also his "Hopi Kachina."

38. Wagner, *Invention*, 105.

39. Americans, Wagner suggests (57), conventionally treat the "innate" as made up, but they also complain about the contrived and made up qualities of things. Thus, one might suppose, they search more intensely for what is natural or "deep." Knowledge that rites are invented rather than given or innate does not necessarily make people more willing to embrace ritual change.

40. Myerhoff, *Number Our Days*, 86.

41. See the films, "Number Our Days" and "In Her Own Time," available from Direct Cinema.

42. Turner, *Forest of Symbols*, 51.

43. A similar critique is developed by Staal in "The Meaninglessness of Ritual." For a critique of Staal and further reflection on Sperber's thesis see Penner, "Language, Ritual and Meaning."

44. Sperber, *Rethinking*.
45. Sperber, *Rethinking*, 83.
46. Sperber, *Rethinking*, 50.
47. Sperber, *Rethinking*, 118.
48. Sperber, *Rethinking*, 148.
49. Sperber, *Rethinking*, 117.
50. Sperber, *Rethinking*, x-xi.
51. Sperber, *Rethinking*, 145.
52. Sperber, *Rethinking*, 113.
53. Sperber, *Rethinking*, x.

Chapter 2

54. Originally delivered in 1990 as a plenary address to the annual meeting of the North American Academy of Liturgy in St. Louis, Missouri, this chapter was subsequently published in the *Proceedings of the North American Academy of Liturgy* (1990: 15-34). Reprinted here with the permission of the Academy.

55. Myerhoff, *Number Our Days*, 86.

Chapter 3

56. This chapter is the revised form of a lecture delivered in 1992 at the University of Notre Dame for a conference entitled "Reclaiming Our Rites." In 1993 the paper was discussed in Albuquerque, New Mexico, at the annual meeting of the North American Academy of Liturgy. It was first published in *Studia Liturgica* (23 [1993]: 51-69) and is here reprinted with permission of the Notre Dame Center for Pastoral Liturgy. I am deeply indebted to Mary Collins, Marjorie Procter-Smith, Lynn Ross-Bryant, S.L. Scott, and Janet Walton for their reflections, critique, and encouragement in writing the original paper.

57. The version printed in the actual program differs slightly from this one.

58. Mitchell, "Americans," 181.

59. Mitchell, "Americans," 182.

60. For an alternative theological view of liturgy that emphasizes its public nature but attempts to overcome this tendency to accord it privileged status see Jennings, "Liturgy" and "Sacrament."

61. Mitchell, "Americans," 180.

62. Kavanagh, *Baptism*, 146.

63. The term is used by Aidan Kavanagh in *Studia Liturgica* (20.1 [1990]: 102) and quoted by Nathan Mitchell in "Americans," 180.

64. The term was originally Roy Rappaport's (*Ecology*, 197). It is used by Nathan Mitchell in "Americans," 182.

65. Rappaport, *Ecology*, 175. In my *Ritual Criticism* (9-14) I have argued against such exclusion by definition.

66. Mitchell, "Americans," 183.

67. Mitchell, "Americans," 184.

68. The terms belong to Geertz, (*The Interpretation of Culture*).

69. Ebaugh, "Revitalization."

70. The idea is borrowed from anthropologist Anthony Wallace.

71. This rhetorical strategy parallels the strategy of the 1992 Republican convention in the United States, namely, blaming all moral ills on "the culture" while maintaining that "America" (the country) is unblemished. I am indebted to S.L. Scott for pointing out this parallel.

72. Laird, "Women and Ritual," 337.

73. Laird, "Women and Ritual," 338.

74. See my *Ritual Criticism* (chapter 9) for more on ritual infelicity.

75. Adams, "Decoding."

76. Procter-Smith, *In Her Own Rite*.

77. See, for example, Paige and Paige, *Reproductive Ritual*.

78. Turner, *Forest*, 93.

79. Adams ("De-coding," 332), who advocates a "baptismal paradigm," ought to take this bias in rites of passage theory into account, since he makes explicit use of the theory.

80. Such as Victor Turner, Clifford Geertz, and Roy Rappaport.

81. Such as Rosemary Radford Ruether, Marjorie Procter-Smith, Janet Walton, Mary Collins, Kathleen Hughes, and the many unknown Renatas.

82. Huntington and Metcalf, *Celebrations of Death*.

83. Kavanagh, *Elements*, 56.

84. Kavanagh, *Elements*, 55. This statement is softened considerably by one that follows: "The liturgical assembly is normally always in the business of absorbing cultural elements into itself in a rich diversity of ways and over long periods of time" (57). Clearly, Kavanagh is aware that the liturgy/culture relation is not a one-way street.

85. The usual distinction is that sexuality is biologically given, whereas gender is socially constructed.

Chapter 4

86. "Portals" is reprinted by permission of Macmillan Publishing Company from *The Encyclopedia of Religion*, Mircea Eliade, Editor in Chief, volume 11, pp. 452-453. Copyright © 1987, Macmillan Publishing Company, a division of Macmillan, Inc. "Procession" is reprinted by permission of Macmillan Publishing Company from *The Encyclopedia of Religion*, Mircea Eliade, Editor in Chief, vol. 12, pp. 1-3. Copyright © 1987, Macmillan Publishing Company, a division of Macmillan, Inc.

87. For more on races and the ritual dimensions of sports see the *Journal of Ritual Studies* (7.1 [1993]), a full issue on the topic.

88. See Davies, *Temples*, 240.

89. Landon, "Hymns," 47.

Chapter 5

90. Jonathan Z. Smith, *Place*, 104.

91. *Maps*, 267.

92. See, for example, Albanese, *Nature Religion*; Ross-Bryant, "Land"; Jonathan Z. Smith, *To Take Place*; and Kliever "Story and Space."

93. A documentary video by Jeannette DeBouzek and Diane Reyna, available from Quotidian Independent Documentary Research, 413 10th St., Albuquerque, NM 87102.

94. Wallace, *Culture and Personality*.

95. Jonathan Z. Smith, *Map*.

96. Jonathan Z. Smith, *To Take Place*.

97. See Tuan, "Geopiety," especially 36, n. 1. The term "geopiety" was originally coined by John K. Wright (*Human Nature*, 250-85) to refer to the natural theology and world systems of American pietistic scholars.

98. For an assessment of Frederick Jackson Turner's frontier hypothesis from the point of view of the Hispanic Southwest see Weber (*Myth and History*, 33-54).

99. Here I am not concerned with an explicit theory like Redfield's but with tacit metaphors.

100. The term proxemic, meaning "spatially determined," was coined and discussed by Edward T. Hall (*The Hidden Dimension; The Silent Language*) in his study of the cultural determinants of space.

101. Marty, *Behavers*, 1.

102. Marty is quite aware of the metaphoric nature of his use of maps: "These maps—which are now only metaphorical and can no longer be rendered cartographically . . ." (5).

103. Marty, *Behavers*, 56.

104. Marty, *Behavers*, 160.

105. Marty, *Behavers*, 204.

106. Marty talks as if maps have no permanent effect on either landscapes or map makers. He imagines maps as transparent (204). But a transparent map is no map at all, and maps with markings on them—even if they are on a transparent background—soon become opaque if layered on top of each other as Marty implies with his palimpsest metaphor. Though he is stretching his metaphors, Marty is probably closer to being right when he says that maps leave "sediments" on landscapes (3) and that new maps are made at the expense of old ones (52).

107. Marty, *Behavers*, 16.

108. Michaelsen, "Red Man's Religion," 675.

109. Michaelsen, "Red Man's Religion," 676.

110. Albanese, "Research Needs," 103.

111. Deloria, "Completing," 279.

112. Ortiz, *Tewa*, 18, 22.

113. Beck and Walters, *The Sacred*, 148.

114. Obvious resources for initiating such a critique would include Montejano (*Anglos and Mexicans*) and Weber (*New Spain; The Mexican Frontier; Myth and History*).

115. A Navajo and a White woman (Beck and Walters 1977) have already attempted this in their book *The Sacred: Ways of Knowledge, Sources of Life*.

116. Carol Smith, *Regional Analysis*.

117. Jonathan Z. Smith, *To Take Place*, 104.

Chapter 6

118. In 1990 a portion of this chapter was delivered as a lecture at the Glenbow Museum in Calgary, Alberta. It was called "Sacred Objects, Junkyard Rubble, and the Booty of Civilizations." Subsequently, it was published in *Studies in Religion/Sciences Religieuses* (21.4 [1993] 419-430). It is reprinted here with the permission of the Canadian Corporation for Studies in Religion.

119. On the relation of religion to art objects and television space see Goethals, *Electronic Golden Calf*.

120. The terms "exegetical" and "positional" are Victor Turner's. See his *Forest*, 50-51.

121. Because scholars of religion are likely already familiar with the literature on the cultural processes of iconoclasm and secularization, I omit consideration of them here. However, I am aware that the term "secularization" introduces a host of problems. Here I mean by the term not "the absence of the sacred" but the ideological and legal attempt to confine sacrality to a particular cultural sphere, "the religious," and the simultaneous dispersal of sacrality into tacit processes and relatively "invisible" forms such as one finds in North American advertising or politics.

122. For a discussion of commoditization see Appadurai, *The Social Life of Things*.

123. See Mayo, *American Material Culture* and Daniel Miller, *Material Culture*.

124. For more on the possibility of violating art objects see Grant, *Pillage*.

125. All these terms are used by Glenbow staff person, Elizabeth Herbert (in her "Art") to describe "Art in the Religions and Myths of Mankind."

126. Herbert, "Art."

127. Richardson, "The Artifact."

128. See Kopytoff, "Cultural Biography."

129. Glenbow Museum, *The Spirit Sings*.

130. For more illustrations of the ways objects, both artistic and sacred, are affected by their contexts see the *Journal of Ritual Studies* (6.1 [1992]), a special issue called "Art in Ritual Context."

131. Grimes, *Ritual Criticism*, 10.

132. As is the case, for example, in Bonifazi's study of sacred objects, *A Theology of Things*.

133. A few of these are more fully described in my *Ritual Criticism*, 135 ff.

134. Sexson, *Ordinarily Sacred*, 5.

135. For more on puja see Baab, *Divine Hierarchy*.

136. I do support, however, the practice of allowing Native North American groups actively to use sacred pipes and masks held in museum collections even when doing so contributes to the deterioration of those objects.

137. Rougemont, "Mission of the Artist."

138. A good source on the meanings of domestic objects is Csikszentmihalyi and Rochberg-Halton, *Things*.

139. On the meaning and importance of play and objects of play see Erikson, *Toys*.

Chapter 7

140. This chapter is based on the Davidson Lecture sponsored by Carleton University in Ottawa, Ontario, in cooperation with the Canadian Museum of Civilization's display, "Masks, Mime, and Transformation." Subsequently, the revised lecture was published as "The Biography of a Mask" in *The Drama Review* (36.3 [1992]: 61-77). It is reprinted here with the permission of MIT Press.

141. See, for example, Crumrine and Halpin, *Masks*.

142. Koptyoff, "Things," 64-91.

143. See, for instance, Young-Laughlin and Laughlin, "Masks."

144. Laughlin and Young-Laughlin, "Masks."

145. Eliade, "Masks," 524.

146. Winnicott "Transitional Objects"; see also Schechner, *Between*, 36.

147. Goffman, *Presentation of Self*, 19.

148. See Grimes, *Beginnings*, 75-85.

149. See the *Journal of Ritual Studies* (4.2 [1990]). The entire issue, on ritual and power, takes up this issue.

150. Pernet, "Masks," 264.

151. Eliade, "Masks."

152. See Miles, *Carnal Knowing*.

Part III

153. Research for the chapters in part three was supported by the Research Office of Wilfrid Laurier University and a sabbatical fellowship grant from the Social Sciences and Humanities Research Council of Canada.

154. Detweiler, *Breaking the Fall*, 38.

155. Lincoln, "Notes."

156. Mailloux, *Conventions*. See Fish, *Self-Consuming, Surprised*, and *Text*; and Iser, *Indeterminacy*, "Reading Process," *Implied Reader*, and *Act of Reading*.

157. Resseguie, "Reader," 317.

158. Myerhoff, *Number Our Days*, 86.

159. See Segal, "Myth" and Hardin, "'Ritual.'"

160. See, for instance, Ashley, *Turner*.

161. See Myerhoff and Metzger, "Journal."

162. See especially Burke, *Literature as Symbolic Action*.

163. Frye, *Anatomy*, 104-105.

164. Frye, *Anatomy*, 106, 161.

165. See Frye, *Anatomy*, 109.

166. See Frye, *Scripture*.

167. Miller, *Fiction*, 114.

168. Miller, *Fiction*, 206.

169. Miller, *Fiction*, 20.

170. See Miller, *Fiction*, 6, 16.

171. Miller, *Fiction*, 68.

172. Brown, *Rhythm*, 28-9.

173. Booth, *Dogma*, 181-182.

Chapter 8

174. Reprint permission has been granted by *Religion and Literature* (21.1 [1989]: 9-26), University of Notre Dame, Notre Dame, Indiana).

175. O'Connor, *Violent*, 19.

176. O'Connor, *Violent*, 76-77.

177. O'Connor, *Violent*, 61.

178. O'Connor, *Violent*, 91-92.

179. O'Connor, *Violent*, 106.

180. O'Connor, *Violent*, 113.

181. O'Connor, *Violent*, 171.

182. O'Connor, *Violent*, 182.

183. O'Connor, *Violent*, 209.

184. O'Connor, *Violent*, 241.

185. As simple as it may sound, my claim is debatable, though I will not enter into the fray here. John May (*Pruning*), for instance, thinks the central dramatic metaphor is that of the seed from the New

Testament parable of the sower, whereas Davies ("Anagogical") thinks it is that of bread from the Eucharist.

186. O'Connor, *Manners*, 111.

187. See O'Connor, *Manners*, 204, 469.

188. Davies, "Anagogical."

189. In O'Connor, *Stories*.

190. By implication, then, I reject O'Connor's own claim that *The Violent Bear It Away* is "a very minor hymn to the Eucharist" (*Habit* 389). Certainly, the author links baptismal imagery to eucharistic imagery, but the former controls the latter, not vice-versa. The Tarwaters hunger for baptizing, not for bread.

191. See O'Connor, *Habit* 352-353.

192. O'Connor, *Manners*, 162.

193. Davies ("Anagogical") argues that O'Connor conflates the medieval anagogical and moral levels.

194. Frye, *Anatomy*, 115 ff.

195. Frye, *Anatomy*, 122.

196. If David Williams (*"Via Negativa"*) is correct about the importance of the *via negativa* for O'Connor, one might surmise that anagogical symbols not only encompass and thereby conserve other kinds of symbols, they also tend to negate or undermine them. This dynamic would account for the torque anagogy exercises on the coherence of a symbol system.

197. Gerhart and Russell, *Metaphoric*.

198. The search leads to some peculiar evasions. Brinkmeyer ("Borne"), for instance, tries to justify the violence of the novel by arguing that O'Connor sees no other way than exaggeration to reach her secularized readers. True as this claim may be, it evades the moral issue internal to the plot. Peter Hawkins ("Overstatement") has pointed out the weaknesses of a novelist's resorting to hyperbole and overstatement in order to get a reader's attention, and he has criticized readers who resort to overinterpretation as a strategy for making texts seem religious.

Another evasion tactic is that of blurring the distinction between the values of critic, character, narrator, and author. For instance, Getz (*Nature and Grace*, 9, n. 9) says ambiguously, "The murder of Bishop seems of little consequence in moral terms. The commission of a murder first confirms Tarwater in evil and then the same act frees him to begin doing good . . ." To whom is the death of Bishop of little consequence? From whose point of view is Tarwater doing good after the death?

Getz and others sometimes cite as their warrant O'Connor's own comment that the murder "is forgotten by God and of no interest to society" (*Habit*, 343). Unless the act scandalizes the reader, however, it loses much of its Christian impact. Regardless of what God and society think, I doubt that the murder is forgotten by either Francis, Rayber, or O'Connor.

199. The best brief summary on the role of ritual in literary criticism is Hardin's "'Ritual.'" The most comprehensive bibliographical survey of the relations between religion and literature is Ruland's *Horizons*.

200. *Crossroads*, 81, 83.

201. "Vision," 35.

202. J. Oates Smith, "Ritual and Violence," 554, 552, 549.

203. J. Oates Smith, "Ritual and Violence," 553.

204. J. Oates Smith, "Ritual and Violence, 552. See, for example, Eggenschwiler (*Humanism*) and McDermott ("Voices").

205. Jonathan Z. Smith, "Bare Facts," 124-5.

206. Gay, "Public," 250.

207. Gay, "Public," 259.

208. On doubling see Rosenfield ("Shadow") and Paulson ("Apocalypse").

209. Bateson, *Ecology*.

210. On various ways that rites fail or otherwise lose legitimacy see Grimes, *Ritual Criticism*, chapter 9.

211. What is true of a rite as a whole is often true of its constituent symbols, namely, that they are irresolvably ambivalent. Getz (*Nature and Grace*, 101) recognizes this fact in her discussion of the multivalent, polarized meanings of fire and water.

Chapter 9

212. Bellow, *Henderson*, 162.

213. Bellow, *Henderson*, 50.

214. Bellow, *Henderson*, 42.

215. Bellow, *Henderson*, 240.

216. Bellow, *Henderson*, 55.

217. Bellow, *Henderson*, 68.

218. Bellow, *Henderson*, 74.

219. Bellow, *Henderson*, 91.

220. Bellow, *Henderson*, 117.

221. Bellow, *Henderson*, 158.

222. Bellow, *Henderson*, 159.

223. Bellow, *Henderson*, 166.

224. Bellow, *Henderson*, 169.

225. Bellow, *Henderson*, 231.

226. Bellow, *Henderson*, 276.

227. Zuesse, "Meditation," 519.

228. Pilgrim, "Ritual," 70.
229. Bellow, *Henderson*, 183.
230. Bellow, *Henderson*, 22.

Chapter 10
231. Genet, *Blacks*, 84.
232. Genet, *Blacks*, 105-106.
233. Genet, *Blacks*, 122.
234. Genet, *Blacks*, 18, 65, 15, 22.
235. See Sartre, *St. Genet*, x.
236. Artaud, *Double*, 12.
237. Genet, *Blacks*, 27-28.
238. Genet, *Blacks*, 3.
239. Genet, *Blacks*, 4.
240. Genet, *Blacks*, 99.
241. Genet, *Blacks*, 100.
242. Genet, *Blacks*, 14, 27.
243. Genet, *Blacks*, 20.
244. Genet, *Blacks*, 116.
245. Genet, *Blacks*, 119.
246. See, for instance, Genet, *Blacks*, 17.
247. Genet, *Blacks*, 36-37.
248. Genet, *Blacks*, 32.
249. Genet, *Blacks*, 58.
250. Genet, *Blacks*, 76-77.
251. Schechner, *Essays*, 46.
252. Schechner, *Essays*, 55 ff.
253. For further discussion of ceremony see Grimes, *Beginnings*, 41-42.
254. Genet, *Blacks*, 12.
255. See Durkheim, *Elementary*, 62.
256. Gluckman, *Rebellion*.
257. Driver, *Quest*, 346.
258. Cited in Booth, *Irony*, 230.
259. Gluckman, *Essays*, 36-37.
260. Booth, *Dogma*, 22 ff.
261. Rappaport, *Ecology*, 193.
262. Booth, *Irony*, 36.
263. Genet, *Blacks*, 58.

Chapter 11
264. Wiesel, *Gates*, 19.
265. Wiesel, *Gates*, 31.
266. Wiesel, *Gates*, 63.

267. Wiesel, *Gates*, 90.

268. Wiesel, *Gates*, 116.

269. Wiesel, *Gates*, 160.

270. Wiesel, *Gates*, 165.

271. Wiesel, *Gates*, 168.

272. Wiesel, *Gates*, 173.

273. Wiesel, *Gates*, 180.

274. Wiesel, *Gates*, 196.

275. Wiesel, *Gates*, 198.

276. Wiesel, *Gates*, 219.

277. Wiesel, *Gates*, vi-x.

278. Wiesel, *Gates*, 219.

279. Wiesel, *Gates*, 189.

Chapter 12

280. Sartre, *Words*, 37-38.

281. Sartre, *Words*, 17.

282. Sartre, *Philosophy*, 58-59.

283. Sartre, *Words*, 20.

284. Sartre, *Words*, 18.

285. This view is even more obvious in Sartre's *St. Genet*. In it he follows Jean Genet's own lead in *A Thief's Journal* by treating crime as a kind of inverted ceremonial of the underworld. As in *The Words*, Sartre's rhetoric is infested with the rhetoric of ritual: Genet's life is a "liturgical drama" shot through with profane "hierophanies" and "fictive communion."

286. Sartre, *Words*, 25.

287. Sartre, *Words*, 28-29.

288. See Rappaport, *Ecology*, 175.

289. Winnicott, "Transitional," 233.

290. Sartre, *Words*, 233.

291. Sartre, *Words*, 40.

292. Sartre, *Words*, 44.

293. Sartre, *Words*, 54.

294. Jonathan Z. Smith, "Bare Facts," 124-125.

295. Sartre, *Words*, 60.

296. The term is from Goffman, *Interaction*.

297. Sartre, *Words*, 65.

298. Sartre, *Words*, 72.

299. Sartre, *Words*, 76.

300. For more on the religiosity of cinema attendance see Bryant, "Cinema," 101.

301. Sartre, *Words*, 104.

302. Sartre, *Words*, 112.

303. Sartre, *Words*, 136.

304. Sartre, *Words*, 124.

305. Sartre, *Words*, 157.

306. Sartre, *Words*, 149.

307. Sartre, *Words*, 158.

308. Sartre, *Words*, 53.

309. Sartre, *Words*, 121-122.

310. Sartre, *Words*, 43.

311. Artaud, *Double*, 111.

312. Sartre, *Words*, 110.

313. Sartre, *Words*, 62.

314. Sartre, *Words*, 149.

315. Sartre, *Words*, 153.

316. See Ong, "Maranatha."

317. Sartre, *Words*, 126.

Chapter 13

318. Assis, *Casmurro*, 11-12.

319. Sartre, *Words*, 38-39.

320. Sartre, *Words*, 123.

321. Sartre, *Words*, 45.

322. Freud, *Works*, 9: 117 ff.

323. O'Keefe, *Lightening*, 349 ff.

324. Assis, *Casmurro*, 82.

325. See Jung, *Memories*, chapters 1-2.

326. Assis, *Casmurro*, 86.

327. Assis, *Casmurro*, 87.

328. Assis, *Casmurro*, 34-35.

329. Assis, *Casmurro*, 33.

330. Assis, *Casmurro*, 157.

331. Assis, *Casmurro*, 111.

332. Assis, *Casmurro*, 133.

333. Assis, *Casmurro*, 94.

334. Assis, *Casmurro*, 127.

335. Assis, *Casmurro*, 109.

336. Assis, *Casmurro*, 111.

337. Assis, *Casmurro*, 125.

338. Assis, *Casmurro*, 39.

339. Assis, *Casmurro*, 53.

340. Assis, *Casmurro*, 118.

341. Schechner, "Restoration," 3.

342. Assis, *Casmurro*, 119.

343. Assis, *Casmurro*, 187.

344. Assis, *Casmurro*, 205.

345. Assis, *Casmurro*, 183.

346. Assis, *Casmurro*, 85.

347. Assis, *Casmurro*, 152.

348. Tillich, *Dynamics*.

349. Austin, *How To Do Things with Words*.

350. Assis, *Casmurro*, 104.

351. See Rougemont, *Love*.

352. Assis, *Casmurro*, 128.

353. Assis, *Casmurro*, 200.

354. Assis, *Casmurro*, 23.

355. Assis, *Casmurro*, 23.

356. Assis, *Casmurro*, 15.

357. Assis, *Casmurro*, 13.

Chapter 14

358. Goffman, *Presentation*, 22.

359. Unless otherwise specified, all references are to Kierkegaard, *Fear and Trembling* and *Repetition*, translated by Howard and Edna Hong, and abbreviated *Repetition*.

360. Fenger, *Kierkegaard*, 21.

361. Mackey, *Poet*, 247.

362. The phrase belongs to Howard V. and Edna H. Hong (in Kierkegaard, *Repetition*, xxi-xxv, 357). They offer it as the best interpretation of Kierkegaard's subtitle, "a Venture in Experimenting Psychology."

363. Fenger, *Kirkegaard*, 183-184.

364. Kierkegaard, *Repetition*, 131.

365. Kierkegaard, *Repetition*, 133.

366. Kierkegaard, *Repetition*, 136.

367. Kierkegaard, *Repetition*, 133-134.

368. Kierkegaard, *Repetition*, 135.

369. Kierkegaard, *Experimental*, 7; compare *Repetition*, 133. Note that the abbreviated title *Experimental* refers to Lowrie's translation, while *Repetition* denotes the Hongs' translation.

370. Kierkegaard, *Repetition*, 136.

371. Kierkegaard, *Repetition*, 141.

372. Kierkegaard, *Repetition*, 142.

373. Kierkegaard, *Repetition*, 142.

374. Kierkegaard, *Repetition*, 145.

375. The last line of the quotation above.

376. Kierkegaard, *Repetition*, xxxiii.

377. Kierkegaard, *Repetition*, 146.

378. Kierkegaard, *Repetition*, 148.

379. Kierkegaard, *Repetition*, 147.

380. Kierkegaard, *Repetition*, 163-164.
381. Kierkegaard, *Repetition*, 161.
382. Kierkegaard, *Experimental*, 165, n. 32.
383. Kierkegaard, *Repetition*, 166.
384. Kierkegaard, *Repetition*, 166.
385. Kierkegaard, *Repetition*, 173.
386. Kierkegaard, *Repetition*, 172.
387. Kierkegaard, *Repetition*, 180.
388. Kierkegaard, *Repetition*, 181.
389. Kierkegaard, *Repetition*, 185.
390. Kierkegaard, *Repetition*, 185.
391. Kierkegaard, *Repetition*, 197.
392. Kierkegaard, *Repetition*, 210.
393. Kierkegaard, *Repetition*, 209.
394. Kierkegaard, *Repetition*, 211.
395. Kierkegaard, *Repetition*, 214.
396. Kierkegaard, *Experimental*, 140; compare Kierkegaard, *Repetition*, 217.
397. Kierkegaard, *Repetition*, 221-222.
398. The term is Gluckman's in *Rebellion*.
399. Kierkegaard, *Repetition*, 222.
400. Kierkegaard, *Repetition*, 226.
401. Kierkegaard, *Repetition*, 228.
402. Kierkegaard, *Repetition*, 230.
403. Kierkegaard, *Repetition*, 188.
404. See Kierkegaard, *Repetition*, 211.
405. Kierkegaard, *Repetition*, 214.
406. Kierkegaard, *Repetition*, 218.
407. Kierkegaard, *Repetition*, 188.
408. Kierkegaard, *Repetition*, 225.
409. Kierkegaard wrote, "Instead of the plot in *Repetition*, I could imagine something like this: 'A young man with imagination and a lot more, but who hitherto has been otherwise occupied, falls in love with a young girl—to use an experienced coquette here is not very interesting psychologically except from another angle. This young girl is of course pure and innocent but very imaginative in an erotic way. He comes with his simple ideas. She develops him. Just when she is really delighted with him, it becomes apparent that he cannot remain with her. A prodigious desire for multiplicity is awakened, and she must be set aside. In a way, she herself had made a seducer of him, a seducer with the limitation that he can never seduce her. Incidentally, it could be very interesting to have him sometime later, at the peak of his powers, improved by experi-

ence, proceed to seduce her as well, because he owed her so much'" (quoted in *Repetition*, 325).

410. Kierkegaard, *Journals and Papers*, 5:43.

411. Kierkegaard, *Letters and Documents*, 90.

412. Kierkegaard, *Letters and Documents*, 115.

413. Kierkegaard, *Letters and Documents*, 121.

414. Kierkegaard, *Letters and Documents*, 136.

415. Kierkegaard, *Letters and Documents*, 115.

416. Kierkegaard, *Letters and Documents*, 124.

417. Kierkegaard, *Letters and Documents*, 93.

418. Kierkegaard, *Letters and Documents*, 33.

419. I have discussed this tendency to remove feminine symbols from the fray and install them on pedestals as motives for action in *Symbol and Conquest*, chapter 5. There I showed how the Santa Fe Fiesta Queen played a role similar to that of the fiance in *Repetition*, namely, that of an unmoved mover, to use Aristotle's term for God.

420. Cited in Kierkegaard, *Repetition*, 379.

421. In these works I think Constantin can safely be equated with Kierkegaard. In *Repetition* Constantin was a character, but here he is a scarcely disguised persona.

422. Kierkegaard, *Repetition*, 292.

423. My use of lower case indicates that I am talking about religious sensibilities, not denominations.

424. See Kierkegaard, *Repetition*, 301.

Postscript

425. See Kierkegaard, *Repetition*, 292, 294.

426. Goethe, quoted by Heiberg and then cited in Kierkegaard, *Repetition*, 34.

427. The phrase is Hutcheon's in *Narcissistic Narrative*.

428. Kliever, "Fictive," 658.

429. See Kliever, "Fictive," 662.

430. Kliever, "Fictive," 659.

References

Adams, William Seth. "De-coding the Obvious: Reflections on Baptismal Ministry in the Episcopal Church." *Worship* 66.4 (1992): 327-338.

Ahlstrom, Sydney E. *A Religious History of the American People.* New Haven, CT: Yale University Press, 1972.

Albanese, Catherine L. *Nature Religion in America: From the Algonkian Indians to the New Age.* Chicago: University of Chicago Press, 1990.

Albanese, Catherine L. "Research Needs in American Religious History." *Council on the Study of Religion Bulletin* 10.4 (1979): 102-107.

Amado, Jorgé. *Tent of Miracles.* Translated by Barbara Shelby. New York: Avon, 1971.

Appadurai, Arjun, ed. *The Social Life of Things.* Cambridge: Cambridge University Press, 1986.

Artaud, Antonin. *The Theater and its Double.* Translated by Mary Caroline Richards. New York: Grove, 1958.

Ashley, Kathleen, ed. *Victor Turner and the Construction of Cultural Criticism: Between Literature and Anthropology.* Bloomington: Indiana University Press, 1990.

Assis, Machado de. *Dom Casmurro.* Translated by Helen Caldwell. New York: Avon, 1980.

Austin, J.L. *How To Do Things With Words.* Edited by J.O. Urmson. New York: Oxford University Press, 1962.

Baab, Lawrence. *The Divine Hierarchy: Popular Hinduism in Central India.* New York: Columbia University Press, 1975.

Babcock-Abrahams, Barbara. "The Novel and the Carnival World." *Modern Language Notes* 89.6 (1974): 911-937.

Badone, Ellen. *The Appointed Hour: Death, Worldview and Social Change in Brittany*. Berkeley, CA: University of California Press, 1989.

Bateson, Gregory. *Steps to an Ecology of Mind*. San Francisco: Chandler, Daniel, and W. Larry Ventis, 1982.

Beck, Peggy V., and Anna L. Walters. *The Sacred: Ways of Knowledge, Sources of Life*. Tsaile, AZ: Navajo Community College Press, 1977.

Beck, Renee, and Sydney Barbara Metrick. *The Art of Ritual: A Guide to Creating and Performing Your Own Rituals for Growth and Change*. Berkeley, CA: Celestial Arts, 1990.

Bellah, Robert. *Varieties of Civil Religion*. San Francisco: Harper & Row, 1980.

Bellah, Robert, and others. *Habits of the Heart: Individualism and Commitment in American Life*. Berkeley, CA: University of California Press, 1985.

Bellow, Saul. *Henderson the Rain King*. New York: Viking, 1974.

Bonifazi, Conrad. *A Theology of Things: A Study of Man in His Physical Environment*. Westport, CT: Greenwood, 1967.

Booth, Wayne C. *Modern Dogma and the Rhetoric of Assent*. Chicago: University of Chicago Press, 1974.

Booth, Wayne C. *A Rhetoric of Irony*. Chicago: Unversity of Chicago Press, 1974.

Brinkmeyer, Robert H., Jr. "Borne Away by Violence: The Reader and Flannery O'Connor." *The Southern Review* 15 (1977): 313-321.

Brody, Hugh. *Maps and Dreams: Indians and the British Columbia Frontier*. London: Norman & Hobhouse, 1981.

Brown, E.K. *Rhythm in the Novel*. Toronto: University of Toronto Press, 1950.

Bryant, M. Darrol. "Cinema, Religion, and Popular Culture." In *Religion in Film*. Edited by John R. May and Michael Bird. Knoxville: University of Tennessee Press, 1982.

Budapest, Zsuzsanna. *The Holy Book of Women's Mysteries*. Berkeley, CA: Wingbow, 1989.

Burke, Kenneth. *Language as Symbolic Action: Essays on Life, Literature and Method*. Berkeley: University of California Press, 1968.

Burke, Kenneth. *The Rhetoric of Religion: Studies in Logology*. Berkeley: University of California Press, 1970.

Carnes, Mark C. *Secret Ritual and Manhood in Victorian America*. New Haven: Yale University Press, 1989.

Clebsch, William A. *From Sacred to Profane America: The Role of Religion in American History*. New York: Harper & Row, 1968.

Connerton, Paul. *How Societies Remember*. Cambridge: Cambridge University Press, 1989.

Cooper, Guy H. "Individualism and Integration in Navajo Religion." In *Religion in Native North America*, 67-78. Edited by Christopher Vecsey. Moscow, ID: University of Idaho Press, 1990.

Crumrine, N. Ross, and Marjorie Halpin, eds. *The Power of Symbols: Masks and Masquerade in the Americas*. Vancouver: University of British Columbia Press, 1983.

Csikszentmihalyi, Mihaly, and Eugene Rochberg-Halton. *The Meaning of Things: Domestic Symbols and the Self*. Cambridge, England: Cambridge University Press, 1981.

Davies, Horton. "Anagogical Signals in Flannery O'Connor's Fiction." *Thought* 55 (1980): 428-438.

Davies, J.G. *Temples, Churches and Mosques: A Guide to the Appreciation of Religious Architecture*. Oxford: Oxford University Press, 1982.

Delattre, Roland. "Ritual Resourcefulness and Cultural Pluralism." *Soundings* 61.3 (1978): 281-301.

Deloria, Vine, Jr. "Completing the Theological Circle: Civil Religion in America." *Regious Education* 71.3 (1976): 278-287.

Detweiler, Robert. *Breaking the Fall: Religious Readings of Contemporary Fiction*. San Francisco: Harper & Row, 1989.

Driskell, Leon, and Joan Brittain. *The Eternal Crossroads*. Lexington, KY: The University Press of Kentucky, 1966.

Driver, Tom F. *Romantic Quest and Modern Query: A History of the Modern Theatre*. New York: Delacourte, 1970.

Durkheim, Emile. *The Elementary Forms of the Religious Life*. Translated by Joseph W. Swain. New York: Free Press, 1965.

Ebaugh, Helen. "The Revitalization Movement in the Catholic Church: The Institutional Dilemma of Power." *Sociological Analysis* 52.1 (1991): 1-12.

Eggenschwiler, David. *The Christian Humanism of Flannery O'Connor*. Detroit: Wayne State University, 1959.

Eliade, Mircea. "Masks." *Encyclopedia of World Art* 9: 520-525. New York: McGraw-Hill, 1964.

Eliade, Mircea. *The Sacred and the Profane: The Nature of Religion*. Translated by Willard R. Trask. New York: Harper & Row, 1961 [1957].

Erikson, Erik. *Toys and Reasons: Stages in the Ritualization of Experience*. New York: Norton, 1977.

Fenger, Henning. *Kierkegaard: The Myths and their Origins*. Translated by George C. Schoolfield. New Haven: Yale University Press, 1980.

Fenn, Richard. *Liturgies and Trials*. New York: Pilgrim, 1982.

Fernandez, James. *Bwiti: An Ethnography of the Religious Imagination in Africa*. Princeton: Princeton University Press, 1982.

Fish, Stanley. *Is there a Text in this Class? The Authority of Interpretive Communities*. Cambridge: Harvard University Press, 1980.

Fish, Stanley. *Self-Consuming Artifacts: The Experience of Seventeenth-Century Literature*. Berkeley: University of California Press, 1972.

Fish, Stanley. *Surprised by Sin: The Reader in Paradise Lost*. Berkeley:

Foster, Steven, and Meredith Little. "The Vision Quest: Passing from Childhood to Adulthood," 79-110. In *Betwixt & Between: Patterns of Masculine and Feminine Initiation*. Edited by Louise Carus Mahdi and others. La Salle, IL: Open Court, 1987.

Freud, Sigmund. *The Complete Psychological Works of Sigmund Freud*. Edited by James Strachey. London: Hogarth, 1959.

Frye, Northrop. *Anatomy of Criticism: Four Essays*. New York: Atheneum, 1968.

Frye, Northrop. *The Secular Scripture: A Study of the Structure of Romance*. Cambridge, MA: Harvard University Press, 1976.

Gay, Volney. "Public Rituals Versus Private Treatment: Psychodynamics of Prayer." *Journal of Religion and Health* 17 (1978): 244-260.

Geertz, Clifford. *The Interpretation of Culture*. New York: Basic, 1973.

Genet, Jean. *The Blacks: A Clown Show*. Translated by Bernard Frechtman. New York: Grove, 1960.

Genet, Jean. *The Thief's Journal*. Translated by Bernard Frechtman. New York: Grove, 1964.

Gennep, Arnold van. *The Rites of Passage*. Translated by Monika B. Vizedom and Gabrielle L. Caffee. Chicago: University of Chicago Press, 1960.

Gerhart, Mary, and Alan Russell. *The Metaphoric Process: The Creation of Scientific and Religious Understanding*. Forth Worth: Texas Christian University, 1984.

Getz, Lorine M. *Nature and Grace in Flannery O'Connor's Fiction*. Toronto: Edwin Mellen, 1982.

Gill, Sam D. "Hopi Kchina Cult Initiation: The Shocking Beginning of the Hopi's Religious Life." *Journal of the American Academy of Religion*, Supplement 45.2 (1977): 447-514.

Gill, Sam. *Native American Religious Action: A Performance Approach to Religion*. Columbia, SC: University of South Carolina Press, 1987.

Girard, René. *Deceit, Desire, and the Novel: Self and Other in Literary Structure.* Translated by Yvonne Freccero. Baltimore: Johns Hopkins University Press, 1965.

Girard, René. *Violence and the Sacred.* Edited and Translated by Patrick Gregory. Baltimore: Johns Hopkins University Press, 1977.

Glenbow Museum. *The Spirit Sings: Artistic Traditions of Canada's First Peoples.* Toronto: McClelland and Stewart, 1987.

Gluckman, Max. *Rituals of Rebellion in South-East Africa.* Manchester: Manchester University Press, 1954.

Gluckman, Max, ed. *Essays on the Ritual of Social Relations.* Manchester, England: Manchester University Press, 1962.

Goethals, Gregor. *The Electronic Golden Calf: Images, Religion, and the Making of Meaning.* Cambridge, MA: Cowley, 1990.

Goffman, Erving. *Frame Analysis: An Essay on the Organization of Experience.* New York: Harper & Row, 1974.

Goffman, Erving. *Interaction Ritual: Essays on Face-to Face Behavior.* New York: Doubleday Anchor, 1967.

Goffman, Erving. *The Presentation of Self in Everyday Life.* Garden City: Doubleday, 1959.

Goody, Jack. "Religion and Ritual: The Definitional Problem." *British Journal of Sociology* 12 (1961): 142-164.

Grant, Judith. *A Pillage of Art.* New York: Roy, 1966.

Grimes, Ronald L. *Beginnings in Ritual Studies.* Washington, DC: University Press of America, 1982.

Grimes, Ronald L. *Ritual Criticism.* Columbia, SC: University of South Carolina Press, 1990.

Grimes, Ronald L. *Symbol and Conquest: Public Ritual and Drama in Santa Fe, New Mexico.* Albuquerque: University of New Mexico, 1992 [1976].

Grimes, Ronald. "Victor Turner's Definition, Theory, and Sense of Ritual." In *Victor Turner and the Construction of Cultural Criticism: Between Literature and Anthropology,* 141-146. Edited by Kathleen M. Ashley. Bloomington: Indiana University Press, 1990.

Gunn, Giles B., ed. *Literature and Religion.* New York: Harper & Row, 1971.

Hall, Edward T. *The Hidden Dimension.* Garden City, NY: Doubleday, 1966.

Hall, Edward T. *The Silent Language.* Garden City, NY: Doubleday Anchor, 1973.

Hardin, Richard R. "'Ritual' in Recent Criticism: The Elusive Sense of Community." *PMLA* 98 (1983): 846-862.

Hawkins, Peter S. "Problems of Overstatement in Religious Fiction and Criticism." *Renascence* 32 (1980): 36-46.

Heilman, Samuel. *Synagogue Life: A Study in Symbolic Interaction.* Chicgo: University of Chicago Press, 1976.

Herbert, Elizabeth. "Art in the Religions and Myths of Mankind." *Glenbow* 9.1 (1989): 4-7.

Hine, Virginia. "Self-Created Ceremonies of Passage." In *Betwixt & Between: Patterns of Masculine and Feminine Initiation*, 304-326. Edited by Louise Carus Mahdi and others. La Salle, IL: Open Court, 1987.

Hine, Virginia. "Self-Generated Ritual: Trend or Fad?" *Worship* 55.1 (1981): 404-419.

Hobsbawn, Eric, and Terence Ranger, eds. *The Invention of Tradition.* Cambridge, England: Cambridge University Press, 1983.

Hultkrantz, Åke. *Native Religions of North America.* San Francisco: Harper & Row, 1987.

Huntington, Richard, and Peter Metcalf. *Celebrations of Death: The Anthropology of Mortuary Ritual.* Cambridge: Cambridge University Press, 1979.

Hutcheon, Linda. *Narcissistic Narrative: The Metafictional Paradox.* Waterloo, Canada: Wilfrid Laurier University Press, 1980.

Iglehart, Hallie Iglehart. *Womanspirit: A Guide to Women's Wisdom.* San Francisco: Harper & Row, 1983.

Imber-Black, Evan, and others. *Rituals in Families and Family Therapy.* New York: Norton, 1988.

Iser, Wolfgang. *The Act of Reading: A Theory of Aesthetic Response.* Baltimore: Johns Hopkins University Press, 1978.

Iser, Wolfgang. *The Implied Reader: Patterns of Communication in Prose. Fiction from Bunyan to Beckett.* Baltimore: Johns Hopkins University Press, 1974.

Iser, Wolfgang. "Indeterminacy and the Reader's Response in Prose Fiction." In *Aspects of Narrative*. Edited by J. Hillis Miller. New York: Columbia University Press, 1971.

Iser, Wolfgang. "The Reading Process: A Phenomenological Approach." *New Literary History* 3 (1972): 272-299.

Jennings, Theodore W., Jr. "Liturgy." *The Encyclopedia of Religion*, 8: 580-583. Edited by Mircea Eliade. New York: Macmillan, 1986.

Jennings, Theodore W., Jr. "On Ritual Knowledge." *The Journal of Religion.* 62.2 (1982): 111-127.

Jennings, Theodore W., Jr. "Sacrament." *The Encyclopedia of Religion*, 12:500-504. Edited by Mircea Eliade. New York: Macmillan, 1987.

Jung, C.G. *Memories, Dreams, Reflection*. Recorded and edited by Aniela Jaffé. Translated by Richard and Clara Winston. New York: Random House, 1965.

Kavanagh, Aidan. *Elements of Rite: A Handbook of Liturgical Style*. New York: Pueblo, 1982.

Kavanagh, Aidan. *The Shape of Baptism: The Rite of Christian Initiation*. Collegeville, MN: Liturgical Press, 1978.

Kierkegaard, Søren. *Fear and Trembling* and *Repetition*. Kierkegaard's Writings, vol. 6. Edited and translated by Howard V. and Edna H. Hong. Princeton, NJ: Princeton University Press, 1983 [1843].

Kierkegaard, Søren. *Kierkegaard: Letters and Documents*. Translated by Henrik Rosenmeier. Princeton, NJ: Princeton University Press, 1978.

Kierkegaard, Søren. *Repetition: An Essay in Experimental Psychology*. Translated by Walter Lowrie. Princeton, NY: Princeton. University Press, 1946 [1843].

Kierkegaard, Søren. *Søren Kierkegaard's Journals and Papers*, volume 5, Autobiography, part 1. Edited and translated by Howard V. and Edna H. Hong, assisted by Gregor Malantschuk. Bloomington: Indiana University Press, 1978.

Kirk, G.S. *Myth: Its Meaning and Functions in Ancient and Other Cultures*. Berkeley: University of California Press, 1970.

Kliever, Lonnie D. "Fictive Religion: Rhetoric and Play." *Journal of the American Academy of Religion* 49.4 (1981): 657-669.

Kliever, Lonnie D. "Story and Space: The Forgotten Dimension." *Journal of the American Academy of Religion*, Supplement 45.2 (1977): 529-563.

Kluckhohn, Clyde. "Myths and Rituals: A General Theory." In *Reader in Comparative Religion*. Third edition. Edited by William A. Lessa and Evon Z. Vogt. New York: Harper & Row, 1972.

Kopytoff, Igor. "The Cultural Biography of Things." In *The Social Life of Things*, 64-91. Edited by Arjun Appadurai. Cambridge: Cambridge University Press, 1986.

Laird, Joan. "Women and Ritual in Family Therapy." In *Rituals in Families and Family Therapy*, 331-362. Edited by Evan Imber-Black and others. New York: Norton, 1988.

Lakoff, George, and Mark Johnson, *Metaphors We Live By*. Chicago: University of Chicago Press, 1980.

Landon, S. "Three Hymns in the Cult of the Deified Kings." *Proceedings of the Society of Biblical Archaeology* 40 (1918): 31-52.

Lasch, Christopher. *The Culture of Narcissism: American Life in an Age of Diminishing Expectations*. New York: Warner, 1979.

Lincoln, Bruce. "Two Notes on Modern Rituals." *Journal of the American. Academy of Religion* 45.2 (1977): 147-160.

Litell, Frank. *The Macmillan Atlas History of Christianity*. New York: Macmillan, 1976.

McDermott, John V. "Voices and Vision in Tarwater's Odyssey." *Renascence* 32 (1980): 214-220.

Mackey, Louis. *Kierkegaard: Some Kind of Poet*. Philadelphia: University of Pennsylvania Press, 1971.

McLaren, Peter. *Schooling as a Ritual Performance: Towards a Political Economy of Educational Symbols and Gestures*. London: Routledge and Kegan Paul, 1986.

Mailloux, Stephen. *Interpretive Conventions: The Reader in the Study of American Fiction*. Ithaca, NY: Cornell University Press, 1982.

Marty, Martin. *A Nation of Behavers*. Chicago: University of Chicago Press, 1976.

May, John R. *The Pruning Word: The Parables of Flannery O'Connor*. Notre Dame, IN: Univeristy of Notre Dame Press, 1976.

Mayo, Edith. *American Material Culture: The Shape of Things Around Us*. Bowling Green, Ohio: Bowling Green State University Popular Press, 1984.

Michaelsen, Robert S. "Red Man's Religion / White Man's Religious History." *Journal of the American Academy of Religion* 51.4 (1983): 667-684.

Miles, Margaret R. *Carnal Knowing: Female Nakedness and Religious Meaning in the Christian West*. Boston: Beacon, 1989.

Miller, Daniel. *Material Culture and Mass Consumption*. Oxford, England: Basil Blackwell, 1987.

Miller, J. Hillis. *Fiction and Repetition: Seven English Novels*. Cambridge, MA: Harvard University Press, 1982.

Mitchell, Nathan. "Americans at Prayer." The *Amen* Corner. *Worship* 66.2 (1992): 177-184.

Montejano, David. *Anglos and Mexicans in the Making of Texas, 1836-1986*. Austin: University of Texas Press, 1987.

Morgan, Sophia S. "On Rituals and Reflection." Unpublished paper prepared for the Wenner-Gren Foundation for Anthropological Research, Burg Wartenstein Symposium Number 76, 1977.

Myerhoff, Barbara. *Number Our Days*. New York: Simon and Schuster, 1978.

Myerhoff, Barbara, and Metzger, Deena. "The Journal as Activity and Genre: Or listening to the Silent Laughter of Mozart." *Semiotica* 3.1-2 (1980): 97-114.

Navajo Curriculum Center, Rough Rock Demonstration School. *Navajo History*. Vol. 1. Many Farms, AZ: Navajo Community College Press, 1971.

Novak, Michael. *Ascent of the Mountain, Flight of the Dove: An Invitation to Religious Studies*. New York: Harper & Row, 1971.

O'Connor, Flannery. *The Complete Stories*. New York: Farrar, Straus, & Giroux, 1971.

O'Connor, Flannery. *The Habit of Being*. New York: Farrar, Straus, & Giroux, 1979.

O'Connor, Flannery. *Manners and Mystery*. New York: Farrar, Straus, & Giroux, 1969.

O'Connor, Flannery. *The Violent Bear it Away*. New York: Farrar, Straus, & Cudahy, 1960.

O'Keefe, Daniel Lawrence. *Stolen Lightning: The Social Theory of Magic*. New York: Continuum, 1982.

Ong, Walter. "*Maranatha*: Death and Life in the Text of the Book." *Journal of the American Academy of Religion* 45.4 (1977): 419-449.

Ortiz, Alfonso. *The Tewa World: Space, Time, Being, and Becoming in a Pueblo Society*. Chicago: University of Chicago Press, 1969.

Paige, Karen Ericksen, and Jeffery M. Paige. *The Politics of Reproductive Ritual*. Berkeley, CA: University of California Press, 1981.

Paulson, Suzanne Morrow. "Apocalypse of Self, Resurrection of the Double: Flannery O'Connor's *The Violent Bear It Away*." *Literature and Psychology* 30 (1980): 100-111.

Penner, Hans. "Language, Ritual and Meaning." *Numen* 32.1 (1985): 1-16.

Pernet, Henry. "Masks: Ritual Masks in Nonliterate Cultures." *Encyclopedia of Religion* 9: 263-269. Edited by Mircea Eliade. New York: Macmillan, 1987.

Pilgrim, Richard. "Ritual." In *Introduction to the Study of Religion*. Edited by T. William Hall. New York: Harper & Row, 1978.

Procter-Smith, Marjorie. *In Her Own Rite: Constructing Feminist Liturgical Tradition*. Nashville: Abingdon, 1990.

Rappaport, Roy A. 1979. *Ecology, Meaning, and Religion*. Berkeley, CA: North Atlantic.

Resseguie, James L. "Reader-response Criticism and the Synoptic Gospels." *Journal of the American Academy of Religion* 52.2 (1984): 307-324.

Richardson, Miles. "The Artifact as Abbreviated Act: A Social Interpretation of Material Culture." In *The Meanings of Things: Material Culture and Symbolic Expression*, 172-177. Edited by Ian Hodder. London: Unwin Hyman, 1989.

Rosenfield, Claire. "The Shadow Within: The Conscious and Unconscious Use of the Double." *Daedelus* 92 (1963): 326-344.

Ross-Bryant, Lynn. "The Land in American Religious Experience." *Journal of the American Academy of Religion* 58.3 (1990): 333-355.

Rougemont, Denis de. *Love in the Western World*. Revised edition. Translated by Montgomery Belgion. Greenwich, CT: Fawcett, 1956.

Rougemont, Denis de. "Religion and the Mission of the Artist." In *Spiritual Problems in Contemporary Literature*, 173-186. Edited by Stanley R. Hopper. New York: Harper & Row, 1957.

Ruether, Rosemary Radford Ruether. *Women-Church: Theology and Practice*. San Francisco: Harper & Row, 1985.

Ruland, Vernon. *Horizons of Criticism: An Assessment of Religious-Literary Options*. Chicago: American Library Association, 1975.

Rulfo, Juan. *Pedro Paramo*. Translated by Lysander Kemp. New York: Grove, 1959.

Sartre, Jean-Paul. *The Philosophy of Jean-Paul Sartre*. Edited by Robert Denoon Cumming. New York: Modern Library, 1965.

Sartre, Jean-Paul. *Saint Genet: Actor and Martyr*. New York: New. American Library, 1963.

Sartre, Jean-Paul. *The Words*. Translated by Bernard Frechtman. Greenwich, CT: Fawcett, 1964.

Schechner, Richard. *Between Theater and Anthropology*. Philadelphia: University of Pennsylvania Press, 1985.

Schechner, Richard. *Essays on Performance Theory, 1970-1976*. New York: Drama Book Specialists, 1977.

Schechner, Richard. "Restoration of Behavior." *Studies in Visual Communication* 7.3 (1981): 2-45.

Segal, Robert A. "The Myth-Ritualist Theory of Religion." *Journal for the Scientific Study of Religion* 19.2 (1980): 173-185.

Sexson, Lynda. *Ordinarily Sacred*. New York: Crossroad, 1982.

Smith, Carol. *Regional Analysis: Social Systems*. Vol. 2. New York: Academic, 1976.

Smith, J. Oates. "Ritual and Violence in Flannery O'Connor." *Thought* 41 (1966): 545-560.

Smith, Jonathan Z. "The Bare Facts of Ritual." *History of Religions* 20.1-2 (1980): 112-127.

Smith, Jonathan Z. *Map Is Not Territory: Studies in the History of Religions*. Leiden: Brill, 1978.

Smith, Jonathan Z. *To Take Place: Toward Theory in Ritual*. Chicago: University of Chicago Press, 1987.

Sperber, Dan. *Rethinking Symbolism*. Translated by Alice L. Morton. Cambridge: Cambridge University Press, 1975.

Staal, Frits. "The Meaninglessness of Ritual," *Numen* 26 (1979): 2-22.

Tambiah, Stanley J. "A Performative Approach to Ritual." *Proceedings of the British Academy* 65 (1979): 113-169.

Thomas, Jim. *Doing Critical Ethnography*. Newbury Park, CA: Sage, 1992.

Thompson, Robert Farris. *Flash of the Spirit: African and Afro-American Art and Philosophy*. New York: Vintage, 1983.

Tillich, Paul. *Dynamics of Faith*. New York: Harper & Row, 1957.

Tuan, Yi-Fu. "Geopiety: A Theme in Man's Attachment to Nature and to Place," 11-39. In *Geographies of the Mind*. Edited by David Lowenthal. New York: Oxford University Press, 1976.

Turner, Victor W. "An Anthropological Approach to the Icelandic Saga." In *The Translation of Culture*. Edited by T.O. Beidelman. London: Tavistock, 1971.

Turner, Victor W. "Dramatic Ritual/Ritual Drama: Performative and Reflexive Anthropology." *The Kenyon Review* [N.S.] 1.3 (1979): 80-93.

Turner, Victor W. *The Forest of Symbols: Aspects of Ndembu Ritual*. Ithaca, NY: Cornell University Press, 1967.

Vargo, Edward P. *Rainstorms and Fire: Ritual in the Novels of John Updike*. Port Washington, NY: Kennikat, 1973.

Vitz, Paul C. *Psychology as Religion: The Cult of Self-Worship*. Grand Rapids, MI: Eerdmans, 1977.

Wagner, Roy. *The Invention of Culture*. Revised and expanded edition. Chicago: University of Chicago Press, 1981.

Walker, Barbara G. *Women's Rituals: A Sourcebook*. San Francisco: Harper & Row, 1990.

Wallace, Anthony F.C. *Culture and Personality*. New York: Random House, 1961.

Warnke, Frank J. "A Vision Deep and Narrow." In *Critical Essays on Flannery O'Connor*, 34-38. Edited by Melvin J. Friedman and Beverly Lyon Clark. Boston: B.K. Hall, 1985.

Watson, James. "The Structure of Chinese Funerary Rites: Elementary Forms, Ritual Sequence, and the Primacy of Performance." In *Death Ritual in Late Imperial and Modern China*, 3-19. Berkeley: University of California Press, 1988.

Weber, David J. *The Mexican Frontier, 1821-1846*. Albuquerque: University of New Mexico Press, 1982.

Weber, David J. *Myth and the History of the Hispanic Southwest*. Albuquerque: University of New Mexico Press, 1988.

Weber, David J., ed. *New Spain's Far Northern Frontier: Essays on Spain in the American West, 1540-1821*. Dallas: Southern Methodist University, 1979.

Wiesel, Elie. *The Gates of the Forest*. Translated by Frances Frenaye. New York: Holt, Rinehart and Winston, 1966.

Williams, David. "Flannery O'Connor and the *Via Negativa*." *Studies in Religion* 8 (1979): 303-312.

Winnicott, D. W. "Transitional Objects and Transitional Phenomena." In his *Through Pediatrics to Psychoanalysis*, 229-242. London: Hogarth and the Institute of Psycho-Analysis, 1975 [1951].

Wright, John K. *Human Nature in Geography*. Cambridge, MA: Harvard University Press, 1966.

Young-Laughlin, Judy, and Charles D. Laughlin. "How Masks Work, or Masks Work How?" *Journal of Ritual Studies* 2.1 (1988): 59-86.

Zuesse, Evan M. "Meditation on Ritual." *Journal of the American Academy of Religion* 43 (1975): 517-530.